D1789468

ADJUDICATING REFUGEE AND ASYLUM STATUS

In this book, an array of legal, biomedical, psychosocial, and social science scholars and practitioners offer the first comparative account of the increasing dependence on expertise in the asylum and refugee status determination process. This volume presents a comprehensive study of the relevance of experts, as mediators of culture, who are called on to corroborate, substantiate credibility, and serve as translators in the face of confusing legal standards that require proof of new forms and reasons for persecution around the globe. The authors draw on their interactions with expertise and the immigration process to provide insights into the evidentiary burdens on asylum seekers and the expanding role of expertise in the forms of country-conditions reports, biomedical and psychiatric evaluations, and the emerging field of forensic linguistic analysis in response to emerging forms of persecution, such as gender-based or sexuality-based persecution. This book is essential reading for both scholars interested in the production of knowledge and clinicians considering the role of experts as mediators of asylum claims.

Benjamin N. Lawrance is the Hon. Barber B. Conable, Jr., Endowed Chair in International Studies in the department of sociology and anthropology at the Rochester Institute of Technology. He has published ten books, most notably *Amistad's Orphans* (2015) and *Trafficking in Slavery's Wake* (2012). Lawrance is a legal consultant and has served as an expert witness for more than 250 West African asylum claims in fifteen countries. His research is situated at the dynamic inter-disciplinary intersection of history, anthropology, and sociology and is focused on international mobilities, including migration, smuggling, trafficking, forced marriage, and refugee movements.

Galya Ruffer is Director of International Studies and the founding director of the Center for Forced Migration Studies housed at the Buffett Center for International and Comparative Studies at Northwestern University. Her work centers on refugee rights and protection, regional understandings of the root causes of conflict and refugee crises, and the rule of law and the process of international justice, with a particular focus on the Great Lakes region of Africa. She serves on the executive committee for the International Association for the Study of Forced Migration and is a vice chair of the American Bar Association International Refugee Law Committee. Aside from her academic work, she has worked as an immigration attorney representing political asylum claimants both as a solo practitioner and as a pro bono attorney.

Adjudicating Refugee and Asylum Status

THE ROLE OF WITNESS, EXPERTISE, AND TESTIMONY

Edited by

BENJAMIN N. LAWRANCE

Rochester Institute of Technology

GALYA RUFFER

Northwestern University

CAMBRIDGE
UNIVERSITY PRESS

CAMBRIDGE
UNIVERSITY PRESS

32 Avenue of the Americas, New York, NY 10013-2473, USA

Cambridge University Press is part of the University of Cambridge.

It furthers the University's mission by disseminating knowledge in the pursuit of education, learning, and research at the highest international levels of excellence.

www.cambridge.org
Information on this title: www.cambridge.org/9781107069060

© Cambridge University Press 2015

First published 2015

A catalog record for this publication is available from the British Library.

Library of Congress Cataloging in Publication Data
Adjudicating refugee and asylum status : the role of witness, expertise, and testimony / edited by Benjamin N. Lawrance, Galya Ruffer.
      pages   cm
Includes bibliographical references and index.
ISBN 978-1-107-06906-0 (hardback)
1. Asylum, Right of.   2. Political refugees – Legal status, laws, etc. 3. Refugees – Legal status, laws, etc.   4. Evidence, Expert – European Union countries.   5. Asylum, Right of – Great Britain.   I. Lawrance, Benjamin N. (Benjamin Nicholas) II. Ruffer, Galya.
K3268.3.A93   2014
261.8–dc20   2014027872

ISBN 978-1-107-06906-0 Hardback

Contents

v

— largely U.S. based from a few institutions
— but high mix of practitioners

About the Contributors

Joanne Ahola, MD, is board certified in psychiatry and on the voluntary faculty of the Weill Cornell Medical College. She maintains a private practice in general and psychodynamic psychiatry. She is Medical Director of the Weill Cornell Center for Human Rights. She has been a member of the volunteer Asylum Network of Physicians for Human Rights (PHR) since 2000. With PHR, she has trained health professionals around the country in evaluating and documenting the psychological effects of torture and other forms of persecution. She has particular expertise in LGBT asylum, the one-year filing deadline, and testifying in court asylum hearings.

Sabrineh Ardalan, JD, is Assistant Director and Lecturer on Law at the Harvard Immigration and Refugee Clinical Program. She previously served as the Equal Justice America Fellow at The Opportunity Agenda and as a litigation associate at Dewey Ballantine LLP. She also clerked for the Hon. Michael A. Chagares of the Third Circuit Court of Appeals and the Hon. Raymond J. Dearie, Chief District Judge for the Eastern District of New York. She holds a JD from Harvard Law School and a BA in History and International Studies from Yale College.

S. Megan Berthold, LCSW, PhD, is Assistant Professor at the University of Connecticut's School of Social Work. A graduate of Harvard, University of Utah, and UCLA, she teaches casework and human rights. Since the mid-1980s she has served as a clinician, forensic evaluator, and researcher with diverse refugees and asylum seekers in the United States and Asia, including with the Program for Torture Victims in Los Angeles. She frequently testifies as an expert witness in U.S. Immigration Court. Her areas of specialization include torture and other traumas, mental health, and human rights. In 2009 the National Association of Social Workers named her Social Worker of the Year.

Khatiya Chelidze   is an MD student at Weill Cornell Medical College. She is Publications Coordinator of the Weill Cornell Center for Human Rights. She graduated from Hunter College with a BA in Comparative Literature.

Taryn Clark   was an MD student at the Weill Cornell Medical College and one of the cofounders of the Weill Cornell Center for Human Rights.

Lisa Dornell,   JD, is a graduate of the University of Texas at Austin School of Law. She currently sits as an Administrative Judge with the Executive Office for Immigration Review and presides over cases at the Immigration Court in Baltimore, Maryland.

Terri Gallen Edersheim,   MD, is Clinical Associate Professor of Obstetrics and Gynecology and Maternal Fetal Medicine at the Weill Cornell Medical College, where she serves as Medical Director of the Weill Cornell Center for Human Rights. She is an AOA graduate of the Albert Einstein College of Medicine, and she completed her residency training in Obstetrics and Gynecology at The New York Hospital. She completed fellowship training in Maternal-Fetal Medicine before joining the faculty in 1986, where she has practiced both on the full-time and voluntary faculties. She has participated in the evaluation of torture victims seeking asylum with HealthRight International and Physicians for Human Rights.

Bruce J. Einhorn,   JD, is Executive Director and CEO of the Asylum Project, Of Counsel at Wolfsdorf Immigration Law Group, and Adjunct Professor of Law at Pepperdine University. He was formerly Director of the Asylum and Refugee Law Clinic. Einhorn served as a Federal Immigration Judge for seventeen years until 2007. Previously, he served as a special prosecutor and as Chief of Litigation for the U.S. Department of Justice's Office of Special Investigations prosecuting fugitive Nazi war criminals. Einhorn received his JD degree in 1978 from New York University Law School and his BA degree, magna cum laude, from Columbia University in 1975, where he was selected for Phi Beta Kappa.

Margaret Fabiszak   is an MD/PhD candidate at the Weill Cornell/ Rockefeller/Sloan Kettering Tri-Institutional MD/PhD Program and serves as the Research Coordinator at the Weill Cornell Center for Human Rights.

David Gangsei,   PhD, is a clinical psychology graduate of Columbia University and licensed psychologist in California, specializing in providing psychological services to refugees, asylum seekers, and torture survivors. He served as Clinical Director of Survivors of Torture International, San Diego, where he oversaw the development of a program serving health, mental health, case management, and asylum support services. He is a consultant developing programs and training for organizations serving trauma victims and survivors. Gangsei is an expert on forensic documentation of the psychological effects of torture and on recognition and management of vicarious trauma for professionals and support personnel.

Anthony Good, PhD, is Professor Emeritus in Social Anthropology at the University of Edinburgh. His principal overseas field research sites are Tamil Nadu, South India, and Sri Lanka. He has served as an expert witness in more than 600 asylum claims, mainly involving Sri Lankan Tamils. He conducted fact-finding visits to assess the human rights situation in Sri Lanka, producing reports for use as evidence in asylum appeal cases. He has conducted research on expert evidence in British asylum courts. He has published numerous books and articles, including *Anthropology and Expertise in the Asylum Courts* (2007).

Christine Hauskeller, PhD, is Senior Lecturer in the Department of Sociology and Philosophy at the University of Exeter. Her work combines critical theory and empirical, hermeneutic research in studies on the interrelation between social institutions, individuals, knowledge formation, and the role of biomedicine in social practices. The combination of conceptual and empirical work characterizes her approach and she has published widely on Foucault and Butler, on torture, on stem cell ethics, and on genetics and identity. She was Director of the U.K. Economics and Social Research Council–funded Centre for Genetics in Society in Exeter.

Jeffrey Herbst is President of Colgate University.

Noé Mahop Kam is a PhD candidate in the Department of Political Science, Social and Communication Sciences at the Catholic University of Louvain–la Neuve and Managing Director of Makano International, an African-language analysis agency based in the Netherlands.

Benjamin N. Lawrance, PhD, is the Hon. Barber B. Conable, Jr., Endowed Professor of International Studies at Rochester Institute of Technology. He has published ten books, notably *African Asylum at a Crossroads* (2015), *Amistad's Orphans* (2015), and *Trafficking in Slavery's Wake* (2012). Lawrance is a legal consultant and has served as an expert witness on more than 250 occasions. Lawrance is the recipient of several national and international awards, including a fellowship from the National Endowment for the Humanities and fellowships at Yale, Harvard, and the University of California.

Stuart Lorin Lustig, MD, MPH, is a child and adolescent psychiatrist currently working for Cigna as a Lead Medical Director. He is Associate Clinical Professor of Psychiatry at the University of California San Francisco School of Medicine and has extensive experience in forensic psychiatry pertaining to the political asylum process. He has collaborated with numerous human rights organizations on clinical and academic endeavors.

Miriam H. Marton, JD, MSW, is Director of the Tulsa Immigrant Resource Network, a post-graduate fellowship program at the University of Tulsa Law School, and assistant visiting clinical professor. Formerly she was the William R. Davis Clinical Teaching Fellow in the Asylum and Human Rights Clinic at the University of Connecticut School of Law. A practicing attorney since 2001, Marton worked for Skadden, Arps, Slate, Meagher & Flom LLP as lead attorney in the representation of asylum applicants as part of Skadden's pro bono program. She holds a JD from Michigan State University College of Law and an MSW from the University of Michigan School of Social Work. Marton had a fourteen-year career as a clinical social worker before pursuing her interest in the law.

Galya Ruffer, JD, PhD, is Director of International Studies and the founding Director of the Center for Forced Migration Studies housed at the Buffett Center for International and Comparative Studies at Northwestern University. Her work centers on refugee rights and protection, regional understandings of the root causes of conflict and refugee crises, rule of law, and the process of international justice. She serves on the Executive Committee for the International Association for the Study of Forced Migration and is Vice Chair of the American Bar Association International Refugee Law Committee.

Nicole Sirotin, MD, is a general internist and served as Assistant Professor in the Department of Medicine at the Weill Cornell Medical College and a medical director of the Weill Cornell Center for Human Rights. She has been conducting medical evaluations for asylum seekers since 2008. She has a particular interest in education and in teaching medical trainees about the health issues of survivors of torture and in the health issues of recently arrived female immigrants. She serves as a volunteer for both Physicians for Human Rights Asylum Network and the HealthRight International volunteer network.

Hawthorne Emery Smith, PhD, is a licensed psychologist and the Clinical Director of the Bellevue/NYU Program for Survivors of Torture. He is also an Assistant Clinical Professor at the NYU School of Medicine. Smith received his doctorate in Counseling Psychology (with distinction) from Teachers College, Columbia University. Smith has also earned a Bachelor of Science in Foreign Service from the Georgetown University School of Foreign Service; an advanced certificate in African Studies from Cheikh Anta Diop University in Dakar, Senegal; and a Master's in International Affairs from the Columbia University School of International and Public Affairs.

Steven Sturdy, PhD, is Professor of the Sociology of Medical Knowledge; Head of Science, Technology and Innovation Studies; and Wellcome Trust Senior Investigator in Medical Humanities at the School of Social and Political Sciences, University of Edinburgh. He has published numerous articles about how developments in medical science have informed and been informed by wider changes in medical practice and medical policy. His current research examines the scientific, technological, social, and political processes that have led, over the past forty years or so, to the current ferment of activity around "genomic medicine."

Richard Tutton, PhD, is Senior Lecturer in the Department of Sociology at Lancaster University. His work examines the social implications of human genetics research, in areas ranging from health and citizenship, biobanking and human tissue collection, enhancement and biomedicalization, and identity formation in the context of genetic knowledge.

Luis Villegas is an MD student at Weill Cornell Medical College.

Patriss Wais Moradi is Clinical Researcher, Weill Cornell Center for Human Rights at Weill Cornell Medical College, and a graduate of the University of California, Davis.

Acknowledgments

As is always the case, an edited volume is much more than the sum of its parts. The editors and authors whose chapters appear in this volume are indebted to the colleagues who shared thoughts and ideas during the Second Conable Conference in International Studies, entitled "Refugees, Asylum Law, and Expert Testimony: The Construction of Africa and the Global South in Comparative Perspective," in Rochester, New York, in April 2011. The authors would also like to thank the reviewers whose insights, we hope, strengthened the text. Thanks also go to John Berger and David Jou at Cambridge; Devasena Vedamurthi at Integra Software Services, who so smoothly guided this project toward completion; and Meridith Murray for the index.

Galya Ruffer appreciates the research support of the Dispute Resolution Research Center at Northwestern University and owes much thanks to her family, Jim, Ari, Jonah, Eli and Sheli, who wait endlessly for her to have a work-free weekend.

Benjamin N. Lawrance would like to thank the several organizations and entities that made the conference possible, namely, the Conable Endowment for International Studies, the Starr Foundation, the Program in International and Global Studies in the Department of Sociology and Anthropology in the College of Liberal Arts at Rochester Institute of Technology, the Weill Cornell Center for Human Rights, and the Department of History at Cornell University. He would also like to thank his family, especially Wilson Silva.

We both thank the various individuals whose contributions ultimately all feature in this final product, including Peter Agree, Penny Andrews, Iris Berger, Judi Byfield, Taryn Clark, Evan Criddle, Susan Dicklitch, Tasha Fain, Paul Finkelman, Barbara Harrell-Bond, Jeffrey Herbst, Tobias Kelly, Christine Kray, Sue Long, Katherine Luongo, Mary Meg McCarthy, Andrea McIntosh, Karen Musalo, Juan Osuna, Tricia Redeker Hepner, Cassandra

Shellman, Meredith Terretta, Robert Ulin, James Winebrake, and the more than 100 participants in the conference.

When we first began serving as expert witnesses for asylum claims, we had no sense of the unspeakable ordeals people are prepared to endure to survive. Jean-Francois Lyotard described the burden-facing asylum seekers as an "ethical tort," an extreme form of injustice insofar as the victim is deprived of means to speak about or prove their persecution. With this book, we are a little closer to some sense of understanding, but there is still much work to be done. We hope this book fosters conversations, activism, and critical scholarship. We offer this book as a vehicle to encourage others to embrace what may be an unrecognized capacity and share their expertise. We are in awe of each and every one of the hundreds of lives we have encountered during our expert witnessing.

We dedicate this book to the refugees and asylum seekers who routinely display profound and unfathomable courage as they are asked by adjudicators to present their case and recount the brutalities and torture they have suffered, even as they are judged in languages and idioms they do not understand.

NOTE

All possible effort has been made to protect the identity and confidentiality of the individuals whose life stories form part of this book. The authors of chapters employ anonymous or pseudonymous monikers consistent with their respective discipline(s) where appropriate. Details, including but not limited to race, ethnicity, and national origin, have been changed where necessary and appropriate.

Foreword

Adjudicating Refugee and Asylum Status is an important collection of essays examining how Western countries have come to use experts while evaluating refugee claims. This book, based on work by an enviable array of scholars and practitioners, provides information on both the mechanics of refugee adjudication and how courts and legal forums have moved in a variety of perhaps unpredictable ways to use the work of experts in deciding whether to grant sanctuary to those with refugee claims. Accordingly, it is also an explicit and extended meditation on how knowledge developed and deployed by Western experts is used to evaluate the particular circumstances of people from poor regions of the world whose lives will be fundamentally altered depending on the ultimate decision about their refugee status. In the settings examined by the authors, knowledge is not retained for contemplation by those in the "ivory tower" but is used to make what may often literally be life-or-death decisions.

The essays also hint at some of the paradoxes of globalization. In the twenty-first-century world, knowledge, as well as data, money, and media, flow across national boundaries with unprecedented ease. However, the flow of people across boundaries has perhaps never been more regulated. In sub-Saharan Africa, the continental home of many refugee crises over the centuries, a common response to unhappiness or crises was for individuals or whole communities to move. It was only in the twentieth century – with the creation of national boundaries developed by the colonialists and subsequently ratified by independence leaders and the ensuing development of notions of citizenship tied to politically defined boundaries – that the concept of "refugee" was even possible. There seems to be every indication that the movement of people will continue to be closely regulated by all nations and those, especially in the West, who have some ability to police their borders will continue to try to control population movements through administrative mechanisms.

At the same time, because knowledge generally flows irrespective of borders, we know, or think that we know, more about the world than ever before. Partially as a result, refugee adjudication relies increasingly on the knowledge that in many cases we have or think that we possess. Yet, reflection, as found in this volume, suggests that the knowledge that we think we have is inevitably complex and sometimes problematic, especially given what is at stake for individuals.

It is likely that the tension between ever-greater regulation of population movements and the desire to adjudicate individual cases through expert knowledge will only increase in the future. There are, as this book makes clear, no easy answers, although there are many important proposals in the individual chapters that should be considered. More generally, a profound understanding of how countries have arrived at their particular reliance on expert knowledge will hopefully allow us to develop in the future systems that are fairer, more transparent, and appropriate, given the consequences of particular decisions. The individual contributions in this book and the intellectual project that the authors collectively contribute to are therefore important and timely and should be appreciated by both other scholars and those practicing in this very difficult area.

Jeffrey Herbst
President, Colgate University

Introduction: Witness to the Persecution? Expertise, Testimony, and Consistency in Asylum Adjudication

Benjamin N. Lawrance and Galya Ruffer

The narratives of refugees and asylum seekers are routinely subjected to scrutiny in a variety of Western jurisdictions, ranging from the administrative courts in the United States and the immigration review board of Canada, to the multiple levels of review in diverse European jurisdictions. Historically, the refugee and asylum adjudication process (henceforth RSD) has been internal, domestic, and more often than not, behind closed doors and not subject to appeal. From the 1980s, however, many legislatures reformed administrative law systems to reflect greater accountability and domestic immigration laws and asylum review procedures were targeted for particular amendment (Alexander 1999). The legacy of these legislative reforms is now becoming apparent throughout North America, Europe, and Australasia. Just as the asylum and refugee adjudication process has become more transparent, denial and deportation rates have risen (Ramji-Nogales et al. 2009). Over the past decade, judges and adjudicators have sought to insulate their decision making by demonstrating sensitivity to evidence and narrative by incorporating external expertise. *Adjudicating Refugee and Asylum Status* explores the increasing evidentiary burdens on asylum seekers and expanding role of a variety of forms of expertise – ranging from country conditions reports, to biomedical and psychiatric evaluations, to the emerging field of forensic linguistic analysis – in refugee decision making.

In its 1979 *Handbook and Guidelines on Procedures and Criteria for Determining Refugee Status (UNHCR Guidelines)*, the UNHCR stated that while "the burden of proof lies on the person submitting a claim," it is often the case that "a person fleeing from persecution will have arrived with the barest necessities and very frequently even without personal documents." Therefore, the UNHCR observed, the "duty to ascertain and evaluate all the relevant facts" is shared "between the applicant and the examiner." The handbook further noted that the "requirement of evidence should thus not be too strictly applied in view of the difficulty of proof inherent in the special situation in which an applicant for refugee status finds" him or herself. Instead, an applicant's fear of persecution should be considered well-founded if he or she "can establish, to a reasonable degree," that his or her "continued stay" in the respective "country of origin has become intolerable." The 2011 reissue of the Handbook reaffirmed these guidelines, and common law countries have generally supported the view that there is no requirement to prove well-foundedness conclusively beyond doubt, or even that persecution is more probable than not. To establish "well-foundedness," persecution must be proved to be reasonably possible (UNHCR 1998).

Notwithstanding this lower threshold, according to Peter Showler, the former Chair of the Canadian Immigration and Review Board, deciding refugee claims is the single most complex adjudication function in Western societies (Rousseau et al. 2002, p. 43). To be a refugee and obtain asylum, an asylum seeker must prove that she is unable or unwilling to return to her country of origin either because she has suffered persecution in the past or because she has a "well-founded fear" of future persecution. The asylum seeker must also prove that her persecutor targeted her on account of at least one of five protected grounds: race, religion, nationality, political opinion, or membership in a particular social group. Whereas in most criminal and civil procedures adjudicators are able to access a range of concrete evidence, asylum cases are marked by a general lack of factual, verifiable evidence (CREDO 2013, p. 11).

The central piece of evidence in an asylum case is the applicant's testimony, in written and/or oral form, where he or she narrates all the information relevant to her/his case. The case, therefore, hinges on whether the adjudicator deems the applicant's testimony to be credible. Documenting the situation in the country of origin, including general social and political conditions, the human rights situation and record, relevant legislation and application of law, the persecuting agent's politics or practices, and particular policies, practices, or attitudes towards persons who are in similar situations as the applicant, are especially important for assessing an individual's credibility (Cohen 2001; Millbank 2009; UNHCR 2013; CREDO 2013). In addition to country of origin information (COI), experts are increasingly called upon to lend credibility and corroborate the applicant's testimony of both events that occurred in the past (past persecution) and the risk that they will occur in the future should the applicant be returned to his or her country of origin (well-founded fear of future persecution). In evaluating the risk of persecution, bureaucrats, tribunals, and courts take into account the personal circumstances of the applicant such as his/her background, experiences, personality, and other personal factors that could expose him/her to persecution. Particularly relevant is whether the applicant has previously suffered persecution or other forms of mistreatment and the experiences of relatives and friends, persons in the same situation.

There is little international guidance on the role of experts in asylum claims. An expert witness is generally a person, who by virtue of education, or profession, or experience, or a combination of all, is believed to have special subject matter knowledge beyond that of the average person sufficient that others rely on him for his opinions. In the U.S. immigration court, a person must qualify as an expert through a series of questions designed to establish expertise on the specific topic in question (*Immigration Court Practice Manual*, ch. 3). In the United Kingdom, if an expert can demonstrate a particular sitting judge has accepted his proficiency by citing a specific adjudication, other judges appear to be more willing to accept the claim of expertise. Although, technically, any person who has lived or travelled in the applicant's country would qualify as experts by definition, the credentials of such witnesses are often problematic in practice, especially if they appear to have a bias or pronounced view about the country, and carry little weight with the judge. The main exception to this generally rudderless context is that of standards and procedures on how to recognize and document symptoms of torture. The International Association of Refugee Law Judges has issued "Guidelines on the Judicial Approach to Expert Medical Evidence" and the Istanbul Protocol, a non-binding document, contains internationally recognized guidelines for assessing the claims of those who allege torture and ill treatment (Iocapino, Ozkalipci, and Schlar 1999; Haagensen 2007). It is widely used – as the chapters in this volume by Khatiya Chelidze et al. and by Hawthorne Smith, Stuart Lustig, and David Gangsei demonstrate – and has been an official U.N. document, "tantamount to a treaty" since 1999, although its utilization is uneven (Grossman 2009, p. 13; Wallace and Wylie 2014, p. 754).

Adjudicating Refugee and Asylum Status has two primary objectives. Collectively, we seek to critique the trend in Western jurisdictions toward the increasing dependence on expert testimony by drawing attention to the ways in which this dependence has distorted the standards, principles, and methods of establishing the facts of refugee claims. The chapters in this anthology examine ways in which expertise is shaped and delimited by immigration determination venues, which operate in a world transformed by greater access to information and technologies, and how knowledge and scholarly disciplines have responded to these challenges. To this end, while speaking to a general need for experts, the volume addresses the concern that these evidentiary demands for unquestionable proof and authenticity point to the specific problems of documentation in Africa, the Middle East, Asia, and other parts of the Global South, where the lack of verified documentation is endemic. Collectively, the volume wrestles with the need for the development of cross-professional collaborations, guidelines, and standards for ways in which experts can become a more holistic asset to the refugee status determination process. Viewed as a conversation among lawyers, social workers, psychiatrists, social scientists and judges with personal experience of the system, this book offers considered reflection and practical guidance on the role of experts in Western countries where claimants may present their claims to an adjudicator and/or are granted an oral hearing in the RSD process. The expanding role of experts in the resource intensive asylum systems discussed in this volume raises the question whether this development, which makes a burdensome process even more demanding, is applicable globally.

More fundamentally, however, the authors in this volume address the epistemological challenges of the production of knowledge across cultures that are accompanying the increase in asylum and refugee claims worldwide. Whereas the original 1979 UNHCR Guidelines may well have emerged from a context of careful and thoughtful intention on the part of international agencies, the UNHCR does not carry sufficient legal authority to level the playing field internationally for asylum seekers (Avery 1983; UNHCR 2013). Instead, national implementation of the convention through domestic processes for RSD continues to reflect pre-existing legal structures and government institutions rather than any input from the UNHCR handbook. The absence of consensus in Western jurisdictions on common evidentiary assessment standards in RSD procedures remains a major obstacle to the development of a just assessment process (Anker 1990; Gorlick 2003; UNHCR 2013). Given the overall climate of immigration restriction in Western countries, the UNHCR Guidelines have become a double-edged sword, providing standards for those who seek to locate new rules, tools, methods, and procedures, for the deployment of, "deference to" (Barnes 2004, p. 352), and exclusion of expert evidence and testimony, often through new case law and precedent (Refugee Review Tribunal 2006; Norman 2007).

These tensions and contradictions are born of a paradox. The UNHCR struggles with its own RSD role, simultaneously enforcing international legal mandates and acknowledging individual national RSD failures (Goodwin-Gill 2002; Barutciski 2002; Kagan 2006). But rather than simplifying the path to an asylum claim for traumatized, vulnerable, and often-undocumented refugees, the UNHCR Guidelines appear to have generated labyrinthine practices and processes tied to heightened securitization measures (Brouwer

2002). The lower threshold for establishing the "credibility" of a claimant is increasingly conflated with the much higher barrier of "proof" (Sweeney 2009). The essays in this collection narrate the experiences of asylum seekers and refugees as they navigate themselves and their families through untested pseudo-science and unverified country conditions claims, many of which imperil their credibility.

The assembled chapters were selected from over forty-five papers delivered at an international conference held in April 2012 in Rochester, New York, that explored the role and experience of the expert and the employment of expert testimony in refugee contexts. Read together, the chapters narrate a broad spectrum about the Global South migrant experience in Western immigration jurisdictions. This volume constitutes the first attempt to offer a comparative account of the globalized professional and clinical practices pertaining to the increasing reliance on experts in refugee law. Although several scholars have raised concerns about expert evidence in asylum cases (Good 2004; Thuen 2004; Piot 2007; Good 2007, 2008; Bloomaert 2009; Squire 2009), new legislation around the globe, such as the 2005 REAL ID in the U.S., and regional coordination (such as common standards in the European Union and in MERCOSUL countries) is contributing to the increasing reliance on experts. We view the time as ripe for serious scrutiny of the increasing dependence on expertise and the impact on the form, quality, and nature of the expertise produced in the context of RSD.

THE ASYLUM DIALECTIC

Adjudicating Refugee and Asylum Status draws on clinical and academic reflections to raise compelling issues about trends in asylum adjudication, the ambivalence of adjudicators toward expert testimony and, in particular, the "hermeneutics of suspicion" that characterizes asylum and refugee proceedings in Western Europe and the United States (Ricœur 1965; Gadamer 1984; Stewart 1989; Kessler 2005). The resulting conversation provides a productive platform with which to evaluate the unfolding nature of the relationship between expert testimony and asylum adjudication. The clinical reflections by trauma specialists, legal advocates, and forensic experts in the first section highlight the significance of sociocultural inconsistencies in testimonies from refugees, and the back and forth between adjudicators and experts struggling to reconcile testimony with "fact." The academic studies reflect on how perceived physiological and psychiatric inconsistencies stimulate the development of new mechanisms and tests to mitigate inconsistencies. Psycho-medico inconsistency provides the vehicle for exploring the particular ways in which the testimony of asylum seekers is imperiled by the adjudication process and the responses of experts to the challenges presented by the refugee status determination process.

An overarching interest of the authors here is in understanding the emerging role of experts and the performance of legal process as the dialectical relationship between asylum adjudicators and expert witnesses. While describing the relationship between a decision maker and a third party in dialectical terms may not meet more conventional deployments of classical dialectics, not the least because the power relation is qualitatively and permanently imbalanced, our observations indicate that the "discursive activity" of the professional asylum collective (here, both adjudicators and expert witnesses) is deeply interwoven in complex and powerful ways (Jones and Smith 2004, p. 387; Hardy and Phillips 1999). And when viewed separately from the narratives of claimants, their advocates, and their opponents, the dialectical asylum collective is at least ostensibly united by a commitment to identifying an underlying "truth," as discovered through reason and logic in discussion.

The value of thinking in terms of dialectic is that it highlights a productive interdependence, and in particular, the ever-deepening nature of the dependency. Both parties appear deeply conscious of their mutually constitutive relationship: adjudicators appear increasingly reluctant to proceed to judgment in contentious cases without requisite expert reports on which their decisions – negative or positive – can partly rest; and experts adhere to guidelines on format and content and directly interface with judicial reasoning. By contrast, they regularly seek each other's counsel as part of the broader project of ostensibly delivering justice to asylum claimants: both parties frequently seek specific answers to questions in the course of deliberation; they appear to recognize what might loosely be described as boundaries of knowledge and the relationship of scholarly knowledge to objective evidence, and both regularly defer to the other's respective fields of knowledge.

We highlight the dialectical relationship because the expansive international architecture of RSD – guidelines, protocols, conventions, agencies, indeed, a high commission – encourages us to locate a supra-analytical apparatus transcending specific domestic legal or constitutional traditions. Whereas the chapters in this volume offer individual national case studies, the patterns of interdependency uncovered are transnational and global. The adversarial framework categorizing many scholarly studies of common judicial procedure has little relevance for understanding the unfolding and constantly expanding deployment of expert testimony in the United States or other common law countries (e.g., Landsman 1983; Barnes 2004, p. 352). Similarly, in some countries employing Roman-Canon inquisitorial traditions, RSD processes have spawned autonomous administrative tribunals where ambiguous stereotypes and social prejudice trump the adherence to law and regulation (Jubany 2011). Moreover, some countries, notably Canada, have created entirely new review boards, decisions of which may remain entirely distinct from the judicial process until a more advanced stage of appeal (Rousseau et al. 2002; Crépeau and Nakache 2008). At the same time, the traditional civil–common law divide appears to break down when RSD is the subject of scrutiny (see Barnes 2004). The "normal civil process" has "no tradition" in asylum jurisdiction (Jones and Smith 2004, p. 388). Common law traditions appear to be subtly infiltrating the RSD process in Europe, and adjudicators operating under common law tradition in the United States and the United Kingdom are increasingly adopting the role of judge-inquisitor or fact-finder (*see* Anker 1992; Jones and Smith 2004).

In addition to the obvious statement that the expert witness is usually a third party whose primary responsibility is, in a very general sense, to the court and governed by rules and procedures, there are several other reasons why a conceptual understanding of the dialectical RSD collective is required. First, the questions adjudicators pose in a refugee status determination, and indeed the manner in which they are posed reflect the global and transnational contexts that give rise to asylum claims as much as they do domestic policy concerns. Second, the individual adjudicators themselves are rarely constitutive of the core demographic of which the wider judiciary is comprised in most domestic jurisdictions. In many countries, the first line of decision making resides in the hands of a government employee, not a judicial officer, and expert testimony is often only solicited after this first stage. It is frequently only on appeal, and before a judge, that an expert statement is submitted. Furthermore, many judges enter immigration tribunals from bureaucratic careers and are rarely career jurists, although this appears to be slowly changing. Third, the venues in which claims are evaluated are often physically quite unlike the classic adversarial geography of the courtroom. In some countries, immigration tribunals or courts look more like boardrooms or meeting rooms, and parties sit in close proximity, but in many cases, the refugee is detained in a remote facility, and appears by video link. And, fourth, in less contentious cases, or when government agents appear to concede the likelihood that a case will prevail in the applicant's favor, government lawyers fail to present. In the United States, experts are frequently required to be available for cross-examination, but in the United Kingdom they are rarely examined on the stand, and when a government lawyer fails to appear, decisions are rendered *ex parte*.

Generally speaking, globally there is agreement that refugee claims constitute neither criminal nor civil law, and that credibility determinations should not rest on "hard" facts, hence our interest in reconceptualizing the relationship by focusing on the mechanisms of knowledge production (Millbank 2009). But the essays in this collection also reveal the detachment from established legal procedure to be a double-edged sword. Adjudicators may base decisions entirely on oral statements and make an assessment of an applicant's subjective account in light of the objective situation in the country of origin, or they may expressly demand the production of an expert report addressing a key element of the claimant's narrative, hence the dialectical relationship. Just as adjudicators are less tied by the constraints of civil or criminal procedure in their respective domestic jurisdictions, as administrative appointments, many are increasingly exposed to the types of domestic pressures attendant to border and identity securitization that characterize the post-9/11 world. Travel documents, for instance, are often not accepted as identification due to the manner in which the date of birth is recorded, while the renewal of documents is often a major problem for refugees unable to meet the expense (Bohmer and Shuman 2015). In addition an absence of documentation is increasingly invoked as grounds for doubting the credibility of an applicant's entire narrative. Combined with a climate of distrust and fear in Western countries about losing control over borders, the project of RSD has departed from the noble rights-based rhetoric post–World War II, and become one of proving identity, credibility, and "genuine" persecution, as distinct from the structural violence and economic inequalities of many countries in the Global South (Hathaway 1984; Kälin 2003).

To be clear, we do not idealize the refugee status determination process. RSD offers perhaps the most clarion example of the entanglement of international human rights obligations with national politics, policy objectives, and domestic anxieties (e.g., for Germany, see Blay and Zimmerman 1994; for Spain and Portugal, see Fullerton 2005; for Australia, see Foster and Pobjoy 2011). And indeed, the chapters in this volume speak to many of the peculiarities and pitfalls associated with this relationship. Whereas the UNHCR Guidelines may have sought to provide clarity and coherence to the proliferation of complex and contradictory domestic adjudication processes, the relationship between adjudicators and experts continues to unfold unevenly worldwide. Courts and lawyers are increasingly straying from these standards by appearing to apply standards that effectively increase the value of and thus burden of proof in asylum cases. In the United States, for example, the 2005 REAL ID Act permits and, some would argue, even encourages immigration judges to find asylum seekers lacking in credibility even if the discrepancies or miscomprehensions in their responses refer to matters ancillary to their particular claim. Indeed, the REAL ID Act has been used, as Bruce Einhorn and Megan Bertholdt state in their chapter, as a "crypto-diagnostic tool by legal professionals," in lieu of the requisite medical and scientific expertise, "to explain the imperfections in testimony of the alleged victims of persecution, often in negative and discrediting terms" (Einhorn and Bertholdt this volume; Galoni 2008; Conroy 2009). Issuance of a negative credibility determination by an immigration judge – often the "fulcrum" of a decision – is similarly one of the swiftest mechanisms to deportation from the United Kingdom (Thomas 2006, p. 79).

The case studies presented in the volume are those of clinicians, academics, experts and adjudicators reflecting on the dialectical RSD collective. In Part I, trauma specialists, legal practitioners, and forensic professionals discuss the contours of expertise emerging both inside and outside courtrooms and tribunals, ranging from new specialized subfields of research to the creation of national directorates for sourcing expert opinion. These chapters highlight the increasing need of experts to resolve sociocultural inconsistencies and offer solutions that speak to the competing responsibilities of lawyers, judges and experts, lack of training of judges, need for cross-cultural understanding, inadequacy of resources and the caseload of lawyers and adjudicators who are unprepared themselves for the stress of asylum cases. In Part II, social scientists examine the treatment of psycho-medico inconsistencies by practitioners, and experts discuss the perils of persecution testimony invoking physiological and psychological harms, ranging from navigating personal relationships and ethical dilemmas to countering the overzealous deployment of pseudo-scientific standards and biomedical technology. We will consider these two analytical frameworks in more detail in this Introduction.

SOCIOCULTURAL INCONSISTENCY AND THE CONTOURS OF EXPERTISE

Refugee status determination requires decision makers to have knowledge of the applicant's particular fear of being returned to countries where they say they are in danger. Given the lack of availability of documents, decision makers have turned to experts to resolve inconsistencies in asylum applicant testimony and shed light on questions of demeanor. The chapters in part one examine the ways in which expert testimony responds to and is drawn into the sociocultural inconsistencies of asylum claims while simultaneously creating and defining the boundaries and contours of expertise. As Western countries continue to place barriers to entry with an underlying presumption that most asylum seeker claims are bogus, the trend has been toward standardization of knowledge that, when combined with the formalism of legal reasoning through which judges apply legal principles to the facts in a case, seeks to remove the discretion of the decision maker (Hart 1961, 1983). Thus, although there has been a greater recognition of the varied sociocultural contexts that contribute to refugee flight, the remedy has sought to increase fairness and professionalism by bringing in experts to help bridge understandings. In this newly forming collaboration between adjudicators and experts, experts both form and shape understandings of particular contexts in the Global South and are redefined by them in ways that need further examination.

Although the figure of the expert may seem relatively straightforward, Anthony Good (2004, 2008) has demonstrated how each specific form of testimony operates within a defined set of parameters and requirements. Judges, for example, may call upon experts when the documentary evidence about persecution is inadequate or credibility imperiled. Immigration lawyers may draw on experts to translate the narrative of a claimant "as a personal trauma into an act of political aggression" (Shuman and Bohmer 2004, p. 396). Experts may be invited to interpret the current status of a domestic statute (such as nationality and citizenship law), and how it pertains to a specific claim of a refugee or asylum seeker, such as statelessness (Lawrance forthcoming). Country conditions experts may level the playing field, as Susan Kerns (2000) argues. Indeed, the tasks of the expert are so wide-ranging that Immigration Judge Gary Malphrus (2010, p. 8) suggests that "what constitutes adequate qualifications to testify as an expert should be broadly defined."

Asylum and immigration experts serve a similar role to that of interpreters in the sense that experts translate the testimony of asylum seekers into vocabularies and images that are legible to decision makers. Absent of sensitivity to the sociocultural background of the asylum seeker, an interpreter can cause misunderstanding. In a general sense, the role of the expert in asylum claims is to testify about the political, cultural, and social climate in the asylum seekers' home countries, and to assess the degree to which a refugee or asylum seeker would be in danger if they were returned. Part of the reason that experts are called upon is to resolve the problem of inconsistency. There is no requirement that a refugee be credible to be granted asylum. Instead, informed by the horrors of World War II, the governing documents require that refugees be given the benefit of the doubt; and, therefore, experts are called to assist adjudicators as they attempt to distinguish the noncredible refugee who has a valid claim for asylum from the noncredible refugee who does not (Kagan 2003). Notwithstanding convention mandates, and, very significantly, eligibility remains in the mind of the adjudicator.

Although "credibility" is not mentioned in the 1951 Refugee Convention or the Statute of the Office of the UNHCR, decisions often hinge on perceptions of the credibility of the refugee applicants, many of whom are rarely in a position to provide corroborating documentation or testimony about the central elements of their claims (Kagan 2003, p. 367). Whereas a trend toward establishing objective principles, standards, and criteria that should govern credibility assessments may be underway, the need to rely on concrete facts and analysis has increased reliance on expert knowledge. The requisite knowledge encompasses everything from the testimony of scholars and field researchers, to reports by national directorates, to the sourcing of expert opinion from companies providing medical reports and "forensic language testing."

In many parts of the world, the existence of a national research directorate has become a core element of the RSD process. The reliance on expert knowledge thus suffers from what B.S. Chimni calls "objectivism" that "disenfranchises the refugee through eliminating her or his voice in the process leading to the decision to deny or terminate protection" (Chimni 1999, p. 7).

> Objectivism is sustained on the mistaken view that there are facts out there waiting to be discovered in order to arrive at a just decision with respect to the denial or termination of protection. Unfortunately, however, facts do not exist outside the world of interpretation. Therefore, most often, what objectivism tends to do is to substitute the subjective perceptions of the State authorities for the experience of the refugee. Its injustice relates above all to the fact that 'all traces of particularity and otherness are reduced to a register of sameness and cognition', whereas fear, pain and death are 'radically singular'; they resist and at the limit destroy language and its ability to construct shared worlds. (Chimni 1999, p. 7)

The substitution of expert knowledge about the experience of the refugee for the experience of the refugee in an attempt to apply objective legal standards of credibility on the basis of factual accounts of country conditions or persecution sharply reveals the limits of sociocultural understandings across borders. Whereas the assumption is that expert knowledge can contribute to the construction of a shared world of understanding, expert knowledge, as it becomes the official understanding of persecution, trauma or pain, may also increase the gap between the subjective perceptions of the state authorities and the experience of the refugee.

Given the nature of cultural divides between the applicant and the adjudicator, the testimony of an asylum seeker may often come across to an asylum officer or immigration judge as fraught with inconsistencies. An applicant's demeanor and ability to recount his or her history of persecution or violence is often compromised in ways that may lead to an adverse credibility determination. Deborah Anker explains that,

> Various factors make it difficult for adjudicators to determine accurately the applicant's credibility. These include differences in cultural norms, the effect of an asylum seeker's past traumatic experiences and flight on her ability to recall events, language barriers, the adversarial nature of the hearing, the asylum seeker's limited access to legal counsel, and the adjudicator's sometimes inaccurate perceptions of foreign culture and politics. (Deborah Anker, cited in Kagan 2003)

But demeanor is particularly relative, and it varies widely depending on many factors, such as reaction to trauma or shame as Miriam Marton's chapter demonstrates. In such situations, expert witnesses familiar with trauma, mental health, anthropology, linguistics, or other specialties and disciplinary perspectives can be a valuable source of evidence for immigration judges in asylum hearings. Adjudicators have come to rely heavily on experts because of a perception that reconciling inconsistencies is part of the asylum and refugee adjudication process. The chapters in Part I engage the need for experts, but also question how experts have altered the refugee status determination process by examining the way in which experts themselves and understandings of expert knowledge in courts and tribunals reflect and shape sociocultural inconsistencies.

Einhorn and Berthold address this codependency, from the perspectives of a retired federal immigration judge and that of a social work professor and clinician who is a trauma specialist and expert witness of torture survivors, in their discussion of the emotional challenges to credibility. They turn to legal pragmatism as a way to resolve the problems introduced by an emphasis on legal formalism. Legal pragmatism places the decision maker in the role of a problem solver, drawing on experts and methods from other social science and the field of health care and therapeutics. Embracing the messiness and open-endedness of fact patterns, the decision maker is called on to examine inconsistencies in the context of the asylum applicant.

Inconsistencies emerge from a broad spectrum of contexts, and subfields and new scholarly trajectories have arisen in tandem with the expanding dependency on expertise. In the Global North there has been a heightened emphasis on identity determinations as part of both post-9/11 security concerns and as a matter of border protection (e.g., Brouwer 2002). Often having fled without identity papers such as a birth certificate or coming from countries where such documents are either expensive or difficult to obtain, asylum seekers find themselves in detention until a verification of their identity can be made. Identity verification is also necessary as part of the status determination process. Identity determination is an example of the way in which the contours of expertise has been redrawn to fill the need for information. Biological and sociological processes to determine applicant identities raise questions concerning reliability and accuracy. Noé Mahop Kam examines language analysis for determining origin (LADO) in cases where the identity of the asylum seeker is in question. Immigration services use a variety of language analysis techniques when the applicant is unable to present appropriate identity documentation. His chapter analyses the role of audio documents as a key element in LADO and a crucial site causing inconsistency in expert evaluations. The desire to standardize the verification of identity gives way, however, to the complexity of language use as embedded in social relationships and hierarchies. Whereas the presumption is of a direct link between a language and a country or nationality, the language as recorded on a compact disc is revealed to be a power struggle based on negotiations and cultural types. In other words, the problem of sociocultural inconsistencies significantly derives from the shortcomings of the listener.

The question of credibility often hinges on the ability of the listener to hear and to be able to bear witness. Testimony of rape and gender-based violence are particularly problematic. What appear to be inconsistencies are often more a reflection of societal understandings of the rape script where rape victims are expected to have a certain demeanor (Buss 2009). Likewise, what may appear to be "inconsistencies" in a rape narrative may only be inconsistencies within a framework that expects linearity and fails to account for survival mechanisms like fragmented memory of a trauma, as Marton argues. Sexual violence is an important site for examining how experts contribute to resolving sociocultural inconsistencies, and several chapters address different dimensions. Galya Ruffer examines the problem of cultural divides and inconsistencies from the perspective of human rights reports and experts that come to be seen as the official narrative of harm such as that of mass rape in the Democratic Republic of the Congo. She examines how these official narratives undermine individual asylum speakers of rape who find their testimony silenced, ignored, and rejected through the asylum process. In asylum cases that involved rape survivors, Marton realized that some barriers to obtaining asylum unmistakably stemmed from how the consequences of rape – the very persecution for which the applicant was seeking relief – conflicted with the evidentiary requirements of the legal system in which asylum cases are adjudicated. She considers the issue of addressing inconsistencies and the concern that the level of detail a rape victim must provide in order to be heard comes at the price of retraumatization. She examines the role of mental health professionals who can become part of a legal team representing rape and ways in which an interdisciplinary approach can reduce harm and encourage empowerment and healing.

Although experts contribute to resolving the internal inconsistencies in asylum seekers' personal narratives of persecution and suffering, they are also called upon to resolve any external inconsistencies about the situation in the country of origin. In an attempt to forestall the introduction of new inconsistency between cases from the same country or similar contexts of persecution, a number of countries have deployed considerable resources toward establishing COI research directorates. Although COI data figures importantly in RSD procedures generally, there are important national differences in how it is produced and used. Good's chapter analyses the use of COI in British asylum decision making, drawing on field research in the courts and the experience of acting as a "country-expert" in over five hundred appeals involving Sri Lankan asylum applicants. Good highlights the tensions between the expectation that experts will be objective toward the evidence in their duty to help judges reach decisions and the adversarial legal process where the lawyers representing asylum applicants are routinely solely responsible for hiring experts. His chapter raises the question of whether expert testimony is "objective" or, in the processes of contextualization, interpretation and construction, "subjective." The United Kingdom has recently adopted criteria for assessing COI that includes "accuracy, independence, reliability, objectivity, reputation, adequacy of methodology, consistency and corroboration," but there is not consistency in how courts apply these criteria across countries or what a factual assessment ought to entail as a matter of a well-theorized legal approach to COI.

Through the examination of sociocultural inconsistencies certain themes emerge and we are able to offer recommendations on how experts might best contribute to the refugee status determination process. Experts are best employed when they are part of an interdisciplinary team contributing to a range of knowledge upon which a decision maker can draw.

THE PRACTICES AND TECHNOLOGIES FOR MEDICO-PSYCHO EXPERTISE

Part II examines the rapid expansion of the deployment of psychological, psychiatric, physiological, medical, and pharmaceutical expertise in refugee determination, and its implication in the development of new practices and technologies for the adjudications of asylum seekers. Until the 1980s, at least

according to Didier Fassin and Estelle d'Halluin, claimants operated within a
climate of "trust, in which the applicant was presumed to be telling the truth."
Today, however, claimants must represent their concerns within "a climate of
suspicion," one "in which the asylum seeker is seen as someone trying to take
advantage of the country's hospitality" (Fassin and d'Halluin 2005, p. 600).
Whereas several decades ago, the production of a medical report documenting
the physical signs of torture was exceptional in an asylum tribunal, today
torture claims are routinely accompanied by medical expertise as "the
evidence of truth" (Fassin and d'Halluin 2005, p. 598).

Medico-psycho matters provide a powerful and personal lens with which
to scrutinize the unfolding relationship between experts and adjudicators
because of perceptions of the lopsided impact of expert reports. The former
vice president of the U.K. Immigration Appeal Tribunal, John Barnes,
argued the "grave responsibilities" of the expert are reinforced by the less
adversarial context of RSD as much as the fact that the U.K. government
rarely has access to country background information beyond that produced
by the "frequently inaccurate and misleading" Country Information Policy
Unit, or in the absence of a report, the U.S. State Department reports (Carver
2003; Barnes 2004, p. 352). Whereas "there will almost always be other
evidence" about country conditions, according to Barnes, there is "no
similar breadth of evidence to assist in the evaluation of expert medical
evidence" (Barnes 2004, p. 354). Barnes distinguishes between medical
evidence of past events, e.g. torture, and evidence for future treatment, for
example, psychotropic medication. The "relevant competence" to make
expert claims about a particular scar, for example, can be considered
"corroborative testimony" (Barnes 2004, p. 355). By contrast, future treatment needs and mental state, coupled with the impact of forced removal,
constitute much greater "problems" for the judiciary. Barnes looks very
cynically at psychiatric expert reports which appear to be commissioned
upon threats of deportation by those who "have no realistic prospect of
showing that return to their own country will lead to any reasonable likelihood of persecution." Venturing into jurisprudence, Barnes asserts that the
mere fact that a medical or psychiatric treatment is "clinically desirable"
does not in and of itself enjoin a humanitarian claim of refugee protection
(Barnes 2004, p. 356).

Medico-psycho matters are also fascinating sites of study for the dialectical
relationship because of the subjective nature of much of the evidentiary base,
such as trauma, stress, and memory. Juliet Cohen's (2001) analysis of
patterns whereby credibility is doubted or diminished based on perceptions
about incorrect or poor memory is particularly illuminating in this regard.

Adjudicators tend to be quite skeptical of incidents described in later interviews with claimants, not mentioned in the first instance. This tendency is at
odds with the UNHCR Handbook, which notes:

> While an initial interview should normally suffice to bring an applicant's
> story to light, it may be necessary for the examiner to clarify any apparent
> inconsistencies and to resolve any contradictions in a further interview, and
> to find an explanation for any misrepresentation or concealment of material
> facts. Untrue statements by themselves are not a reason for refusal of refugee
> status and it is the examiner's responsibility to evaluate such statements in the
> light of all the circumstances of the case. (UNHCR 2011, p.199)

Indeed, Cohen surveys memory research to demonstrate that memories of past
persecution and trauma are very likely to change after repeated recollection.
Memories are rarely detailed, accurate, and consistent across successive
reports. Perhaps even more important for our study here, the interrogative
limited detail closed questioning framework, which is often the basis for the
first interview with a refugee, has been shown to cause shifting responses under
repeated questioning (Cohen 2001, p. 296).

Perceptions about the medical and psychological state of the asylum applicant filter into decision making, and the rapid escalation in the submission of
medico-psycho expert reports is directly tied to the unscientific assertions of
adjudicators subsequently challenged by refugees' legal counselors. Barnes
infamously claimed that appellate immigration judges had their "own level of
expertise" including a capacity to consider and evaluate medical reports
(Barnes 2004, p. 349). Good (2004a) and Jones and Smith (2004) pushed
back against this blurring of the "separation of roles," reminding us that
"credibility rests significantly on the testimony of the claimant" (Jones and
Smith 2004, pp. 381–3). Although few adjudicators possess the requisite
medical or psychological training to disentangle the effects of torture, sleep
deprivation, or rape, for example, on the ability of an Iraqi woman to narrate
the details of her persecution, the "tension" of the assessment system within
which they operate demands that they do precisely this, and not infrequently
deliver "nonsense" assessment of claims (Jones and Smith 2004, pp. 386, 396).
On the one hand, adjudicators openly react with skepticism to claims of, for
example, post-traumatic stress disorder (Barnes 2004). By contrast, studies
suggest that asylum seekers massively underreported the actual incidence of
conditions, such as post-traumatic stress disorder (Ramsay et al. 1993).

There is a peculiar irony in the observation that the scientific reports, and
not country conditions assessments, are the site of some of the most intense
contestation between experts and adjudicators. Cohen argues that a detailed

history and examination by an independent medical expert is the "simplest" and "most important element" in the quantification and documentation of conditions affecting memory and thus credibility (Cohen 2001, p. 306). And she concludes that, "there are strong grounds for arguing that lack of consistency *per se* cannot be used to give any negative weight to the assessment of credibility" (Cohen 2001, p. 308). Jones and Smith (2004, p. 397) observe that because the UNHCR states that the benefit of the doubt resides with the claimant, only when "*significant* doubt" arises is the "validity" of the expert report "potentially undermined." Notwithstanding, the increase in evidentiary demands, including forensic medical and psychological expert evidence to bolster credibility and corroborate applicant's testimony of harm and fear, is having unanticipated effects on the asylum adjudication process. The chapters comprising Part II examine a variety of these effects and outcomes via case studies of practices and technologies. One consequence of the increasing reliance on expertise is the emergence of collaborative relationships between medical experts and asylum lawyers. Sabrineh Ardalan's chapter considers this new collaborative arrangement as an important site for scrutiny; these individuals see their respective work and view "evidence" through different optics. Psychological and medical expertise differ in their approach to diagnosing and treating injuries, trauma and other conditions, but the collaboration with legal professionals is now an essential element of the asylum process.

Another key impediment to the effective representation of asylum and refugee claims is the availability of skilled medical and psychiatric personnel. Chelidze et al. also address the collaborative arrangement between experts and legal counsel from the perspective of the training of medical professionals. Their chapter addresses an important ethical dimension, namely, the intersection of training and testifying. They demonstrate that barriers that inhibit the use of medical expert testimony, such as lack of trained evaluators, varying quality of written medical affidavits, and minimal to nonexistent institutional support for providers performing evaluations, should take a backseat to the hands-on training of physicians and clinicians capable of testifying to the physiological markers of torture. By drawing on the widely employed U.S. law school clinic model, the Cornell Weill Center for Human Rights is transforming the role of medical professionals, and expanding the capacity for expertise. The scaling up afforded by the clinic model will also likely provide a platform for the type of macro-analysis of patterns of medical and psychiatric presentation previously unavailable.

Equally frustrating to immigration practitioners is the wide variation in psychological treatment and care for asylum seekers who are victims of brutal violence. Courts and tribunals have played a powerful role in the development of standards and practices associated with the psychological evaluation of asylum seekers. But one unfortunate consequence of the early adoption of standards and regulations for psychological and psychiatric expertise is that standards vary considerably among mental health practitioners and between jurisdictions. Smith, Lustig, and Gangsei endeavor to expand the discourse so that more clinicians and adjudicators speak the same language and work from the proverbial "same page" when considering challenging cases. Their chapter addresses the issue of bias in mental health assessments and the standards in the field of addressing inconsistencies in testimony.

As governments have struggled to counter the deluge of expert testimony in immigration tribunals and courts, they have occasionally overstepped. Within a climate of increasing criminalization of asylum seekers, the use of expert technology to "prove" the nationality of asylum applicants has come under scrutiny. Richard Tutton, Christine Hauskeller, and Steve Sturdy discuss the short-lived Human Provenance Pilot Project (HPPP) of the U.K. Border Agency (UKBA), which aimed to evaluate the possible utility of genetic and isotope testing as means of corroborating asylum seekers' accounts of their nationality. Although the UKBA announced that the tested techniques would not be introduced into asylum procedures, HPPP is emblematic of a wider campaign to subject individuals to biometric and other identification practices established in the treatment of crime suspects. They argue that HPPP needs to be examined against scholarly and lay understandings of basic human rights and a state's responsibility to protect the most vulnerable.

Because government legal counsel in courts and tribunals frequently challenges medical and psychological testimony, the final chapter of Part II examines how country conditions experts may become the last safeguard for a humanitarian protection claim. The U.K. Medical Foundation does not consider reports on medical care availability to be "medical evidence." Without "real knowledge of what is available," such a report would be "speculative" (Jones and Smith 2004, pp. 398, 405), hence the need for country conditions expert. Benjamin Lawrance examines how migrants pursuing humanitarian protection invoke the poor quality and limited accessibility of medical and psychiatric treatments in their home countries as grounds for refugee status or humanitarian protection with differing degrees of success. Under sustained legal assault by the UKBA, human rights claims become detached from the bio-medical narration of the claimants own deteriorating conditions, but the dynamic role of expert testimony re-tethers the specificity of claims (Lawrance 2013). Lawrance's chapter focuses on the strategies of legal practitioners in the context of the unstable terrain of European human rights law. With important implications for the study of medical humanitarianism, the expert country conditions report is revealed to be a key difference between the experiences of two *causes celèbres* in the United Kingdom.

CONCLUSION

From a global transnational perspective, the asylum determination venue plays a central role in constructing and delimiting the contours of expertise. But it is equally important as a site of innovation in knowledge production. We offer the chapters in *Adjudicating Refugee and Asylum Status* as, what we hope, will become a fruitful and lively discussion of the relationship between adjudicators and experts. There is no question that the role of the expert witness in asylum and refugee assessment has expanded dramatically in recent years. Many of the authors in this volume have served as expert witnesses. Others have served as counselors to claimants or judges in adjudicatory capacities, and have both read and evaluated expert reports, and cross-examined expert witnesses. We have assembled this complex, contrasting and complementary set of essays with the primary goal of scrutinizing this unfolding relationship.

The role of expert witnesses will only continue to expand in asylum adjudication. As more countries adopt regularized screening measures and establish purpose-built tribunals or courts, refugee rights activists will strive to provide greater protection and better representation of asylum applicants' interests. Expert witnessing arose from a perceived need on the part of RSD adjudicators to address questions beyond their areas of specialization and knowledge. But whereas the UNHCR provided early guidance on how asylum claims should be evaluated, the precise relationship between adjudicators and expert witnesses has been left to individual domestic jurisdiction. One consequence of this has been a varying array of conflicting and sometimes competing mechanisms for the deployment of expert testimony.

This book draws attention to the ways in which the increasing dependence by immigration determination venues is distorting the standards, principles, and methods of establishing the facts of refugee claims as idealized by the UNHCR. Individual authors also provide recommendations about how experts can better assist the refugee status determination process. This collection of essays provides two analytical frameworks for thinking about the expanding role of expert witnesses, focusing on the construction of expertise and the innovation in knowledge production. It is our hope that this will stimulate others to think about asylum adjudication as a critical site for new knowledge about the lived experiences of survivors of trauma and suffering.

REFERENCES

Agamben, Giorgio. 2003. *Stato di Eccezione. Homo Sacer, 2,1.* Turin: Bollati Boringhieri Trans. Kevin Attell as *State of Exception* (2005).

Alexander, M. 1999. "Refugee Status Determination Conducted by UNHCR." *International Journal of Refugee Law* 11.2: 251–89.

Anker, Deborah E. 1990. "Determining Asylum Claims in the United States Summary Report of an Empirical Study of the Adjudication of Asylum Claims Before the Immigration Court." *International Journal of Refugee Law* 2.2: 252–64.

Anker, Deborah E. 1992. "Determining Asylum Claims in the United States: A Case Study on the Implementation of Legal Norms in an Unstructured Adjudicatory Environment." *N.Y.U. Review of Law & Social Change* 19.3: 433–528.

Avery, Christopher L. 1983. "Refugee Status Decision-Making: The Systems of Ten Countries." *Stanford Journal of International Law* 19.2: 235–356.

Barnes, John. 2004. "Expert Evidence – The Judicial Perception in Asylum and Human Rights Appeals." *International Journal of Refugee Law* 16.3: 349–67.

Barutciski, M. 2002. "A Critical View on UNHCR's Mandate Dilemmas." *International Journal of Refugee Law* 14.2–3: 365–81.

Bettinson, V. and Jones, A., 2009. "The Integration or Exclusion of Welfare Rights in the E.C.H.R.: The Removal of Foreign Nationals with H.I.V. after *N. v. U.K.*" *Journal of Social Welfare and Family Law* 31: 83–94.

Blay, Sam and Andreas Zimmermann. 1994. "Recent Changes in German Refugee Law: A Critical Assessment." *The American Journal of International Law* 88.2: 361–78.

Bloomaert, Jan. 2009. "Language, Asylum, and the National Order." *Current Anthropology* 54.4: 415–41.

Bohmer, Carole and Amy Shuman. 2015. "Cultural Silence as an Excuse for Injustice: The Problems of Documentary Proof." In Iris Berger, Benjamin N. Lawrance, Meredith Terretta, Jo Tague, and Tricia Redeker Hepner, eds., African Asylum at a Crossroads: Activism, Expert Testimony, and Refugee Rights. Athens: Ohio University Press.

Brouwer, Evelien. 2002. "Immigration, Asylum and Terrorism: A Changing Dynamic Legal and Practical Developments in the EU in Response to the Terrorist Attacks of 11.09." *European Journal of Migration and Law* 4: 399–424.

Buss, Doris E. 2009. "Rethinking 'Rape as a Weapon of War'." *Feminist Legal Studies* 17.2: 145–163.

Carver, N. 2003. "Home Office Country Assessments: An analysis." London: Research and Information Unit, Immigration Advisory Service.

Chimni, B. S. 1999. "From resettlement to involuntary repatriation: Towards a critical history of durable solutions to refugee problems." UNHCR, New Issues in Refugee Research, Working Paper No. 2.

Cohen, Juliet. 2001. "Questions of Credibility: Omissions, Discrepancies and Errors of Recall in the Testimony of Asylum Seekers." *International Journal of Refugee Law* 13.3: 293–309.

Conroy, Melanie A. 2009. "Real Bias: How REAL ID's Credibility and Corroboration Requirements Impair Sexual Minority Asylum Applicants." *Berkeley Journal of Gender, Law & Justice* 24: 1–56.

CREDO (2013). *Hungarian Helsinki Committee, Credibility Assessment in Asylum Procedures – A Multidisciplinary Training Manual*, Volume 1.

Crépeau, François and Delphine Nakache. 2008. "Critical Spaces in the Canadian Refugee Determination System: 1989–2002." *International Journal of Refugee Law* 20.1: 50–122.

Douzinas, Costas and Ronnie Warrington. 1995. "A Well-Founded Fear of Justice: Law and Ethics in Postmodernity." In Jerry Leonard, ed., *Legal Studies as Cultural Studies*. 197–229. New York: State University of New York Press.

Eastmond, Marita. 1998. "Nationalist Discourses and the Construction of Difference: Bosnian Muslim Refugees in Sweden." *Journal of Refugee Studies* 11.2: 161–81.

Fassin, Didier and Estelle d'Halluin. 2005. "The Truth from the Body: Medical Certificates as Ultimate Evidence for Asylum Seekers." *American Anthropologist*, 107.4: 597–608.

Fassin, Didier. 2012. *Humanitarian Reason: A Moral History of the Present*. Berkeley: University of California Press, 2012.

Foster, Michelle and Jason Pobjoy. 2011. "A Failed Case of Legal Exceptionalism? Refugee Status Determination in Australia's 'Excised' Territory." *International Journal of Refugee Law* 23.4: 583–631.

Fullerton, Maryellen. 2005. "Inadmissible in Iberia: The Fate of Asylum Seekers in Spain and Portugal." *International Journal of Refugee Law* 17.4: 659–87.

Hardy, Cynthia and Nelson Phillips. 1999. "No Joking Matter: Discursive Struggle in the Canadian Refugee System." *Organization Studies* 20.1: 1–24.

Gadamer, Hans-Georg. 1984. "The Hermeneutics of Suspicion," In Gary Shapiro and Alan Sica, eds., *Hermeneutics: Questions and Prospects*, 54–65. Amherst: University of Massachusetts Press.

Galloni, Tania. 2008. "Keeping It Real: Judicial Review of Asylum Credibility Determinations in the Eleventh Circuit After the REAL ID Act." *University of Miami Law Review* 62: 1037–1062.

Goodwin Gill, Guy S. 1999. "Refugee Identity and Protection's Fading Prospect." In Frances Nicholson and Patrick Twomey, eds., *Refugee Rights and Realities: Evolving International Concepts and Regimes*. Cambridge: Cambridge University Press.

Good, Anthony. 2004a. "Expert Evidence in Asylum and Human Rights Appeals: An Expert's View." *International Journal of Refugee Law* 16.3: 358–80.

Good, Anthony. 2004b. "'Undoubtedly an Expert'? Anthropologists in British Asylum Courts." *Journal of the Royal Anthropological Institute* 10: 113–33.

Good, Anthony. 2007. *Anthropology and Expertise in the Asylum Courts*. London: Routledge.

Good, Anthony. 2008. "Cultural Evidence in Courts of Law." *Journal of the Royal Anthropological Institute* 14 (April).

Gorlick, Brian. "Legal Elements in Assessing Claims to Refugee Status." *International Journal of Refugee Law* 15.3: 357–376.

Grossman, Claudio. 2009. "The Normative Value of the Istanbul Protocol." In Susanne Kjær and Asger Kjærum, eds., *Shedding Light on a Dark Practice: Using the Istanbul Protocol to Document Torture*, 11–13. Copenhagen, Denmark: International Rehabilitation Council for Torture Victims.

Haagensen, Jan Ole. 2007. "The Role of the Istanbul-Protocol in the Uphill Battle for Torture Survivors Being Granted Asylum in Europe and Ensuring the Perpetrators Pay." *Torture*, 17.3: 236–39.

Hart, H. L. A. 1961. *The Concept of Law*. Oxford: Oxford University Press.

Hart, H. L. A. 1983. *Essays In Jurisprudence and Philosophy*. Oxford: Oxford University Press.

Hathaway, James C. 1984. "The Evolution of Refugee Status in International Law: 1920–1950." *International and Comparative Law Quarterly* 33.2: 348–80.

Iacopino, V., O. Ozkalipci, and C. Schlar. 1999. "The Istanbul Protocol: International Standards for the Effective Investigation and Documentation of Torture and Ill Treatment." *Lancet* 354 (9184): 1117.

International Association of Refugee Law Judges. 2011. "Guidelines on the Judicial Approach to Expert Medical Evidence." http://www.iarlj.org/general/images/stories/working_parties/guidelines/medicalevidenceguidelinesfinaljun2010rw.pdf. Accessed February 26, 2014.

Jones, David Rhys and Sally Verity Smith. 2004. "Medical Evidence in Asylum and Human Rights Appeals." *International Journal of Refugee Law* 16.3: 381–410.

Jubany, Olga. 2011. "Constructing Truths in a Culture of Disbelief: Understanding Asylum Screening from Within." *International Sociology* 26.1: 74–94.

Kagan, Michael. 2003. "Is Truth in the Eye of the Beholder? Objective Credibility Assessment in Refugee Status Determination." *Georgetown Immigration Law Journal* 17: 367–415.

Kagan, Michael. 2006. "The Beleaguered Gatekeeper: Protection Challenges Posed by UNHCR Refugee Status Determination." *International Journal of Refugee Law* 18.1: 1–29.

Kälin, W. 2003. "Supervising the 1951 Convention on the Status of Refugees: Article 35 and Beyond." In E. Feller, V. Turk, and F. Nicholson, eds., *Refugee Protection in International Law: UNHCR's Global Consultations on International Protection*, 613–666. Cambridge: Cambridge University Press.

Kerns, Susan K. 2000. "Country Conditions Documentation in U.S. Asylum Cases: Leveling the Evidentiary Playing Field." *Indiana Journal of Global Legal Studies* 8.1: 197–222.

Kessler, Amalia D. 2005. "Our Inquisitorial Tradition: Equity Procedure, Due Process, and the Search for an Alternative to the Adversarial." *Cornell Law Review* 90: 1181–1275.

Landsman, Stephan. 1983. "Brief Survey on the Development of the Adversary System." *Ohio State Law Journal* 44: 713–39.

Lawrance, Benjamin N. 2013. "Humanitarian Claims and Expert Testimonies: Contestation over Health Care for Ghanaian Migrants in the United Kingdom." *Ghana Studies*. 15–16: (Special Double Issue, "Health and Health Care") 251–86.

Lawrance, Benjamin N. forthcoming. "De jure? De facto? Denied, Deported: State-Effected Statelessness." In Benjamin N. Lawrance and Jacqueline Stevens, eds., *Citizenship-in-Question: Evidentiary Encounters with Blood, Birthright, and Bureaucracy*. Philadelphia: University of Pennsylvania Press.

Malphrus, Garry. 2010. "Expert Witnesses in Immigration Proceedings." *Immigration Law Advisor* 4.5: 6–10.

McColl, Helen and Johnson, Sonia. 2006. "Characteristics and Needs of Asylum Seekers and Refugees in Contact with London Community Mental Health Teams: A Descriptive Investigation." *Social Psychiatry and Psychiatric Epidemiology* 41: 789–95.

Meffert, Susan M., Musalo, Karen, McNiel, Dale E. and Binder, Renée L. 2010. "The Role of Mental health Professionals in Political Asylum Processing." *Journal of the American Academy of Psychiatry Law* 38.4: 479–89.

Millbank, Jenni. 2009. "'The Ring of Truth': A Case Study of Credibility Assessment in Particular Social Group Refugee Determinations." *International Journal of Refugee Law* 21: 1–30.

Musalo, Karen. 1998. "Ruminations on *In re Kasinga*: The Decision's Legacy." *U.S.C. Review of Law and Women's Studies* 7: 35–37.

Musalo, Karen. 1996. "*In re Kasinga*: A Big Step Forward for Gender-Based Asylum Claims." *Interpreter Releases* 73 (July): 853–67.

Norman, S. 2007. "Assessing the Credibility of Refugee Applicants: A Judicial Perspective." *International Journal of Refugee Law* 19.2: 273–92.

Piot, Charles. 2007. "Representing Africa in the Kasinga Asylum Case." In Ylva Hernlund and Bettina Shell-Duncan, eds., *Transcultural Bodies: Female Genital Cutting in Global Context*. New Brunswick, NJ: Rutgers University Press.

Piwowarczyk, Linda. 2001. "Seeking Asylum: A Mental Health Perspective." *Georgetown Immigration Law Journal*. 16: 155–71.

Ramji-Nogales, Jaya, Schoenholtz, Andrew I. and Schrag, Philip G. 2009. *Refugee Roulette: Disparities in Asylum Adjudication and Proposals for Reform*. New York: New York University Press.

Ramsay, R., C. Gorst-Unsworth and S. Turner. 1993. "Psychiatric Morbidity in Survivors of Organised State Violence Including Torture. A Retrospective Series." *British Journal of Psychiatry* 162: 55–59.

Refugee Review Tribunal (Australia). 2006. "Guidance on the Assessment of Credibility."

Ricœur, Paul. 1965. *Freud and Philosophy: An Essay on Interpretation* [English trans. 1970].

Rose, A. M. 1956. "The Social Scientist as an Expert Witness." *Minnesota Law Review* 40: 205–218.

Rosen, Lawrence. 1977. "The Anthropologist as Expert Witness." *American Anthropologist* 79.3: 555–78.

Rousseau, Cécile, François Crepeau, Patricia Foxen, Francé Houle. 2002. "The Complexity of Determining Refugeehood: A Multidisciplinary Analysis of the Decision-Making Process of the Canadian Immigration and Refugee Board." *Journal of Refugee Studies* 15.1: 43–70.

Shuman, Amy and Carol Bohmer. 2004. "Representing Trauma: Political Asylum Narrative." *Journal of American Folklore* 117: 394–414.

Speed, Shannon. 2006. "At the Crossroads of Human Rights and Anthropology: Towards a Critically-Engaged Activist Research." *American Anthropologist* 108.1: 66–76.

Squire, Vicki. 2009. *The Exclusionary Politics of Asylum*. Basingstoke: Palgrave-Macmillan.

Stewart, David. 1989. "The Hermeneutics of Suspicion," *Literature and Theology* 3(3): 296–307.

Stevens, Dallal. 2010. "Asylum Seekers and the Right to Access Health Care." *Northern Ireland Legal Quarterly* 61.4: 363–90.

Sweeney, James A. 2009. "Credibility, Proof and Refugee Law." *International Journal of Refugee Law* 21.4: 700–26.

Thomas, Robert. 2006. "Assessing the Credibility of Asylum Claims: EU and UK Approaches Examined." *European Journal of Migration & Law* 8: 79–96.

Thuen, Trond. 2004. "Anthropological Knowledge in the Courtroom: Conflicting Paradigms." *Social Anthropology* 12.3: 265–87.

Ticktin, Miriam. 2006. "Where Ethics and Politics Meet: The Violence of Humanitarianism in France." *American Ethnologist* 33.1: 33–49.

Ticktin, Miriam. 2011. *Casualties of Care: Immigration and the Politics of Humanitarianism in France*. Berkeley: University of California Press.

Tuitt, Patricia. 1996. *False Images: The Law's Construction of the Refugee*. London: Pluto Press.

Watters, Charles. 2001. "Emerging Paradigms in the Mental Health Care of Refugees." *Social Science and Medicine* 52: 1709–1718.

UNHCR 1979. *Handbook and Guidelines on Procedures and Criteria for Determining Refugee Status under the 1951 Convention and the 1967 Protocol Relating to the Status of Refugees*. Reissued December 2011, HCR/1P/4/ENG/REV. 3, http://www.refworld. org/docid/4f33c8d92.html. Accessed April 17, 2013.

UNHCR 1998. "Note on Burden and Standard of Proof in Refugee Claims," December 16, 1998.

UNHCR 2013. "Beyond Proof: Credibility Assessment in EU Asylum Systems," May 2013.

Wallace, Rebecca M. M. and Karen Wylie. 2014. "The Reception of Expert Medical Evidence in Refugee Status Determination." *International Journal of Refugee Law* 25: 749–767.

PART I

SOCIOCULTURAL INCONSISTENCY AND THE CONTOURS OF EXPERTISE

1

Reconstructing Babel: Bridging Cultural Dissonance between Asylum Seekers and Adjudicators

Bruce J. Einhorn and S. Megan Berthold

During a particularly contentious asylum proceeding in 2005 over which a United States Immigration Judge presided, the Ethiopian litigant was asked by government counsel in what year she allegedly had been detained and tortured by her country's security police. "Nineteen-ninety five," she replied. The government's counsel went positively apoplectic. "Your Honor," he declared, "she's lying! Lying like a rug. On her written asylum application, she wrote that she had been arrested and beaten in December 2002!" The date-based discrepancy constituted a potentially material inconsistency that threatened to torpedo the litigant's chances of obtaining asylum relief. It was only the intervention of the court's Amharic language interpreter that saved the Immigration Judge from facing a decision that could have sent the asylum seeker for further persecution back in Ethiopia. As the interpreter, herself an Ethiopian immigrant, explained, the ancient, Coptic-based Ge'ez calendar is used as the official calendar in Ethiopia. The Ge'ez calendar has twelve months with thirty days each, and a thirteenth month called Pagume with five or six days, depending on the year. After some not very quick calculations, we all agreed that 1995 as referenced under the Ge'ez calendar referred to December 2002 under ours. The Amharic interpreter's conclusions were confirmed by an expert witness, a political scientist with a specialization in Africa, who, fortunately and with some cajoling from the court, appeared in court at no expense to the asylum seeker. The litigant received asylum, and the government did not appeal the grant. But for the intervention of a cross-culturally fluent interpreter and pro bono expert, a manifest injustice would have befallen an already tormented soul.

When assuming the post of Immigration Judge, Bruce J. Einhorn did so with a not inconsiderable amount of hubris. After all, he was one of the drafters of the United States Refugee Act of 1980, the modern law of asylum. (Unless otherwise stated in this chapter, the words "Immigration Judge" refer to the co-author, Bruce J. Einhorn.) The case of the Ethiopian asylum seeker, however, and many more like it, taught him what legal texts alone could not. They taught him context, tolerance, and the need to recognize that while we may all be created equal, we are surely not the same.

Judge Einhorn has informally calculated that in his 17 years on the immigration bench, he heard cases from 144 different nationalities, including over 36 nationalities of those claiming asylum in the United States. In the course of hearing thousands of asylum cases, he was presented with claims involving over two dozen religions, over fifteen political ideologies, and, perhaps most importantly, over 30 different physical and emotional disorders arising from alleged persecution. The walls of his file cabinets containing his private notes reveal that except for those asylum cases where the majority of the asylum seekers' claims went uncontested (and where the issues for decision involved technical matters such as filing deadlines), about one-half of the asylum grants he issued came after he heard both eyewitness and expert witness testimony. The eyewitness testimony almost always included the testimony of the asylum seekers, usually without the testimony of other fact witnesses. The expert witnesses included physicians, therapists, historians of foreign conflicts, scholars of religion, political science specialists on country conditions, gender specialists, cultural anthropologists, and even linguists with expertise in the idioms of foreign tongues as spoken by different ethnic and educational groups within the same country. In the Immigration Judge's seventeen years on the bench, he only found four proposed experts unqualified to take the stand. He would be ashamed to admit how many marginally competent lawyers he tolerated during those same seventeen years. His experience on the bench with experts led him to retain an expert – whether a healthcare professional or a cross-cultural specialist, a political scientist or an historian – in every single case he has supervised while directing the Asylum and Refugee Law Advocacy Clinic at Pepperdine University in Southern California. In every single clinical case, the client has obtained asylum, and the expert witness has been cited by the adjudicator as an important basis for finding the asylum seeker's claim credible. Judge Einhorn's commitment to encouraging interdisciplinary cooperation in asylum cases between non-legal experts, on the one hand, and advocates and adjudicators, on the other, is complete.

INTRODUCTION

Credibility determinations in asylum hearings often call on the adjudicator to use his or her discretion. Frequently, the asylum officer or immigration judge must do so with only scant documentary evidence available. The lack of available documents has been particularly common in recent years with asylum seekers coming from countries in Africa, the Middle East, Asia, and other parts of the Global South. The testimony of some asylum seekers is fraught with inconsistencies and their demeanor and ability to recount their history of persecution is often compromised in ways that may lead to an adverse credibility determination. Expert witness testimony from trauma, mental health, cultural, and other specialties provide an invaluable source of evidence for immigration judges in asylum hearings that may provide context and explain some of the inconsistencies and unexpected demeanor found in respondents. Immigration judges must reach into disciplines outside their own formalist understanding of the law in order to fight cultural dissonance in asylum proceedings and understand and rule on the claims of the traumatized asylum applicants they encounter in court.

This chapter explores the benefits of expert witness testimony in mediating the cultural and emotional challenges to credibility from the perspectives of a retired Federal Immigration Judge, now a professor of international refugee and U.S. immigration law, a director of a law school clinic for the representation of indigent asylum seekers, and an author of the modern U.S. law on asylum, and from a social work professor and clinician who is a trauma specialist and has served as an expert witness in many asylum hearings of torture survivors. Those benefits include a clearer cross-cultural competency on the part of asylum adjudicators, which then leads to a clearer comprehension of the claims of asylum seekers. Avoiding cultural misunderstandings eliminates a cultural imperialism whereby Western judges impose a credibility checklist on litigants who demonstrate physical and verbal expressions that require expert interpretation to be accurately assessed. Without the intervention of cultural and country experts and therapists to explain the context of an asylum seeker's communications to those who represent her and those who judge her, her case may be doomed by the confusion of counsel and court. Additionally, frustrations on the part of lawyers and adjudicators may occasion an anger by both that may constitute a grave assault on the dignity and health of a litigant already injured and traumatized by her experiences in her homeland. In short, without cross-cultural competency, those who seek refuge from persecution – such as the Ethiopian woman from the Immigration Judge's own courtroom experience – may well be persecuted again, however unintentionally, by our own justice system. This chapter will enrich the dialogue on the legal basis of credibility and the substantiation and proof of torture and other persecution claims.

THE CHALLENGE: BUILDING CROSS-CULTURAL COMPETENCY
TO AVOID MISJUDGMENTS OF CREDIBILITY

> So the Lord scattered them abroad from there [Babel] over the face of all the
> earth, and they left off building the city. Therefore its name was called Babel,
> because there the Lord confused the language of all the earth; and from there
> the Lord scattered them abroad over the face of all the earth. (*Genesis* 11:1–9)

In the adjudication of asylum cases, with their potential life-and-death repercussions, we are all truly children of Babel, struggling to overcome the
linguistic, racial, religious, ethnic, sexual/gender, and, in general, the psychological and cultural divides in order to facilitate communication on critical
issues between asylum seekers and asylum judges. At the heart of most asylum
cases is the issue of credibility: if the asylum seeker's testimony and representations are found credible, then s/he is likely to receive refugee status and
protection. However, many factors of psychology and culture (including those
already mentioned as well as past trauma and deep fear and suspicion of
authority figures, such as judges) often cause a disconnect in communication
and comprehension that can and does interfere with fair and full credibility
resolution. Take, for example, the case of the Ethiopian asylum seeker
described earlier in this chapter. Absent the intervention of the interpreter
and the expert witness, there was no feasible way for the litigant to explain the
seven-year discrepancy between the date of her persecution as reported by her
in her written asylum application and the year of the same events as stated by
her in her testimony. When the discrepancy was raised rather vociferously by
government counsel, the asylum seeker appeared utterly confused – almost as
confused as her judge was. Her confusion then gave way to fear, evidenced by
her literally shaking in her winter boots. Absent expert assistance, her physical
distress may have been misinterpreted as the demeanor of a liar caught in the
web of her own deceptions. The lessons of that litigant's case were not lost on
the Immigration Judge as he continued his tenure as an immigration judge.
He also taught that very same lesson to his students in the Asylum and Refugee
Clinic he directed at Pepperdine University School of Law. In training those
students for representing indigent asylum seekers before immigration judges
and other federal government adjudicators, he told and retold the story of the
Ethiopian woman whose case illustrates the need to be culturally sensitive to
what may at first appear to be the muddled and less than credible statements of
clients from backgrounds radically different than those who were tasked with
advancing their claims. In many, many cases in immigration court, however,
cultural misunderstandings caused by a lack of cross-cultural competency have

remained the norm. The frustration and even anger these misunderstandings occasion toward asylum seekers by adjudicators has been found to account for up to an 1,820 percent difference in grant/denial rates of asylum between judges deciding similar claims even in the same city (Ramji-Nogales, Schoenholz, and Schrag 2011).

The challenge is, therefore, to figure out how the asylum adjudication system can best mediate these psychological and cultural factors in order to promote clearer communication, comprehension, and fairer and more consistent credibility determinations. That challenge is made more critical by the existence of the REAL ID Act, which allows, and even encourages, immigration judges to find asylum seekers lacking in credibility even if the discrepancies or miscomprehensions in their responses refer to matters ancillary to their asylum claims. Sadly, the REAL ID Act has been used as a crypto-diagnostic tool by legal professionals, most of whom lack the requisite medical and scientific expertise to explain the imperfections in testimony of the alleged victims of persecution in anything but negative and discrediting terms. The same legal professionals are often unfamiliar with the jurisprudential philosophy of pragmatism, articulated in the work *The Growth of the Law* and other writings by the late, great U.S. Supreme Court Justice Benjamin Cardozo, which acknowledges and even demands the assistance of such medical and scientific expertise. These legal professionals also often lack the training necessary to having the cultural sensitivity necessary to a compassionate comprehension of the confused but often credible representations of asylum seekers. Far too many of Judge Einhorn's colleagues on the immigration bench have admitted to him that they continue to insist on applying the formalistic and rigid philosophy that because it is the asylum seeker who must advance her claim for asylum relief, she must overcome any communication problems without adjudicators having to engage in extralegal, interdisciplinary habits, and without encouraging much less recruiting expert witnesses to bridge cultural divides. The rigidity of far too many adjudicators, and their sad lack of curiosity, is inadequate to the task at hand – to judge the credibility of those whose language and demeanor were shaped by experiences different than those learned in the comfortable cloisters of law libraries.

Examples abound in relevant litigation from courts other than Judge Einhorn's own of the "credibility gap" caused, not by deliberate deceit or willful misrepresentation but, rather, by the impact of psychological stress and/or cultural differences on asylum seekers in their attempts to communicate with asylum adjudicators. In one case, for example, a woman seeking asylum in the United States and born in the African nation of Togo, Fauziya Kassindja, was interviewed by an asylum officer of the U.S. Department of

Homeland Security (DHS). During the interview, Kassindja, who was schooled in Ghana, confused the configuration (but not the colors) of the flag of the country of birth with that of her country of education. She also had problems drawing the Togo flag while her hand was shaking. With no concern for whether Kassindja's partial problem with these peripheral matters of memory was occasioned by repression, dissociation, trauma, or just a bad case of nerves, the asylum officer accused the asylum seeker of not being from Togo but, rather, from being from – of all countries – Nigeria (Chaudhary 2010). It is a shame that posterity neither tested nor recorded whether the asylum officer, who did not carry the physical and emotional baggage of a persecuted person, could describe and draw the flag of her own agency, DHS. The authors would be prepared to wager real money that the answer is no.

In another case, *Mousa v. Mukasey*, 530 F.3d 1025 (9th Cir. 2008), an Iraqi Chaldean Christian, was denied asylum by both the U.S. Immigration Judge (IJ) and the U.S. Board of Immigration Appeals (BIA), despite her testimony "that she and her family members . . . had been harassed and pressured to join [Saddam Hussein's] Ba'ath party, and that she and her brother [had been] imprisoned in a Ba'ath Party compound for forty-seven days," during which time she was raped by the party's representatives. Both the Judge and the Board found as a fatal flaw in Mousa's credibility her failure to mention her rape on her pretestimonial, written asylum application. However, the U.S. Court of Appeals for the Ninth Circuit reversed those findings, noting that "the assumption that the timing of a victim's disclosure of sexual assault is a bellwether of truth is belied by the reality that there is often delayed reporting of sexual abuse." In remanding Mousa's proceedings and concluding that her claim of rape was a credible one, the Court of Appeals added that "[m]any victims of sexual assault feel so upset, embarrassed, humiliated, and ashamed about the assault that they do not tell anyone that it occurred." The Court of Appeals cited evidence that the lower courts ignored that emphasized that the psychology behind the reluctance to report rape becomes more pronounced when the country of the sexual assault – in this case, Iraq – is one "where reported rapes often go uninvestigated, and where rape victims are sometimes murdered by members of their own families because they have 'dishonored' their families by being raped." The Court of Appeals concluded that in addition to her demonstrated psychological stress, "Mousa provided a compelling explanation for her failure to mention her rape at an earlier time in the proceedings: her cultural reluctance to admit the fact that it had occurred." In the end, Mousa received asylum – but only after years of anguish while her case was appealed and appealed.

Still another example of psychological and cultural dissonance may be found in the case of *Zhou v. Gonzales*. Zhou had applied for asylum because of his opposition to the Chinese government's policies of coercive population control. Both the IJ and the BIA found against Zhou's claim and his credibility. The IJ concluded that Zhou had testified inconsistently about whether he and his wife suffered forced sterilization in China. The U.S. Court of Appeals for the Second Circuit disagreed, however, and in remanding the proceedings found that "this purported inconsistency appeared to be the result of a translation error rather than an attempt to mislead the IJ." More specifically, the Second Circuit cited to what it regarded as "a nonsensical translation of Zhou's testimony on this exact point: 'I said they forced me to be sterilized and had not been sterilized.'" The Second Circuit then proceeded to criticize the IJ for relying on the translation to reject Zhou's credibility rather than reject the interpreter." The Circuit Court concluded its criticism of the IJ by observing that his adverse credibility determinations "seemed to reflect a lack of cultural sensitivity by treating what were obvious translation difficulties as evasiveness that 'flavored the entire hearing'." Once again, cultural miscommunication led to erroneous findings of fact and years of corrective litigation (Einhorn 2010).

Like every immigration judge, Bruce Einhorn was tasked with proofing for grammatical and spelling accuracy the transcripts of the hearings over which he presided. However, most immigration judges do not take the time (of which they have precious little) to compare the audio recordings of hearings with the resulting transcripts of those hearings. Judge Einhorn did, at first mainly out of intellectual curiosity. However, his curiosity soon turned into concern. In a real sense, transcripts do not always translate the formal record of hearings into the heated passions, contentions, and conflict that constitute the real and relevant substance of courtroom hearings. Although the editorial mistakes in the transcripts were generally minor and easily subject to correction, the differences between the "feel" of the paperwork and the sound of the recordings, with all the levels of nuance revealed by the latter, were remarkable. Invariably, in hotly contested asylum cases in which the asylum seekers' credibility was at issue, the transcripts did an injustice to the genuine tone and the demeanor of the litigants, and provided little clues as to any cultural confusion. After seventeen years as an immigration judge, and six years as a clinician supervising law students in their asylum cases, Einhorn is convinced that a failure to pay attention to the sounds and sights of a hearing as it occurs is a recipe for injustice. No subsequent paper review of a case can make up for the failure of an adjudicator to appreciate the intricacies of an asylum hearing as it happens, and recognize, and with the necessary expert assistance seek to correct, the miscommunication problems that come from an abundance of culture and not from a lack of credibility. Cross-cultural competency and attention to the impact of trauma on asylum seekers' testimony cannot be taught by transcript alone. It must be experienced.

IMPACT OF TRAUMA ON TESTIMONY

There are a number of factors that can negatively influence the ability of traumatized asylum applicants to provide a consistent and coherent narrative account of their relevant experiences in their written and/or oral testimony or otherwise testify effectively in immigration proceedings (Herlihy, Jobson, and Turner 2012).[1] A serious and pervasive impediment to fair credibility assessments is the failure of legally trained judges and attorneys to recognize and account for medical injuries such as head trauma. A history of head trauma can compromise an asylum applicant's functioning and ability to testify (Archiniegas et al. 2013; Mollica 2010). The nature of the traumas they experienced, such as acts that leave them feeling ashamed, as well as resulting symptoms of distress and the associated negative impact on their functioning, may also make them less than effective witnesses. The complexity, scope, and severity of the traumas experienced by asylum applicants may make it exceedingly difficult for them to readily or concisely summarize their experiences in any language, which in turn complicates the ability of adjudicators to understand and make their determinations (Bohmer and Shuman 2008; Mollica 2006; Rousseau et al. 2002).

The process of applying for asylum is often quite retraumatizing and compromises the functioning of asylum applicants in their asylum interviews or court testimonies (Herlihy et al. 2012). This is made worse if they are struggling with symptoms of psychological distress and mistrust toward government officials and authorities as a result of their experiences of persecution in their homelands. Having to testify in immigration or other legal proceedings in front of government authorities can trigger reminders of their persecution, instill fear in them, and negatively affect their functioning in court (Berthold and Gray 2011).

When torture and other human rights violations cause individuals to flee their homelands to seek safety elsewhere, they often face significant challenges

---

[1] The observations described throughout this chapter derive from the literature as well as the experiences of the authors and their colleagues in connection with asylum seekers and their hearings before immigration judges and other adjudicators. In addition, observations and conclusions are based on the more than two decades of clinical experience of co-author Dr. Megan Berthold's work with asylum seekers and refugees.

in communicating their experiences to officials. The impact and nature of the trauma itself frequently has a profound effect on the asylum seeker's memory and overall psychological state, as well as their ability to fill out an asylum application, write a declaration, and testify about their experiences. Trauma can alter the applicant's perception of time (affecting their report of time sequence and date) (Terr 1983). The ability to concentrate and accuracy of an applicant's spacial perception may also be negatively affected by trauma (Pynoos and Nader 1989). The perceived coherence of the applicant's persecution story may be negatively affected if they have memory blocks and/or dissociate such that their experience is not integrated and memories are stored as isolated, disconnected fragments of a variety of affective or emotional states and sensory perceptions (Berthold and Gray 2011; Gyulai et al. 2013).

There are many possible sequalae of exposure to trauma (Berthold and Gray 2011; Briere and Scott 2006). Two of the most common psychological outcomes of trauma are post-traumatic stress disorder (PTSD) and depression. Refugees who have resettled in Western countries have been found to be approximately ten times more likely to have PTSD, according to one literature review, than their age-matched counterparts from the general population in the countries where they are residing (Fazel, Wheeler, and Danesh 2005). In a random community sample of Cambodian refugees in the United States traumatized by the Khmer Rouge regime more than two decades earlier, 62 percent had PTSD, 51 percent were depressed, and 42 percent had both PTSD and depression in the previous year (rates six to seventeen times higher than the U.S. national average for adults) (Marshall et al. 2005). PTSD, depression, and comorbid PTSD and depression are the most common diagnoses found in torture survivors, with rates of psychiatric disorders ranging from 14 to 74 percent (Kinzie, Jaranson, and Kroupin 2007), generally higher than the rates of similar conditions in matched nontortured trauma survivors. High rates of suicide have been found in torture survivors and refugees, in particular in those with PTSD. One study of refugees found that 40 percent of those with PTSD had made suicide attempts (Ferrada-Noli et al. 1998).

Clinicians who work with asylum seekers in the United States note that, before engaging in services with them (often in the context of an evaluation for their asylum proceedings), many survivors have not discussed the details of their experiences with others, including family members. Survivors often find it too painful to talk about these experiences (Mollica 2006). In many cultures, mental illness is stigmatizing. Stigma is one factor that contributes to the traditional lack of seeking mental health services unless the situation is extreme. Furthermore, in some communities mental health services, such as those found in the West, do not exist or are not readily available. Thus, many asylum seekers may not have had the opportunity to formally discuss or get help with their traumatic experiences.

Even in the absence of trauma, one's ability to recall details about all aspects of their life experiences tends to be compromised over time (Gyulai et al. 2013). This ability may be further damaged with trauma due, in part, to avoidance and the inability to recall aspects of one's traumatic experiences as a result of the impact of trauma on memory (Brewin 2011). These are two possible and common symptoms of PTSD (Briere and Scott 2006). One of the hallmarks of PTSD for many survivors is going to great lengths to try to avoid reminders of their traumas, including avoiding talking or thinking about one's traumas, generally because they cannot tolerate the distress that results when flooded with traumatic memories and sensations. Trauma survivors who have strong symptoms of avoidance may not have had the opportunity to revisit the details of their traumas or integrate their memories sufficiently to be able to accurately recount them (Gyulai et al. 2013; Mollica 2006). As with any symptom of distress, individual differences exist in the extent to which survivors are distressed and their ability to tolerate their distress and function adequately. The strong desire among many survivors to avoid revisiting their traumas may further challenge their ability to recall and recount relevant aspects of these experiences in an asylum interview or court hearing (Berthold and Gray 2011). Avoiding thinking and talking about their traumas may serve as a self-protective mechanism that enables them to reduce the risk of being flooded with intrusive traumatic memories and minimize their fear and other painful emotional responses to their traumatic experiences. This mechanism can become a strategy for survival, promoting a survivor's ability to function more successfully in their daily life. In order to testify about their traumatic experiences in an asylum hearing or Immigration Court, this survival strategy has to be suppressed. An asylum applicant who has survived significant trauma often will not volunteer distressing material without being asked with particularity and sensitivity about their experiences (Bohmer and Shuman 2008). Moreover, the credibility of such a testimonially reticent asylum applicant often hinges on the expert testimony of a therapist with experience in the treatment of survivors of persecution or torture.

Additional post-traumatic and depression symptoms commonly found in asylum applicants who have been traumatized have also been observed in court settings. These symptoms can interfere with successful courtroom proceedings. Sleep disorders are common in trauma survivors as a result of being persistently on guard and/or having nightmares or intrusive memories that keep them from sleeping. Exhaustion from sleep deprivation can impair the ability of the survivor to testify effectively by leading to or intensifying their irritability, poor concentration, and/or memory loss. Poor concentration is a common symptom of both PTSD and Major Depressive Disorder, conditions that afflict some asylum applicants. Respondents who have difficulty concentrating often struggle to focus on lengthy and complex questioning of the sort they encounter in asylum interviews and court hearings, and may find it challenging to respond with all of the relevant facts. Court personnel, including adjudicators, may be alienated by a respondent's irritability or outbursts of anger in court. Substance abuse, sometimes used to self-medicate and manage a survivor's distress, may also interfere with their performance in court. In the course of recalling and narrating their traumatic experiences in an asylum proceeding, a survivor may experience a flashback, feeling as though he or she is reliving the trauma in the present. Flashbacks can be disruptive to the asylum proceeding and be confusing to adjudicators and trial attorneys who witness them. Asylum applicants who demonstrate partial or intermittent memory loss in court may be perceived by adjudicators to be lying and deemed not credible, unless understood by the adjudicator as evidence of the applicant's symptoms of post-traumatic distress.

Although many traumatized asylum seekers suffer from post-traumatic stress or depression symptoms that could interfere with their functioning in their immigration proceedings, not all survivors of torture or other severe traumas develop these conditions. Even if a traumatized respondent (i.e., asylum applicant) does not meet the full criteria for PTSD or depression, their ability to testify effectively may be compromised by symptoms of their distress such as difficulty concentrating, shame, and difficulty remembering details of aspects of their trauma. These challenges may contribute to the respondent's testimony being found to be not reliable or credible. The consequence of this may result in the survivor being ordered deported back to the country where they fear that they will be persecuted again and, in some cases, tortured and/or killed. Given the gravity and difficulties in some cases of asylum determinations, it is vital that the court be knowledgeable or educated about these issues. In such cases, the immigration judge may find it relevant and helpful to have expert psychological testimony provided by someone who has examined the respondent to help the judge better understand the respondent's functioning and psychological state as related to their life experiences and their demeanor in court (Keast 2005).

IMPACT OF TRAUMA ON MEMORY

In addition to gaining knowledge about the post-traumatic responses that asylum applicants may have, asylum adjudicators will benefit from understanding the different types of memory and how trauma affects memory (see also Chapter 6 in this volume). This knowledge may assist adjudicators in comprehending some of the ways that traumatized asylum applicants present in court and provide insights into alternative explanations for memory deficits and inconsistencies in respondents who they may otherwise find not credible (Gyulai et al. 2013; see also Chapter 8 in this volume).

Autobiographical memories involve a person's recollection of normal everyday events from their personal history. The construction of normal autobiographical memories involves very different mechanisms than traumatic memories and these differences are relevant to a trauma survivor's ability to testify. In a person without significant cognitive impairment due to head trauma or other factors, normal memory involves the construction of a verbal narrative about routine things such as what the person's activities were the day before or what they did on vacation last summer. The construction of this narrative is generally elective and relatively easy and the account includes a clear beginning, middle, and end. An exception to this is when the event is associated with high levels of emotion. In such instances, a person may exhibit impaired memory of a nontraumatic event (Herlihy and Turner 2007). Examining collateral information such as photos of their vacation may help them refresh or update their memory of a nontraumatic event. In cases of normal memory, it is clear to the individual that the event is one that happened in the past (Herlihy and Turner 2006).

In contrast, memories of traumatic events are often experienced by the survivor as current experiences rather than as memories of past events. Although normal memories tend to be intentionally recalled, this is typically not the case with traumatic memories. When a trauma survivor encounters something that reminds them in some way of their past trauma, the memory of this trauma can be automatically triggered or provoked. Traumatic memories involve emotions and sensations, and are sometimes referred to as *implicit* memories. It is not necessary for the trigger to be completely similar to the original trauma. The trigger may only include one or more aspects of the original trauma (e.g., a similar tone of voice, the smell of cologne, or the size of the room). The survivor often is not able to provide a complete verbal narrative of their traumatic experience, at least not initially. Instead, their memory may consist of fragments of sensory impressions, such as smells, tactile sensations, emotional states, sounds, and/or images of the trauma event.

If asked to testify about their experiences of persecution in an asylum proceeding, trauma survivors may find it exceedingly difficult to provide a coherent and consistent verbal narrative account of their experiences in part given that traumatic memories are typically encoded as sensory fragments

(Herlihy et al. 2012). Traumatic memories are commonly triggered, and therefore the asylum applicant may recall or emphasize different aspects of their
experience depending on the specific trigger in the asylum proceeding. This
may result in discrepancies in some of the details of the account in their
testimony versus what is contained in their asylum application and declaration. The asylum seeker may only report fragments or impressions of the events
that are likely to evoke similar feelings as those they felt at the time of the
original trauma (Herlihy, Scragg, and Turner 2002). Some of the common
feelings that may be aroused are anxiety, fear, sorrow, anger, guilt, humiliation, and/or shame.

In addition, asylum applicants are sometimes asked questions about aspects
of their experiences that they do not perceive to be salient and are redirected or
cut off when they try to provide testimony about other parts of their experiences deemed by the court not to be relevant or responsive to the question at
hand. This can be frustrating and confusing for the survivor, especially when
they are asked to speak about details that seem out of context to them or are not
in chronological order. The ability of traumatized asylum seekers to testify
about their traumatic experiences is frequently compromised due to these
factors as well as the inherent stress of the court proceeding, including having
to testify in front of powerful officials.

Research conducted in London with those who had already been granted
refugee status concluded that inconsistencies in the details of the traumatic
events are commonly found among torture and other trauma survivors with no
reason to fabricate or embellish an account for secondary gain (Herlihy and
Turner 2006). Furthermore, these inconsistencies were particularly common
among those who suffered from PTSD, the longer the time between interviews, when the person had suffered multiple traumas in which there are some
commonalities across incidents, for details that the person themselves views as
less central to their experience, and at times when the survivor is under a lot of
stress and is anxious. When recounting a traumatic experience, the trauma
survivor is more likely to focus on details they perceive to be central (e.g.,
major themes that were most meaningful to the survivor, the emotional
content of the narrative, the essence of the experience) rather than on specific
details that in their experience were peripheral (e.g., exactly how many lashes
he or she received during a whipping, the exact number of people in the mob
who beat them, every question they were asked during an interrogation, and
the exact order of the questions). Asylum applicants may struggle when asked
to provide details that were peripheral to their experience of the events.
Asylum adjudicators may have a different impression or opinion about what
should have been central to the survivor's experience, and thus able to be

remembered and recounted in court. An adjudicator may easily come to an erroneous conclusion about the applicant's credibility if they rely on their own benchmark regarding what is central or reasonable to recall by trauma survivors. Herlihy and Turner's (2006) research findings led them to conclude that adjudicators should not assume that asylum seekers are fabricating histories of trauma and persecution solely on the basis of discrepancies between interviews, even when the interviews take place only weeks apart. Asylum applicants who have been subjected to the most severe trauma may appear as the most incredible to asylum adjudicators. A seemingly vague response by an asylum applicant to a question about important elements of their claim may be perceived to be lying to the adjudicator when the applicant's vague response may be due to their attempts to avoid talking about painful aspects of their trauma or a reflection of dissociation.

Dissociation is "a failure to integrate aspects of identity, memory, perception, and consciousness" (Spiegel 1997, p. 225). Information about one's trauma that is dissociated is unavailable to consciousness at that time, yet the person can become distraught when exposed to something that shares some similarity with the original trauma (Spiegel 1991). Asylum applicants may have dissociated during and for some time after their traumatic experiences as a type of psychological protection mechanism. In doing so, their experience of the trauma would be stored in their memory as disconnected, isolated fragments of sensory perceptions and emotional states. They may not be able to consciously remember or recount some or all aspects of their trauma as a result, including aspects that the adjudicators believe is most salient to the asylum proceedings. This problem may be made worse when the person dissociates in court. Their distress may present in the form of a flashback, as difficulty concentrating on the proceedings, blanking out, getting lost in a trance-like state, or sometimes as a state of speechless terror. Any of these reactions could have a negative impact on the asylum applicant's ability to testify in court.

Trauma can have an impact on the memory of survivors many years after the original trauma, due to symptoms of persistent posttraumatic dissociation or other distress. When trauma memories are reactivated, such as when respondents testify in their asylum proceedings, those who have a history of dissociation may unconsciously use this protective mechanism again to try to reduce their level of psychological distress during the hearing (Briere 2004). Testifying about one's traumatic experiences is a situation that tends to invoke high arousal and defensive strategies in the survivor in an attempt to address this activation of distress. This is especially common if the survivor is feeling threatened such as during aggressive cross examination reminiscent of interrogation they may have gone through during torture, or if the accuracy of their memories or veracity of their experiences is questioned. Trauma and its after effects can influence what an asylum applicant reveals and does not disclose. Post-traumatic symptoms in an applicant who was raped, for example, may lead them to not initially include the rape in their application (Bohmer and Shuman 2008; see also Chapter 4 in this volume).

CULTURAL CHARACTERISTICS AND CONTEXT

In addition to the impact of trauma on memory and disclosure, cultural characteristics and context play a big role in shaping what information is shared and with whom, as well as the presentation of asylum seekers in court proceedings. The context refers to the meaning and consequences of the trauma in the socio-political-historical-cultural-spiritual setting of the survivor. In a society and culture that blames the survivor of a rape, such as in the experience of many torture survivors served by one of the authors, it is not uncommon for the survivor who is seeking asylum to leave his or her experience of rape out of his or her initial asylum application or testimony – even more so if the survivor's religious or spiritual tradition deems them to be a sinner for having sex outside of the context of marriage, even in the instance of rape. For example, one Ethiopian woman explained to her social work clinician, one of the authors, that she could not face what she knew would happen if she mentioned her rape in her asylum application. The woman stressed that if others from her community knew of her rape she would be ostracized, it would bring shame to her family, and her husband would leave her. Within her context, that would ruin her and her family members' future prospects for leading a safe and secure life of dignity and respect. She feared being blamed if her father's business lost customers and if her siblings could not find anyone to marry them due to her bringing disgrace upon them. If an applicant's previously undisclosed rape is later revealed in the asylum process, the applicant's credibility often is called into question. Reports or testimony from experts may be able to shed light on why the applicant acted as he or she did and why this is one common response found in rape survivors from the applicant's culture and society.

An expert needs to consider the various ways that an applicant's experiences and account of their experiences are culturally and contextually constructed, including regarding the expression of persecution, grief, tragedy, and their exile, as well as how their accounts can be influenced by the bureaucratic and legal culture of the immigration proceedings and administrative structures (Shuman and Bohmer 2004). Although members of a given cultural group share certain cultural characteristics, there can be individual differences between members of that culture including in their cultural beliefs, practices, and the meaning and ways of relating their experiences of various events. In addition, there can be significant individual differences between cultures in the expression of distress. It can be risky to make assumptions or interpret the applicant's demeanor and behavior based on one's own life experience or cultural lens. Unless these factors are presented by an expert in a way that is understandable to adjudicators not trained about trauma, memory, or culture or in such disciplines as psychology, social work, or anthropology, the asylum adjudicator may come to an erroneous credibility determination that may lead to the applicant being ordered deported.

EXPERT TESTIMONY FROM THE PERSPECTIVE
OF THE ADJUDICATOR

Expert witnesses should keep in mind the perspective of the asylum adjudicator when approaching their assessment and preparing their testimony. Most helpful to the asylum adjudicator is when a psychological trauma expert can assess the particular asylum applicant and discuss the relevance and impact of factors such as trauma and memory on him or her, both in terms of possible evidence of persecution but also related to issues that may be taken into consideration when the adjudicator makes a credibility determination for that applicant. One of the areas that may be useful for a psychological trauma expert to document and testify about is the applicant's demeanor. A number of factors can affect the asylum applicant's demeanor and presentation in asylum proceedings, such as the applicant's life experiences, type or extent of education, historical and societal context, culture, personality, and coping strategies (see Rousseau et al. 2002).

An example drawn from research and work with Cambodian refugees will be used to illustrate this concept. During the genocidal reign of the Khmer Rouge in Cambodia from 1975 to 1979, Cambodians learned very quickly that it was dangerous to express any emotion, even in the face of seeing their loved ones taken off to be killed or die in front of them. They typically were forced to leave their loved one's corpse and go to work rather than being allowed to bury them. Generally, they were also not allowed to properly mourn their dead. Numerous unmarked mass shallow graves accumulated throughout Cambodia during this time. Cambodians learned that they might be beaten or killed if they showed anger or other strong emotions. Many of the Cambodians who were able to survive the Khmer Rouge regime, some as young children during formative stages of their development, trained themselves not to cry. They learned to be "blank" (completely numb with blunt affects) in order to avoid punishment or death. Some Cambodian survivors, including those treated by one of the authors, describe that they had to train themselves not to feel and become the "walking dead" in order to survive. The fall of the Khmer Rouge in 1979 did not bring an end to trauma for many Cambodians and the survival coping mechanisms they learned over the nearly four years of the Khmer Rouge reign persisted for many survivors.

At present, more than thirty years after the Khmer Rouge were defeated by the Vietnamese and thrown out of power, some Cambodian survivors of the Khmer Rouge regime have attained a sufficient sense of safety and stability that enables them to fully feel and express their emotions. Other survivors, however, have not achieved this state. If called on to testify in front of an asylum officer or in immigration court about their traumatic experiences, they may appear emotionally numb as they speak about their traumatic experiences, appearing distant and detached from their emotions. Their old defense mechanisms that served them well and protected them during the Khmer Rouge regime may not be adaptive in the face of the stress and threat they perceive in their asylum proceeding. Their demeanor may lead the adjudicator to erroneously conclude that they did not experience the events they are describing. One of the authors has witnessed several immigration judges question an applicant's credibility, or find them not credible, because they recounted their traumatic experiences with a flat or blunt affect and emotionally numb demeanor. These judges indicated that the applicant did not emote as much as they thought a person would or should if they had actually experienced the traumatic events they recounted. A psychological trauma expert who has examined the applicant can weigh in on his or her particular demeanor and response to recounting their traumas. In some cases, the expert may note a given person's variable demeanor at different times of revisiting their traumas.

Not all traumatized asylum seekers will appear numb or detached during their trauma proceedings. Some may have considerable difficulty containing or controlling their strong emotions if asked about their traumas or the consequences of those experiences during an evaluation session with a mental health expert or in court. They may display intense overt signs of physiological suffering and distress as they struggle to verbally articulate their experiences of trauma. This type of reaction is likely to be more commonly expected or understood by an asylum adjudicator. Some immigration judges, however, in cases that one of the authors was involved with as an expert, have made comments that in their opinion a visibly distraught asylum applicant was acting hysterical or overly emotional. In such cases, the adjudicator may believe the applicant is making up or embellishing his or her account of trauma and/or the consequences for some kind of secondary gain. The judge may conclude that any of the types of demeanor described here demonstrates that the person is lying.

Trauma professionals, by contrast, understand that a trauma survivor may not behave as one would expect them to, especially under the stressful conditions of a court hearing or asylum interview. The various demeanors described here are possible post-traumatic reactions and need to be considered in the context of the asylum applicant's psychological condition, history, and ability to regulate their emotions under stress. Differences may manifest across and within individuals in terms of their demeanor over time and in different contexts when recounting a trauma story. An expert witness may have observed an asylum applicant display various demeanors during the course of their psychological evaluation of the applicant and can testify about this in court.

The cases described here illustrate that, among Western adjudicators of asylum claims, "[t]he attitude of decision makers and the techniques used to discredit and disbelieve applicants' testimony has been especially problematic" (Sweeney 2009, p. 702). It is as if those adjudicators have an "agenda of disbelief" (Ensor, Shah, and Grill 2006). This mind-set does not arise in a vacuum but, rather, comes from the jurisprudential philosophy of "legal formalism."

LEGAL FORMALISM

The "classic" view employed by judges in their decision-making processes, in immigration law and elsewhere, is one of formalism – also known as the casebook method of legal reasoning, taught in virtually all U.S. law schools. Formalism, also called legal fundamentalism, holds that from a set of legal precedents, that is, of written and published court opinions under the same set of statutes, is distilled a general set of rules and a specific judgment in a specific case-in-controversy. In such a case, judges and lawyer-advocates should examine previously decided cases for those that are similar to the controversy at bar, and then how they should affect resolution of the present proceedings. Judges should then rely on the previous sources and the arguments of counsel in deciding the case-in-controversy. Put another way, formalism states that once a previously decided case is found similar to one in controversy, legal reasoning is a matter of drawing a logically valid deduction from the former's statement of the law (the major premise) and then applying it to the facts of the latter (the minor premise). Legal formalism is precedent-intensive and is predicated on a very insular and rationalistic view of legal institutions. Formalism originated with the preindustrial, prepluralistic development of the English common law and is very much in play in all English-speaking countries such as the United States (Scalia 1989).

The major problem with a fair and professional determination of credibility in asylum cases – one that incorporates mediating tools from the medical, psychological, and cultural communities – lies with the limits that judges impose on themselves in their conscious or almost otherwise mechanical application of the formalist model in their assessment of litigant claims.

THE WEAKNESSES OF FORMALISM IN AN ASYLUM CONTEXT

Formalism is a very "pretty" and "pleasing" form of legal reasoning. It is self-satisfying because it is academically rigorous but almost monastically removed from other disciplines and the larger, messy, and often irrational choices of humankind (Sim 2004). Like fundamentalist theology, legal formalism is a closed system of strict, almost absolute adherence to precedent as revealed truth (Thomas 2006). The pioneer legal pragmatist and Supreme Court Justice Oliver Wendell Holmes Jr. called formalism's obsessive reliance on precedent "the hobgoblin of small minds" (Mendenhall 2012). Formalism's parochial approach harkens back to a more uniform profession and a simpler, less diverse culture. In short, it is not equipped to deal with the legal and factual complexities and the cultural clashes of the immigration system (Einhorn 2010).

Specifically, a formalistic approach to asylum adjudication ignores the critical element of *context* – that is, the psychological and cultural factors that make asylum cases unique and render ineffective the insular abstractions of the casebook method. A strict adherence to precedent, and an overly strict application of the REAL ID Act, without the mediation of context provided by expert psychocultural testimony and an interdisciplinary worldview for judges, almost guarantees that communication challenges will always be deemed evidence of deception or at least insufficient credibility in asylum proceedings, where asylum seekers, no matter how traumatized and foreign to Anglo-American norms, bear the burden of proof. For example, the peasant farmer from Central America who averts his eyes from the immigration judge while testifying about his alleged persecution may be deemed incredible under the REAL ID Act because of his "suspicious" demeanor, when in fact his refusal to look at the court officer may be a cultural gesture of respect. More complex examples exist and are subject to wholesale misconstruction under a formalist mind-set (Ramji-Nogales, Schoenholtz, and Schrag 2011). Such a mind-set makes it difficult for Western adjudicators to appreciate the "[c]ultural factors that have an impact on the construction [and communication] of asylum applicants' narratives" (Shuman and Bohmer 2004, p. 402). Such a mind-set creates problems of understanding that require a pragmatic, not mechanistic, solution.

LEGAL PRAGMATISM AS REMEDY

Legal Pragmatism, which emphasizes experimentation as an arbiter of truth and context as a precondition to truly rational judgments, is an outgrowth of the philosophic school of thought espoused by the educator John Dewey and the post–Industrial Revolution jurisprudential school of legal realism articulated by Supreme Court Justices Holmes and Cardozo.[2] The pragmatic/realist school emphasizes the need for law, lawyers, and judges to look to economics, history, and the social and health sciences in litigating and deciding cases-in-controversy. Pragmatism is antifoundational and antiformalistic, inasmuch as it rejects the proposition that correct outcomes can be deduced from some overarching principle(s). Rather, pragmatism emphasizes *inductive reasoning*, or jurisprudence by problem solving – by trial-and-error, tests, and revisions. Although legal precedents are important starting points in legal analysis, they must often give way to the contemporary and future worldly implications of their applications, particularly where new cultural factors and personalities are present, as in asylum cases from developing nations.

Gone under pragmatism is the cloistered life of the law. The challenges of multiculturalism demand that judges and lawyers end their intellectual isolation and matriculate with other professionals who have different and helpful worldviews. The ancient regime of legal formalism must give way to a discipline that employs experts and methods from other social sciences and from the field of health care and therapeutics. Pragmatism accepts and even embraces the messiness and open-endedness of fact patterns, and perforates the insularity of legal reasoning to allow for an interdisciplinary approach to lawyering and judging. For example, to the formalist mind, the REAL ID Act permits the discrediting of an asylum seeker for ancillary misstatements and

---

[2] In his seminal work, *The Growth of the Law* (1924) at 65, Cardozo writes that "we must spread the gospel that there is no gospel [of legal formalism] that will save us from the pain of choosing at every step. There are times when precedents lead to harsh or bizarre conclusions, at war with social needs ... divorced from the realities of life. In such junctures, judges would do well to keep before them as a living faith that a choice of methods is theirs in the shaping of their judgments." The Cardozo approach comports with the observation of Roger Cotterrell to the effect that, "law is part of social life ... the centre of gravity of legal development lies not in legislation nor judicial decisions but in society itself" (Cotterrell 2006, p. 29). It also comports with the view of noted legal realist, Karl Llewellyn, insofar as "law needed to be studied at the level of detailed particulars ... the 'law-ways' of groups and subgroups" (Mehrotra 2001, p. 750).

demeanor differences. To the pragmatic mind, the REAL ID Act permits a more positive and nuanced road of reasoning: it allows for the examination of testimonial and representational inconsistencies *in the context* of an alien's culture, religion, gender, and state of mental and physical health. To the formalist, the REAL ID Act narrows the contours of credibility by expanding an emphasis on every small inconsistency of fact telling. To the pragmatist, the REAL ID Act calls for a therapeutic jurisprudence designed to autopsy both the details and the whole of an asylum seeker's story, with the aid of medical and social sciences. For the philosophically pragmatic judge, the REAL ID Act is a starting point, not an end point, to the challenge of credibility adjudication.

This chapter, and indeed this book, is a testament to pragmatism, to the critical application of interdisciplinary studies in advancing fairness in the asylum adjudication process. There are no simple asylum cases, because there are no simple societies or simple people, either among the persecuted or the persecutors. Collaboration among jurists and lawyers, on the one hand, and experts in language, in comparative culture and religion, in international and regional political systems, in gender studies, and in psychotherapy, on the other, is often the only safe method of ensuring that what the asylum seeker intends to share at her hearing is understood in Western courts and adjudicative agencies. Cross-cultural competency through an interdisciplinary approach best affords the truthful asylum seeker – the one whose communication skills are compromised not by deliberate deceit but by differences of background, by physical and emotional damage, and by fear – a fair hearing and a just result. Judges, lawyers, and all professionals involved with asylum seekers need to have the humility to ask for each other's help in achieving the twin aims of fairness and justice for the broken souls who desperately cling to our shores.

PRAGMATISM'S CONCRETE PROPOSAL FOR IMPROVED ASYLUM ADJUDICATIONS IN THE UNITED STATES

Given the need for interdisciplinary collaboration in immigration court, the institutional framework for asylum adjudications in the United States needs to be revamped along pragmatic lines. Judges with a pragmatic bent best suited to hearing asylum cases need to have their court restructured to encourage cross-cultural competency and accommodate interdisciplinary expertises. Currently, there exists a unitary U.S. Immigration Court, which hears all cases of aliens (the unfortunate term used in U.S. law for foreign-born persons) whose removal/deportation the DHS seeks and whose claims for relief (including but not limited to asylum) are heard as part of their proceedings before immigration judges. This framework impractically has the same judges who hear the cases of long-standing resident aliens (many of whom speak English, have at least partial U.S. educational backgrounds, make no claim of past or future persecution, and sometimes possess criminal records) also hear the cases and claims of asylum seekers (who are recent arrivals, speak little if any English, have little or no support system in the United States, generally possess no criminal records, and because of past abuse suffer from medical and psychiatric disorders). Pragmatism as a means to fairness requires that the immigration court be split in two, with asylum cases heard before a special-ized, expert-friendly U.S. Asylum and Refugee Court ("USARC"). USARC judges ought to be trained in the school of Legal Pragmatism, and should be regularly oriented in basic issues of cross-cultural communications, post-traumatic stress disorders and other health consequences of persecution and torture, cultural anthropology, world geography, and current political events. Furthermore, lawyers who seek to represent asylum seekers before the USARC should be required to receive interdisciplinary training as the judges of that court do, in order to facilitate a full presentation of their clients' cases.

The need for such counsel in asylum cases, especially those involving the poorest and most injured and dysfunctional asylum seekers, is as great as the need for specially trained judges. Still, however, at present, there is no con-stitutional or statutory right to counsel in U.S. immigration court proceedings. The 1963 U.S. Supreme Court holding in *Gideon v. Wainwright*, which constitutionally mandates a right to counsel (provided by the government at no fee to the indigent) in criminal cases, should be extended by statute to impoverished asylum seekers. Moreover, counsel seeking to practice before the USARC should be required to undergo the same training and continuing legal and inter-disciplinary education expected of the judges of that Court. Also, given the critical effect expert witnesses may have in asylum cases, the USARC should have the authority to appoint and pay such expert witnesses in cases where asylum seekers are indigent and the issues surrounding refugee eligibility are complex, especially as they relate to matters outside the four corners of the law (e.g., in regard to political science or psychology).

USARC judges may find evidence from experts, whether in the form of documentary evidence or testimony, to be valuable in helping to inform their decisions. Such evidence, for example, may be informative in determining whether or not a respondent has met his or her burden of proof (Malphrus 2010). In addition, the use of evidence from expert witnesses in explaining factors that may compromise an applicant's ability to testify may contribute, in part, as a means to fairer credibility determinations and thus fairer decisions.

All efforts and judicial discretion should be exercised to allow bail or release on one's own recognizance for detained asylum seekers, whose reticence to speak and whose mental states are aggravated by custodial status and stress.

Just as USARC judges should look to the testimony of experts, so should they look to sister institutions in the West that have adopted more enlightened approaches for credibility determinations in cross-cultural settings. For example, the USARC should cast a careful eye on the Canadian system of asylum adjudication, which is heavily engaged in reforms designed to enhance a pragmatic and sensitive approach to asylum cases. Canada's Immigration and Refugee Board (IRB) operates as that country's USARC. The IRB has published an *Assessment of Credibility in Claims for Refugee Protection*, available to both its judges and practitioners, as well as to the public at large. The *Assessment* requires that judges in asylum cases "consider all of the evidence, both oral and documentary [and] not just selected portions of the evidence." Adjudicators are admonished that they "should not selectively refer to evidence that supports [their] conclusions without referring to evidence to the contrary." The *Assessment* additionally warns that in cases "[w]here the claimant provides personal documentary evidence or medical reports, specific to and corroborative of his claim, it is not sufficient to simply make a blanket statement, without explanation, that no probative value was assigned to this evidence because of a general lack of credibility on the part of the claimant." Lastly, the *Assessment* cites a major Canadian appeals case, *Maldanado v. Canada*, which ruled that "[w]hen [a claimant] swears to the truth of certain allegations, this creates a presumption that those allegations are true unless there be reason to doubt their truthfulness." This presumption now enshrined in Canadian law is derived from the United Nations Convention and Protocol on the Status of Refugees and the U.N. High Commissioner for Refugees Handbook on Procedures and Criteria for Determining Refugee Status. The U.S. asylum statute that Judge Einhorn helped draft also tracks the language of the U.N. Convention and Protocol. It is therefore common sense that the Canadian *Assessment* would track the presumption of credibility advocated by UNHCR. It would equally be common sense for U.S. law to do the same. "The [Canadian] *Assessment* is national in scope, and thus supports less deviation and eccentricity in judicial findings on credibility" (Einhorn 2010, p. 163). The United States would be well advised to employ a similar mandate to avoid the wild and cynical swings in credibility assessment that punctuate U.S. asylum adjudications. No credible argument has ever been advanced for not doing so. The absence of a counterargument speaks volumes.

Another source of guidance may be found in the *Asylum Policy Instruction* (API) used in credibility determinations by asylum adjudicators of the United

Kingdom Border Agency, the equivalent of our U.S. Customs and Border Patrol. Specifically, the API's *Assessing Credibility in Asylum and Human Rights Claims* (Asylum Policy Instruction, 2006) provides instructions on examining the internal credibility, external credibility, and plausibility of an asylum seeker's claims. With regard to internal credibility, the API admonishes adjudicators that in addition to the level of detail and the nature and number of inconsistencies in an asylum seeker's testimony, mitigating circumstances must be considered in gauging the witness's credibility. Such mitigating circumstances include "mental or emotional trauma, inarticulateness, fear, mistrust of authorities, feelings of shame, [and] painful memories, particularly those of a sexual nature." With regard to external credibility, asylum adjudicators are instructed to put before the asylum seeker any and all inconsistencies between his testimony and objective country evidence. The asylum seeker should be given the opportunity to account for the inconsistencies before the adjudicator assesses his credibility. The API also cautions the adjudicator that the absence of objective country conditions in support of a testimonial claim by an asylum seeker does not necessarily mean that such a claim is untrue. Lastly, with regard to plausibility, the API reminds the adjudicator not to measure the credibility of the asylum seeker's claims against what would be plausible in the United Kingdom. In short, the setting for the asylum hearing should not be substituted for the actual setting in which the asylum seeker's story arises. Adjudicators must never ask whether they believe the asylum seeker; rather, they must only determine whether there is a reasonable basis for the asylum seeker to be believed (Kagan 2003).

A pragmatic approach to credibility determinations makes for a fairer and fuller hearing in which asylum seekers, however damaged by their experiences abroad, feel empowered. It is this empowerment that asylum seekers appear to value, even above the outcome of their hearings (Wexler and Winick 1996). It is this empowerment that may improve the dynamic between asylum seeker and asylum adjudicator.

CONCLUSION

The solutions proposed in this chapter to the often serious but correctable misunderstandings between asylum seekers and adjudicators are therefore, at bottom, intended to mediate "the variable of power" that exists between the psychologically and culturally vulnerable former vis-à-vis the latter (Donovan 2008). Our solutions are in keeping with the foundations of American democracy, which have always advanced pluralism and cultural integration. "The national motto, *E Pluribus Unum*, displayed from the republic's start that whatever singularity the nation achieved was to be constructed out of diverse materials" from which emerged "a new, amalgamated people" (Hollinger 2000, pp. 86–87). The writer and philosopher Ralph Waldo Emerson hailed this "asylum of all nations" (Emerson 1909–1914). So do we.

REFERENCES

Archiniegas, David B., Nathan D. Zasler, Rodney D. Vanderploeg, and Michael S. Jaffee, eds. 2013. *Management of Adults with Traumatic Brain Injury*. Arlington, VA: American Psychiatric Publishing.

Asylum Policy Instruction. 2006. *Assessing Credibility in Asylum and Human Rights Claims*. London, United Kingdom: U.K. Border Agency.

Berthold, S. Megan, and Gerald Gray. 2011. "Post-Traumatic Stress Reactions And Secondary Trauma Effects At Tribunals: The ECCC Example." In Beth Van Schaack, Daryn Reicherter, and Youk Chhang, eds., *Cambodia's Hidden Scars: Trauma Psychology in the Wake of the Khmer Rouge*. Phnom Penh, Cambodia: Documentation Center of Cambodia: 92–120.

Bohmer, Carol and Amy Shuman. 2008. *Rejecting Refugees: Political Asylum in the 21st Century*. London/New York: Routledge.

Brewin, C. R. 2011. "The Nature and Significance of Memory Disturbance in Posttraumatic Stress Disorder." *Annual Review of Clinical Psychology* 7: 203–27.

Briere, John. 2004. *Psychological Assessment of Adult Posttraumatic States: Phenomenology, Diagnosis, and Measurement*. 2nd edn. Washington, DC: American Psychological Association.

Briere, John, and Catherine Scott. 2006. *Principles of Trauma Therapy: A Guide to Symptoms, Evaluation, and Treatment*. Thousand Oaks, CA: Sage Publications.

Cardozo, Benjamin N. 1924. *The Growth of the Law*. New Haven, CT: Yale University Press.

Cotterrell, Roger. 2006. *Law, Culture and Society*. Aldershot, UK: Ashgate Publishing.

Donovan, James. 2008. *Legal Anthropology*. New York: Alta Mira Press.

Einhorn, Bruce J. 2010. "The Gift of Understanding." *Albany Government Law Review*. 3:149–68.

Emerson, Ralph. *Journals of Ralph Waldo Emerson (Boston 1909–1914)* 7: 115–16.

Ensor, J., A. Shah, and M. Grillo. 2006. "Simple Myths and Complex Realities – Seeking Truth in the Face of Section 8." *Immigration, Asylum and Nationality Law* 20: 95.

European Council on Refugees and Exiles. 2006. "Guidelines on the Treatment of Iarqi Asylum Seekers and Refugees in Europe." *International Journal of Refugee Law* 18:452.

Fazel, M., J. Wheeler, and J. Danesh. 2005. "Prevalence of Serious Mental Disorder in 7000 Refugees Resettled in Western Countries: A Systematic Review." *Lancet* 365(9467): 1309–14.

Ferrada-Noli, M., M. Asberg, K. Ormstad, T. Lundin, and E. Sundbom. 1998. "Suicidal Behavior After Severe Trauma. Part 1: PTSD Diagnoses, Psychiatric Comorbidity, and Assessments of Suicidal Behavior." *Journal of Traumatic Stress* 11(1): 103–12.

Gideon v. Wainwright. 1963. 372 U.S. 335.

Gyulai, Gabor, Michael Kagan, Jane Herlihy, Stuart Turner, Lilla Hardi, and Eva Tessza Udvarhelyi. 2013. *Credibility Assessment in Asylum Procedures – A Multidisciplinary Training Manual. Volume 1.* Budapest, Hungary: Hungarian Helsinki Committee.

Herlihy, Jane, Laura Jobson, and Stuart Turner. 2012. "Just Tell Us What Happened to You: Autobiographical Memory and Seeking Asylum." *Applied Cognitive Psychology* 26(5): 661–76.

Herlihy, Jane, Peter Scragg, and Stuart Turner. 2002. "Discrepancies in Autobiographical Memories – Implications for the Assessment of Asylum Seekers: Repeated Interviews Study." *BMJ* 324: 324–27.

Herlihy, Jane, and Stuart Turner. 2006. "Should Discrepant Accounts Given by Asylum Seekers Be Taken as Proof of Deceit?" *Torture* 16(2): 81–92.

Herlihy, Jane, and Stuart Turner. 2007. "Asylum Claims and Memory of Trauma: Sharing Our Knowledge." *British Journal of Psychiatry* 191: 3–4.

Hollinger, David. 2000. *Postethnic America.* New York: Basic Books.

Immigration and Refugee Board of Canada. 2004. *Assessment of Credibility in Claims for Refugee Protection.* Ottawa, Canada: Government of Canada.

INS v. Cardoza-Fonseca. 1987. 480 U.S. 421.

Kagan, Michael. 2003. "Is Truth in the Eye of the Beholder? Objective Credibility Assessment in Refugee Status Determination." *Georgetown Immigration Law Journal.* 17:367–415.

Keast, Rachael. 2005. "Using Experts for Asylum Cases in Immigration Court." *Interpreter Releases: Report and Analysis of Immigration and Nationality Law* 82(30): 1237–43.

Kebebe v. Ashcroft. 2004. 366 F.3d 808 (9th Cir.).

Kinzie, J. David, James M. Jaranson, and G. V. Kroupin. 2007. "Diagnosis and treatment of mental illness." In Walker, P. F., and E. D. Barnett, eds., *Immigrant Medicine.* Philadelphia, PA: Saunders Elsevier: 639–51.

Maldanado v. Canada (Minister of Employment & Educ.), [1980] 2 F.C. 302 (Can.).

Malphrus, Garry. 2010. "Expert Witnesses in Immigration Proceedings." *Immigration Law Advisor* 4 (5):1–3 and 8–14. Retrieved November 26, 2013, from http://eoirweb/library/lib_index.htm.

Marshall, Grant N., Terry L. Schell, Marc N. Elliott, S. Megan Berthold, and Chi-Ah Chun. 2005. "Mental Health of Cambodian Refugees 2 Decades After Resettlement in the United States." *Journal of the American Medical Association* 294: 571–9.

Mehrotra, Ajay. 2001. "Law and the Other: Karl N. Llewellyn, Cultural Anthropology, and the Legacy of the Cheyenne Way." *Law and Social Inquiry* 26: 750.

Mendenhall, Allen. 2012. "Dissent as a Site of Aesthetic Adaptation in the Work of Oliver Wendell Holmes, Jr." *British Journal of American Studies* 1: 517–50.

Mollica, Richard F. 2006. *Healing Invisible Wounds: Paths to Hope and Recovery in a Violent World.* Nashville, TN: Vanderbilt University Press.

Mollica, Richard F. 2010. "History and Evidence of Traumatic Head Injury." Webinar hosted by the National Capacity Building Project of the Center for Victims of Torture, St. Paul, MN.

Mousa v. Mukasey. 2008. 530 F.3d 1025 (9th Cir.).

Paramasamy v. Ashcroft. 2004. 366 F.3d 808 (9th Cir.).

Putnam, Frank W. 1993. "Dissociative Phenomenon." In Spiegel, David, ed., *Dissociative Disorders: A Clinical Review*. Lutherville, MD: Sidran: 1–16.

Pynoos, Robert S., and Kathleen Nader. 1989. "Children's Memory and Proximity to Violence." *Journal of the American Academy of Child & Adolescent Psychiatry* 28(2):236–41.

Ramji-Nogales, Jaya, Andrew I. Schoenholtz, and Phillip G. Schrag, eds. 2011. *Refugee Roulette: Disparities in Asylum Adjudication and Proposals for Reform*. New York: NYU Press.

REAL ID Act. 2005. *Statutes at Large*. Vol. 119, p. 302.

Refugee Act of 1980. 1980. Pub. L. No. 96–212, 94 Stat. 102.

Rousseau, Cécile, Crépeau, Francois, Foxen, Patricia, and Houle, France. 2002. "The Complexity of Determining Refugeehood: A Multidisciplinary Analysis of the Decision-Making Process of the Canadian Refugee and Immigration Board." *Journal of Refugee Studies* 15(1): 43–70.

Scalia, Antonin. 1998. *A Matter of Interpretation: Federal Courts and the Law*. Princeton, NJ: Princeton University Press.

Shuman, Amy, and Carol Bohmer. 2004. "Representing Trauma: Political Asylum Narratives." *Journal of American Folklore* 117(466): 394–414.

Sim, Stuart. 2004. *Fundamentalist World: The Dark Age of Dogma*. Thriplow: Icon Books.

Spiegel, David. 1991. "Dissociation and Trauma." In A. Tasman, and S. M. Goldfinger, eds., *American Psychiatric Press Review of Psychiatry* 10: 261–75. Washington, DC: American Psychiatric Press.

Spiegel, David. 1997. "Trauma, Dissociation, and Memory." *Annals of the New York Academy of Sciences* 821(1): 225–37.

Sweeney, James. 2009. "Credibility, Proof and Refugee Law." *International Journal of Refugee Law* 10:701.

Tambadou v. Gonzales. 2006. 466 F.3d 298 (2d Cir.).

Terr, Lenore. 1983. "Time Sense Following Psychic Trauma: A Clinical Study of Ten Adults and Twenty Children." *American Journal of Orthopsychiatry* 54: 244–62.

Thomas, E. W. 2005. *The Judicial Process: Realism, Pragmatism, Practical Reasoning, and Principles*. Cambridge: Cambridge University Press.

United Nations High Commissioner for Refugees. 1992. *Guidelines of the United Nations High Commissioner for Refugees Handbook on Procedures and Criteria for Determining Refugee Status under the 1951 Convention and the 1967 Protocol Relating to the Status of Refugees*. UN doc. HCR/IP/4/ENG/REV, 1. 2nd edn. Geneva, Switzerland: UNHCR.

United States Department of State. 1967. *United Nations Convention Relating to the Status of Refugees*. TIAS 6577.

United States Department of State. 1967. *United Nations Protocol Relating to the Status of Refugees*. TIAS 6577.

Wexler, David B., and Bruce J. Winick. 1996. *Law in a Therapeutic Key: Developments in Therapeutic Jurisprudence*. Durham: Carolina Academic Press.

Zhou v. Gonzales. 2006. 193 F. Appx. 98 (2d Cir.).

2

Recovering the Sociological Identity of Asylum Seekers: Language Analysis for Determining National Origin in the European Union

Noé M. Kam

"WATERSIDE"

In 2004, I received a phone call from a lawyer representing a young asylum seeker from Liberia. The lawyer explained that his client had just undergone "language identification" that resulted in his client's origin identified as Nigeria instead of Liberia. He informed me further that he had already contacted some experts, and they all knew that the language spoken by the young woman was not familiar in Liberia as was initially believed. However, the lawyer told me that in analyzing his conversations with his client, he had the strong belief that she was from Liberia, as she claimed. Finally, he asked me if I wanted to give a second opinion on this case. I answered in the affirmative; the case offered an interesting opportunity to investigate the Liberian "Waterside" dialect, and to interact with other researchers, including a linguist, an ethnolanguage therapist, a psychologist, a sociologist, and, finally, an anthropologist. The results of the various expert reports were striking.

The first finding, conducted by a linguistics graduate, was cautious and circumspect. He explained:

> At the moment, we can only say one thing with certainty, and that is that the interviewee comes from [Anglophone] West Africa (Ghana, Sierra Leone, Liberia and Nigeria). What is surprising, is that of these four countries, it is only in Liberia that you find people (today) that have not, or will not, speak dialect. And the interviewee does not speak any dialect on this audio document, even when the official irritated her, she gets angry on several occasions, without uttering a single word of an African dialect or "Waterside" like all of Liberia's population. Based on this recording, it is premature to say that she is from Liberia. Before I give you the methodology to conduct this expertise, I would like to say that for a simple linguist, this expertise could be counter-productive because there is a lack of mother tongue that is usually

used to start the analysis. And pushing a descriptive study of existing relationships between linguistic units, as well as functions that are attached to them, you realize that the interviewee cannot come from Liberia. And that is what happened with my three students, who analyzed the recording, without forgetting to mention that geographical knowledge was not taken into account in the linguistic process.

After studying these first results, I decided to subject the digital audio file to further scrutiny.

I sent the compact disc to a linguist still living in Liberia. His conclusion was less equivocal, but nonetheless striking. He observed:

> It is surprising that she does not speak even a little Waterside-English [and she is] unlike most of the population of Liberia. Based purely on linguistic elements, I can conclude that the person is probably not from any region in Liberia. And on the basis of geographical knowledge and culture of the country, it is possible that she was originally from Liberia.

This second report, although more assertive than the first, still did not allow for a definitive conclusion about the girl's origin.

I can assure you that I listened to this audio document more than fifty times. At times it seemed to me as though this recording had replaced the music normally playing in my car as I went about town. At some point, after listening for the umpteenth time, I realized something was obscuring my deeper understanding; it became clear to me that to truly understand such complexity required competencies beyond linguistics. I decided to approach a psychiatrist familiar with African languages. Without answering the question about her identity, his conclusions demonstrated my concern was warranted. He observed, "[while] it is true that I have not had the young woman in my office, I am convinced, from listening to the audio document, that she suffers from a psychological problem that must be treated at its root cause."

The psychiatrist, who specialized in the ethnic dimensions of mental illness, focused on a particular moment in the interview. He drew my attention to the fact that when the interviewing immigration officer asked her, "What ethnicity are you?" she replied, "I was not part of it." The officer continued, "You mean the Waterside?" To which she responded, "It is not me." The psychiatrist explained that:

> She is confused, absent from the interview, but still shows that she has been raised in a good family. This is her only identity and I would say her only nostalgia that she has left. Instead of referring to her community or her people in the interview, she resigns herself and finds refuge in the education she received at home as her first identity. It is at this point that it becomes

disturbing, because for any insider [familiar with] the tradition and linguistic culture of Liberia, you know immediately that something bad had happened in Monrovia. She has not only rejected all her people, but she also asked questions about her existence [. . .] and shortcomings. It seems obvious to me that this interview would not have happened (the person mean "should not have happened"). As a specialist, I must strongly advise you to refer this young patient to a clinical ethno psychiatrist because it is essential to find the etiologies so that she can find life again.

After this report, the lawyer sent the young girl to see a psychologist.

After a few months of treatment, the psychologist submitted an expert report. He explained that "[i]t was as if she was dead. She was completely apathetic, no longer able to live." He diagnosed her multiple symptom presentation as a severe form of post-traumatic stress disorder, accompanied by a major depressive disorder with psychotic features, including depersonalization phenomena, and somatic trauma as a result of rape and abuse in Liberia and the refugee camp in Côte d'Ivoire. He explained that she suffered from "unprocessed trauma, especially from rape." I shall refrain from further discussion of the diagnosis here, particularly the trauma and its impact on the behavior of the girl, because Bruce Einhorn and Megan Berthold discuss these matters at length in their chapter in this book. But her narrative resonates with Galya Ruffer's chapter examining the use of rape as a "weapon of war" in central Africa.

After reviewing the multiple expert reports, the lawyer was still unable to confirm the young woman's identity. The central office of the Swiss UNHCR then conducted an empirical study; the woman had lived under UNHCR protection for approximately a dozen years and her documentary record became the focus of scrutiny. A UNHCR anthropologist and sociologist attempted to deconstruct her identity based on chronologically different stages of socialization. The UNHCR archives were searched for any records of her reception or screening, and additional interviews were conducted at various refugee camps in Liberia and Côte d'Ivoire. After several years the young woman was revealed to have originated in Monrovia, Liberia.

To better understand this "Waterside-English" case study, some cultural knowledge is useful. The young woman's narrative was set in the early 1980s, in a Liberia gripped by political tension; she was born into a young family that lived attuned to the culture of the United States. Her family was a classic "Americo-Liberian" family, the descendants of former American slaves who established themselves in Liberia in the nineteenth century. Until the 1980s, this elite group, comprising only 2.5 percent of the population, had always ruled Liberia; but a coup d'état brought the ethnically indigenous Samuel Kanyon Doe to power on April 2, 1980.

In the context of the subsequent Liberian civil wars (1989–1996, 1999–2003), the young girl fled Monrovia at the age of eleven years. Separated from her family, she was to live alone in various refugee camps over a period twelve years, before she had an opportunity to the Netherlands, where she sought political asylum in 2004. Once in The Netherlands, she had, through language analysis, identified herself as a Monrovia Liberian. Although she did not speak any recognizable form of any of Liberia's many languages, her identification as Liberian was possible using a spectrum of expert reports. The "Waterside-English" case study cautions us to be mindful of the use of Language Analysis for Determining Origin (known colloquially as LADO) by governments, immigration services, and adjudicators. The young lady's experience demonstrates the inadequacy of LADO in isolation, and casts doubt on its purported reliability.

INTRODUCTION

Efforts to interpret the sociological identities of asylum seekers in the European Union offer an opportunity to further scrutinize the use of LADO by immigration officials and the weight it is often given by adjudicators. LADO has two applications pertinent to the process of identification for the purposes of immigration, namely: identifying the origin of an illegal immigrant in order to return him to the county of which he holds nationality; and, identifying the origin of an asylum seeker (applicant) in order to examine the forms of persecution suffered by this person.

This chapter focuses on identifying the origin of an applicant for two reasons. First, I have worked for more than a decade in the field of applicant identification in The Netherlands. The second reason is that the legitimacy of this type of identification is based on the Geneva Convention of 1951 and its various protocols, whereas the illegal immigrant who is identified does not enjoy legal protection. The convention requires the host country to first verify that the applicant has the nationality of the country or region in which the persecution took place before moving on to consider that persecution. Thus it is necessary for the host country to determine the identity of the applicant and sometimes attribute a legal nationality to that person.

During my work with the applicants, I identified two processes with which to determine their identities – biological (e.g., analysis of DNA, age) and sociological (analysis of language, documents, and socialization). As a complement to the chapter by Richard Tutton, Christine Hauskeller, and Steve Sturdy in this volume discussing biological identity claims, this study examines sociological identity, focusing on language analysis. Language analysis has emerged as a central element in asylum adjudication, because many Western adjudicators still believe that language is a fundamental mirror of an applicant's identity, as an individual speaks the language of the social group into which he is socialized.

An identification process is initiated, usually as a matter of domestic immigration regulation, when an applicant is unable to present appropriate documentation to identify him or herself. It is common for the host country's immigration services to use an analysis "technique" known as LADO. The Swedish immigration board first employed LADO as a pioneering method in 1988 (Hedebris 2010). The purpose of LADO is to determine the linguistic identity of the applicant and, thereafter, allocate this identity to a geographic area of a country where s/he could linguistically and socially belong. This national or domestic site (e.g., Liberia) then becomes the context within which an asylum claim is scrutinized against available country of origin information. Thus, the place where the applicant has spent most of his or her youth is the site of socialization (BLT 2007).[1]

The methodologies associated with LADO are the site of considerable scholarly controversy. One consistent grounds for criticism is that frequently one expert cannot reach the same conclusion of a second; despite following and reproducing the same linguistic technique, the result itself is often not replicable. An Australian study provided a good illustration of this debacle (Erard 2003).[2] The study demonstrated that LADO is an arbitrary method that does not respect the established, peer-reviewed methods of scientific language analysis. Furthermore, according to my own tests and interviews of thirteen linguists and forty-eight native speakers experts (2010), no single expert is able to provide an account of rules, which, when followed, support the conclusion. Indeed, a wholly unscientific and unscholarly method is revealed whereby conclusions appear based primarily on the linguist's feelings and the native speaker's intuition.

According to current Dutch jurisprudence, an applicant's legal representative has few avenues for a counterdefense when LADO is presented as evidence.[3] Several studies have highlighted this situation (Blommaert 2008, 2009, 2010; Bronsdijk 2006; Detailleur 2010; Eades 2009; Kam 2009). However, no study has yet examined the role of the digital audio file on compact disc.[4]

---

[1] The work document of the Dutch immigration LADO office.

[2] The report of a group of Australian linguists states, "The reports of these companies contradicted the applicants' claims in 48 of 58 cases. But when those 48 applicants appealed, 35 of them were granted asylum. In some cases, the adjudicators considering those appeals expressed concerns about the accuracy of the tests."

[3] To relevant decision are: case number 200607305/1; JV 2007, 230, published March 29, 2007; and case number 201107996/1/VI; LJN: BW1428, published March 22, 2012.

[4] The immigration officer has a system that allows him to record the interview with the applicant, in sequence calls tracks, on an audio compact disc. Thus, no changes can be made on the disk

This chapter analyzes the digital audio file produced in the context of LADO and reveals that the very creation of this digital audio file is the origin of many the sites of controversy identified in scholarship focused on methodology. My research is informed by three theoretical frameworks: the first framework reveals the failure of the LADO to accurately record the very *"language"* of the asylum seeker; the second framework underscores how the participants ("actors") in the recording process are implicated in decision making; and, the third and final framework shows the cultural negotiation embedded in the digital audio file. Before addressing these theories, it is also important to present the several and various methods of recording an applicant's *"language"* that LADO analysis employs for different immigration boards and commercial offices.

THE MODE OF RECORDING THE DIGITAL AUDIO FILE

Table 1 shows how countries that use LADO record the digital audio file that is analyzed afterward, depending on the recording method, by an expert. The table includes three columns, titled with acronyms. Each group of acronyms is a method of recording a digital audio file and also represents the group of actors who are mobilized for the method. Thus, the column applicant (APP), immigration agent (IMA), and interpreter (I) is the first method of recording shown in Table APP + IMA + I. The second method consists of APP + IMA + IP (interpreter on the phone). The third method consists of APP + NSAI (native speaker analyst and interpreter).

It is important to note the absence of data from some countries (e.g., Australia, Germany, and New Zealand) in this table. Unfortunately, I was not able to collect data from these countries because they did not return the questionnaire. Table 1 shows that there are three modes of digital audio file recordings used by the countries mentioned. Questions asked of staff in charge of recordings show that the choice of modes used is largely arbitrary and depends on the possibility of obtaining an NSAI, IP, or I. An essential fact concerning the dual roles of NSAI and IP in countries that use several modes of recordings – such as Sweden – is an additional important consideration. Here, we notice that the I or IP appears to self-transform into an analyst insofar as s/he assists the Swedish linguist, who does not know how to read or write the applicant's language, and thus is unable to write a report. As for the NSAI, s/he conducts the questioning of the APP, establishes the report, and passes it on to the linguist. Only The Netherlands mandates the consistent use of only one

or even making copies as the number of tracks and minutes are known and the information is magnetically recorded.

TABLE 1: *The mode of digital file recordings*

Countries	APP+IMA+I	APP+IMA+IP	APP+NSAI	Experimentation
Austria	X	X		
Belgium	X	X		X
Canada	X	X		X
Denmark	X	X	X	X
Finland	X	X	X	X
Luxembourg	X	X		X
Netherlands	X			
United Kingdom	X	X		
Sweden	X	X	X	
Switzerland	X	X		

NSAI = Native speaker analyst and interpreter
APP = Applicant
IMA = Immigration agent
I = Interpreter
IP = Interpreter on the phone

mode, ostensibly for coherence in the norms of analysis. This chapter will focus on the Dutch use of LADO.

METHODS OF DIGITAL AUDIO FILE ANALYSIS

Table 2 shows how the digital audio file, once recorded, is analyzed. Each acronym group represents an analysis system and the actors who are mobilized for that system. Thus, the column "linguist with no specialization in the language to be analyzed" (L) and "native speaker" (NS) is the first analysis system shown in Table L + NS. It is important to note that NS has no linguistics background and there is some debate about the "native speaker" appellation. For example, as most Africans speak more than two languages the question arises in what way can a person be considered a "native speaker"? (e.g., Cook 1999; Coppieters 1987; Davies 1991, 2003). Also, L does not often speak or write to any significant degree the language being analyzed. The second analysis system is "linguistic specialist in the language analyzed" (LS). Notwithstanding holding an academic degree in the study of a language, LS is often not able to speak the language to any significant degree; thus, the method employed most often is that of a written report, which is the weak point of NS. The third analysis system is "linguistic specialist who is a native speaker" (LSNS). The debate surrounding of the suitability of the "native

TABLE 2: *LADO analysis system by country*

Country	L+NS	LS	LSNS	NS	Commercial Offices
Austria	X	X	X		
Belgium	X	X	X	X	
Canada	X	X	X	X	
Denmark	X	X	X	X	X
Finland	X	X	X	X	X
Luxembourg	X	X	X		
Netherlands	X				X
United Kingdom	X	X	X	X	X
Sweden	X	X	X	X	X
Switzerland	X	X	X		

L = Linguist with no specialization in the language analyzed
LS = Linguist specialized in the language analyzed
LSNS = Linguistic specialist who is also a native speaker
NS = Native speaker

speaker" appellation combined with the lack of academic teaching in most African languages means that the LSNS analysis system is usually entirely unavailable. And the final analysis system is NS, or native speaker.

Table 2 presents the different systems of language analysis done by each country. We note that some countries (Denmark, Finland, and Sweden) conduct instant analysis; in the sense that during the digital audio file recording (Table 1), NSAI, IP, and I play the role of the IMA and, at the same time, question the APP. They produce a statement, make notes about the interview and write a language analysis report. Once again, all countries except The Netherlands use multiple systems of analysis.

Table 3 demonstrates that the two Swedish commercial enterprises use L+NS. Dutch services do not use this system for two reasons. The first is that whereas Dutch jurisprudence insists on the use of LS who have demonstrable independent judgment, the BLT did not meet these standards (BLT 2007).[5] Second, the name and the academic background of Dutch commercial office "experts" must be published and available to the public, whereas those of BLT and Swedish offices are not.

Another understanding from this table is that the two Dutch bureaus are the only ones that use the services of LS and NS. The reason for using LS and the

---

[5]   Bureau Land en Taal (known as BLT) is the Netherlands Immigration LADO unit.

Noé M. Kam

TABLE 3: *LADO analysis system by commercial offices*

Commercial Expertise Offices	L+NS	LS	LS+NS	LSNS	LSNS +NS	LSNS+NS +ASEE	LS+NS +ASEE
Makano International, The Netherlands			X	X	X	X	X
Spraakab, Sweden	X	X			X		
Taal Studio, The Netherlands		X	X	X			
Verified, Sweden	X	X		X			

ASEE = Anthropologist/sociologist/ethnologist/ethnopsychiatrist

NS is jurisprudential.[6] However, some adjudicators believe that despite the academic level of LS, the NS's participation makes the report reliable. This may be true, but other serious methodological problems still remain (see social regulation theory later in this chapter). Moreover, the Swedish offices play the same role as those in Table 2 because the Swedish government has entrusted them with this task.

Uniquely, one bureau in The Netherlands uses all three systems to produce reports. Having noticed the lack of detail of other analysis systems mentioned earlier, which may lead to nonreliability of language reports, Makano International put in place this system in 2004. Moreover, this system has helped in understanding the origin of LADO problems (Kam 2012b).

THE DIGITAL AUDIO FILE AS THE SITE OF ORIGIN FOR PROBLEMS WITH LADO

In general, when an institution begins an investigation, its purpose is to seek to resolve a situation lacking clarity, such as immigration services who doubt an applicant's self-identification as a particular national subject. It remains a matter of debate as to whether LADO actually allows the identification of an applicant. One way to approach this debate is to test LADO methods against three theoretical frameworks. This will enable a discussion of the repercussions of LADO methods, the role of the digital audio file in the very production of LADO reports, and the highlight the potential impact of the methodologies for the role of the asylum adjudicator. However, it is first necessary to demonstrate how sociologists understand the processes whereby

[6] Nr. 200703619/1, August 7, 2007.

an individual internalizes the accumulated life experiences of one or multiple communities and how this presents in the context of interviewing, what is conventionally referred to in linguistic theory as socialization.

The Socialization Process

The process of socialization may be interpreted as the course of an individual from conception to death. During this process, the individual stores life experiences which reflect how he inserted himself into all the communities in which he lived. The outline below (Figure 1) shows how this presents during the context of the interview.

Internalize, applicant

Result of the internalization, applicant

Individual (African, applicant)

Experience, past ↓

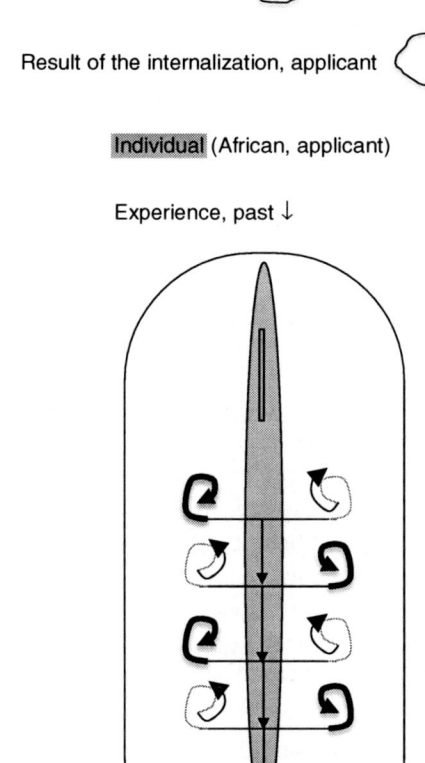

FIGURE 1: Outline of the Theoretical Process of Socialization. Source: Kam (2009).

The above schematic of the theoretical process of socialization (Figure 1) defines socialization as a process whereby members of a society learn, internalize, and give back in the form of patterns of behavior consistent with cultural values of their environment (Ly 1985, p. 417).

The first confrontation with socialization is at birth, and reflects the pressures of "prenatal socialization" (Maurer 2004, p. 44). In African society, prenatal skills are developed by women through rituals around the expectant mother, or through haptonomy in so-called modern society (Dumonteil-Kremer 2003, pp. 28–29). This beginning socialization mirrors the society in which the individual begins his life. Socialization at this point includes talk of a sense of belonging to a society that will always require certain skills to be acquired (Ly 1985; Dubet and Martuccelli 1996). This period marks the start of learning a lifestyle, in the sense that the social makeup of the individual is learned through adaptation to social structures such as the values of the culture, rules of behavior, institutions, social divisions, class, family types, and so on (Martuccelli 2005). The fundamentals that are integrated during "prenatal socialization" represent an individual's weapon of defense throughout all future phases of socialization, enabling him to develop a psychocultural identity (Kam 2009).

The second and final confrontation that brings the socialized individual into being is illustrated by the thick and thin black loops in Figure 1. When an individual is confronted with a situation, such as an interview for linguistic analysis, the questions in the thick loop will be internalized. The individual asks himself questions based on previous experience (downward arrow), meaning experience based on their learning. The result of these questions is that he returns to the society in which he lives (via the thin loop). The society in which he finds himself at that moment will, in turn, accept or reject the result. This social assessor (such as the interpreter or immigration official) allows the individual to assess his degree of belonging to the new society. This increases the feeling of self-value for the individual. This cycle is repeated throughout the individual's life – it is the very essence of the constant confrontation of socialization. I shall now consider the specific situation of applicants in The Netherlands and the linguistic theory supporting this particular approach to language analysis.

Before presenting the three theories here, a note of caution about the digital audio file is in order. Scholarly convention suggests that the interpretation and analysis of the content of a digital audio file requires not only the skills of linguistic science, but also other social sciences (e.g., psychology, sociology, anthropology, and ethnology). But Dutch jurisprudence appears to have closed the door to the employment of social scientific knowledge in the interpretation of the digital audio file. As the door closes, other experts have sought new configurations to account for the role of the audio file, some of which they cannot explain. By way of illustration, one adjudicator, who appointed three experts to facilitate decision making, and received three reports, each with entirely different conclusions.[7]

Framework One: Ferdinand de Saussure

Research on the linguistic identity of an applicant is based on their *"language"* that is recorded on the digital audio file and analyzed by experts. How do the experts extract asylum seeker *"language"* from another actor's *"language"* and analyze this? What do the experts analyze in the recording: is it *"language," "the language"* or the *"speech"*? What is included in linguistics and why? In answering these questions, the origin of points of discord between BLT and second opinion experts is clarified. The arbitrary nature of both methods of analysis is also brought to light, showing confusion and a lack of understanding among the actors involved. These inconsistencies make the adjudicators' work very difficult.

Linguistic theory demonstrates that the insights of linguistics are multi-interpretational (Malmberg 1991, pp. 405–419). The phenomenon of language may be divided by use – speaking the language known as *"speech"* (*parole*) and the language system – the instrument known as *"the language"* (*langue*) (Komatsu and Harris 1993, pp. 66–83). Until today, many research language systems such as LADO do not take into account a person's language use and their social relationships.

In De Saussure's research applied (Vilkou-Pustovaïa 2002) the division of systems known as – *competence* and use, known as – *performance* (Normand 1978, p. 66). This division, illustrated in Figure 2, forms the basis of many theories about *language*.

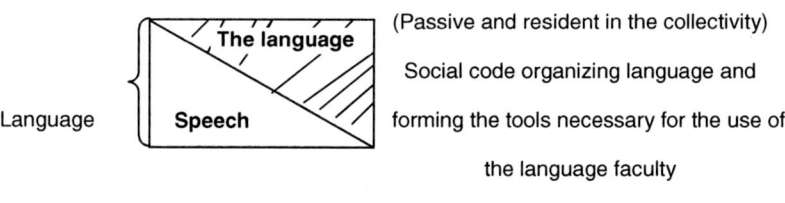

FIGURE 2: Language Division of Saussure. Source: Claudia Mejia (1998: p. 78).

---

[7]   De uitspraak van de Afdeling Bestuursrechtspraak van de Raad van State d.d. 9 September 2013 (zaaknr 201211522/1/V1).

A second insight of De Saussure's interpretation is that *"the language,"* meaning the instrument of *speech*, is a material and physical thing, built in a structured way from a finite set of the smallest units that differ only slightly in meaning. As a simple illustration, the Somali word "tali" (decide, do, etc.) means something different than "bali" (pond, puddle, etc.). There is a mean- ingful distinction between the "t" and the "b" in Somali language that is not only the purely physical characteristics of the sounds (Lesemans 2010). I contend that, as phonemes are part of a phonemic system, they follow certain rules to create a phonological system – one that can be used by language users to produce all words, sentences, and texts of that language (De Mauro 1984, pp. 55–83). As a result, no experts were able to explain the relevance of an applicant replacing "b" with "t" or the repercussion of this action.

Another implication of De Saussure is that *language* is a physical and resonant representation in the area of auditory perception in the brain, at the levels of phonemes, words, sentences, and texts that may indicate meaning, but do not have meaning in themselves (Irigaray 1974, p. 37). Words from BLT reports serve as examples: *groentiga* = vegetable; *mey* = no; *madara- sadda* = the Koranic school (Kam 2010). These examples demonstrate a well-established difference in language structure, namely, the difference between "signifier" and "signified." The former is clearer the object of the study of linguistics; the later is the variously and unspecifically the domain of psychologists, anthropologists, sociologists, and others. Figure 3, adapted from De Saussure (1911), provides an account of the production of the digital audio file.

This schematic diagram in Figure 3 shows the digital audio file is clearly produced using social facts. The digital audio file is a composition of the talking ability of three actors, though only the talking ability of the applicant is analyzed. Furthermore, the study makes no distinction with respect to talking ability. The core argument here is that there is an arbitrary relationship between *"signifier"* and *"signified."* There is a completely random link between the physical sounds that a word or sentence makes and what is being expressed, or to what the word is referring. Typically, it is the users of a language who set the relationship between *"signifier"* and *"signified."* Precisely how this occurs is not a subject of linguistic study (Normand 1978, pp. 66–90; Médina 1978, pp. 17–23).

Following De Saussure, I argue that, by expressing their individual thinking, an individual is not required to conform to the demands of their contemporaries. This is because socialization, as described Ly, Dubet, and Martuccelli, is first an individual process before it becomes a collective process (Winch 1958, p. 30). The BLT collects its own data and engages in

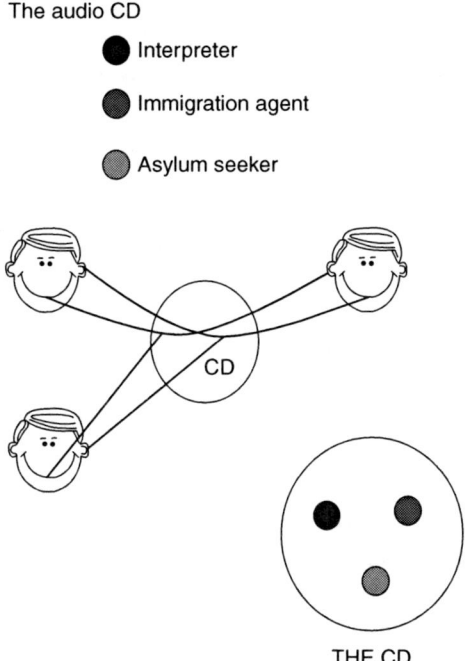

FIGURE 3: The Production of the Digital Audio File. Source: De Saussure (1911).

its own research and translation. In so doing, they disregard the analysis of the language system of the applicants. From 1999, instead of analyzing the language system of applicants, the BLT has analyzed the speech (parole), a site of study currently outside the domain of linguistics (Teubert 2010). It remains a matter of puzzlement to me and many other scholars as to how the BLT can focus on a non-existant linguistic function and yet purport to have made linguistic conclusions. The same may be true for second opinion experts, who follow the BLT method instead of methods that have been subjected to scholarly scrutiny by linguistics. One of the few "experts" who attempted this, first prevailed in on court, but was later reversed on appeal to the High Court.[8]

During a second case, held on April 27, 2012, in Zutphen, I was invited by a court to serve as expert witness to explain and interpret the report of this second opinion expert. During the hearing the second opinion expert was accused by the BLT of not using the examples provided in the BLT report. The second opinion expert, whose report I was engaged to explain, is a university professor and research director in one of the largest institutions of

[8]   Case ABRvS, 201007310/1/V1, published on January 17, 2011.

language studies in Europe. He has published more than one hundred articles, some of which were cited in the linguistic argumentation. He is the editor of two dictionaries of 1400 and 1600 pages of the dialect he analyzes, and he was born and grew up in the country in which the dialect he analyzes is spoken. He taught the dialect in the country before joining the European institution. The explanations of both parties (the BLT linguist and me) during the trial diverged completely. I tried to explain to the adjudicator, with the help of literature, the fact that the words and phrases used by BLT in its report were not appropriate in a language report, but also that these words meant nothing in terms of identification. I then demonstrated, with the perspective of sociolinguistic analysis, that even when considering the example words in the BLT report, the identity of the applicant could not, according to anthropological linguistics, belong to the region indicated by BLT

As a BLT linguist, two elements form the basis for legitimizing the report: the competence of the analyst and jurisprudence. The BLT contends that its analysts are regularly trained and tested in specific dialects, although an analyst may not have academic degree in the dialect (the law does not require the analyst to have academic degree, but it does require such for the second opinion expert). In addition, the BLT argued that its analyst had made two visits to the region over a period of three years where he witnessed the use of the words in his report. The BLT analyst further held that the second opinion expert as a matter of law improperly ignored the sample words, insofar as an analyst he had already been declared competent before the court. Finally, the BLT linguist indicated that he did not find it important to reconsider any new examples given by the second opinion expert or my explanations. In spite of his defence, the second opinion expert's report was rejected by the court because BLT was able to reach a conclusion using speech.[9] In other words, the second opinion expert was effectively told he ought to apply nonexistent linguistic science to reach conclusions in asylum cases.

The implication of this decision is that the BLT recognized that they are not able to analyze the language of the applicant based on the digital audio file. The BLT observed that *"the linguist, but not the language analyst, usually looks at the first interview of the asylum procedure in order to make an estimate of the expected language of an applicant."*[10] This statement contradicts established language recording protocol. More important, by operating in this way, the BLT misleads the applicant (see definition of the

---

[9] Case AWB09/47150, published on May 30, 2012.
[10] Case AWB09/47150, published on May 30, 2012.

problem later in this chapter). The *"signified"* (parole) part of *"language"* is not generally considered a site of linguistic study. An analysis of words, such words as *"groentiga, mey, or madarasadda,"* has no place in BLT linguistics reports. Thus, in this way, the BLT never extracts *"the language"* from *"language."* Social regulation increasingly shows that in the case of asylum seekers, this extraction is necessary and can no longer be neglected.

Framework Two: The Social Regulation Theory of Jean-Daniel Reynaud

To initiate a recording by digital audio file, certain social coventions or rules are engaged or followed. The fulfillment of the task of creating a recording creates a social negotiation, something Reynaud called social regulation. As stated by Alter (2003, p. 78), "One of the perceptions of social regulation leads to considering the analysis of collective activities" by actors "to ensure the transformation of established rules." During the recording, each actor recognizes and uses his power to change the rules, as established by the protocol, to his own advantage, by following three stages of negotiation: definition of the problem, the discussion of the issues, and bargaining (De Terssac: 2003, p. 117).

Definition of the Problem

Explaining the concept of the "definition of the problem" is made possible by recourse to an actual recording of a language analysis interview. The following is an excerpt from such an interview:

> Today it is February 3, 2012, the time is 11am, location is Immigration Zwolle. We begin with a linguistic analysis in case immigration number 0976. My name is officer [XXX], I am working at the immigration office and I would like to explain why you are invited to this meeting. As you can see, this discussion will be taped. This interview is held because of doubts about the origin you specify. This interview gives you the opportunity to make plausible your claimed origin through a demonstration of your language skills. I ask you to speak in your own language. So you can demonstrate that you speak the language as spoken in your home country. I ask you to speak as natural as possible, as you are used to in your country of origin. I also ask you to speak all languages that you have mastered during this interview. This interview today is independent of all previous interviews you have given. This recording will be assessed by people who have not previously been involved in the investigation of your case. During the interview, I will ask you questions that may have already been asked. I request you to answer each question as

thoroughly as possible. Based on the record of this interview, a language analysis will be carried out by an expert. This expert will write down his findings in a reasoned report. The interpreter is present at this interview and whatever you say, he/she will translate. The interpreter has a neutral position in this process and will not be involved in further investigation of your case. About the results of this investigation, you will be informed by your lawyer. If you or your lawyer do not agree with the outcome of the investigation, he/she can call for a contra-expertise by an independent expert. This interview is intended to clarify obtained data about your origin. I therefore request you not to talk about your travel route or asylum motives. I request you not to mention your own name nor the names of your family members or friends during this interview. You have during this interview the opportunity to speak all languages that you have mastered [. . .]. This interview will now start.

This sample text demonstrates how rules are articulated from the outset of the interview in the context of the presentation of the problem, namely, the implausibility of a specific identity claim. It also shows how particular methodological and intellectual claims are conveyed unproblematically, giving rise to specific issues that subsequently become the site of negotiation.

Issues of Negotiation

The immigration officer asks preprepared questions. The interpreter culturalizes the questions and forwards them to the applicant. The applicant's culturalized answers are conveyed in return and in so doing the interpreter reifies the problem. The statement *"the interpreter has a neutral position in this investigation"* appears ironic to the applicant because an interpreter who speaks his language and/or dialect is assumed to share cultural values (Wasow and Arnold 2005). As many asylum seekers emerge from conflicts with ethnic implications, the culturalizing of language during the interpretation is highly problematic. Indeed, the impact of culturalization is most often unconscious because actors frequently continue and internalize the ideological contestation that gave rise for their initial flight in their host-country (Kam 2009, p. 78). Henceforth, from that moment, during recording, the responsibilities of the immigration officer are restricted only to controlling the recording time and ask questions. In the eyes of the applicant, the interpreter has the greater authority.

The recording protocol and culturalization lead to another unspoken understanding, namely, that *there is doubt about the origin of the applicant. The applicant is thus thrust into the realization that they have in front of them someone who "knows" or may have an ability to "know" them. The negotiation*

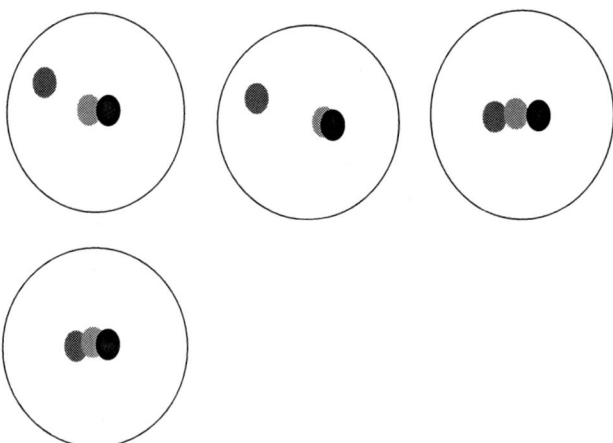

FIGURE 4: The Level of Language Corruption or Imitation

underway compels the applicant to behave as if s/he were in his/her home country, and to take action to demonstrate that s/he is not a liar. Again, Somali claims provide a useful illustration of these problem. Based on my experience, the majority of Somalis fleeing war and seeking asylum countries come from the marginal caste *Waable.* They have no social status and are dependents of noble castes, namely, *Waranle* and *Wadaad.* They have no clan identity, other than the clan on which they depend, they must speak in a manner acknowledging the presence of their master and they must adapt to presence of others. *Waable* groups are designated according to their trades and have different names in different regions (Abdi Mohamed 2000).

To be sure, the process of socialization among Somalis in the early 2000s suggests that it would be unwise to focus solely on the cultural interpretation of behavior. Somalia has been devastated by war and radical Islam from foreigners (Abdi Mohamed 2003). It is important to be cognizant of the current Islamic outlook of the interpreter and applicant. In order to understand and resolve these problems, we must focus on where "the authority" lies – who has authority over whom in the context of the interview (Ramadan 2009). It is difficult for anybody to master how alliances between (clan) groups are formed in Somalia. In fact, the negotiation operates as a means whereby the actors may position themselves linguistically, and a focus on this process provides insight into who is dominant and who is imposing their particular expressive form. The schematic diagrams in Figure 4 illustrate this problem.

Each of the four diagrams in Figure 4 shows, in order, how the interaction between the interpreter, the immigration officer, and the applicant would promote a rational language corruption (imitation) of the applicant. Each figure consists of three interlocutors. The applicant (gray) is always in the middle of the immigration officer (also in gray) and the interpreter (black) because he must answer the questions asked by the other two. The first figure shows an interaction without pressure, of one of the parties, which would result in all cases a consenting rational linguistic corruption of the interpreter and the applicant. Because there is no pressure on the applicant, he does not focus on the immigration officer and, therefore, the latter plays no role in the composition of the language of the applicant. The second figure shows a rational applicant's submission to the interpreter. This means that the applicant speaks rationally as the interpreter. The last two figures represent the alternatives to the second figure: the emancipation of the applicant. The emancipation of the applicant creates a tension with the interpreter, forcing the immigration official to use his authority to complete the interview. As the applicant is on the offensive, he takes into account everything that is said by his two protagonists. Thus, the degree of rational language corruption of the applicant depends on the degree of tension between him and his two protagonists. Also, I noticed while listening to the digital audio file that the immigration officer often suspended the interview in order to lighten the mood. (For more reading on the linguistic corruption during the interaction, see Delvaux et al. 2010; Krauss and Pardo 2006; Pardo et al. 2010.)

The Bargaining Process

The third part of the analysis focuses on bargaining. Bargaining ultimately focuses on analyzing the capacity of actors to develop new rules through the interaction of those who take the initiative (Reynaud 2003, p. 103). Dressen (2003, p. 94) explains that "[t]he issue of taking the initiative by the actors is the awarding of a degree of autonomy." Reynaud highlights three forms of regulation that are of particular interest to scholars of asylum interviews. The following case illustrates the different forms of regulations. The interpreter and the asylum seeker are both from Afgooye, a district of Xaawa Taako, of the caste Waable, and group Jaaji. Their respective lineages are Axmed Faarax and Gacal Dheere.

Bottom → Bottom

The immigration officer allows the interpreter to ask questions directly; direct questioning is not prohibited. In addition, both the interpreter and asylum seeker are under the protection of the same religious leader, *Wadaad*. It is reasonable to assume that they will automatically help each other, one unconsciously using expressions and linguistics of the other as they share the same socialization and internal ideology (Kam 2012).

Interpreter:	"Khudrad ma lagu gadaa?" – Do they sell vegetable?
Applicant:	"Haa, bataato" – Yes, potatoes.
Interpreter:	"Bataato maxa waaye"? – What is Bataato ?
Applicant:	"Baradhada weeye" – It's potatoes (Baradhada is potatoes).

According to the Maxamed Cabdi dictionary (1986), "Bataato" is a Somali language term though in North-Somali, one uses the term "baradho." The interpreter assumes "Bataato" is South-Somali and associates it with a marker of the South (waaye). The applicant replied with the term and North-Somali marker (baradho and weeye): *waaye* "he/she/it is", "they are" with a long vowel [ǎ:] orthographically **aa** in the first syllable vs. *weeyaan* with the long [ǎ:], orthographically aa in the second syllable in the Daarood dialects and *weeye* which includes a long vowel [o̞:], orthographically **ee** in the first syllable in the Northern Somali in its proper sense.

This exchange shows an adaptation effort and mutual assistance among members of marginal castes in a situation without a significantly uneven power ratio. There is no attempt to control; it is an example of autonomous regulation of the first type, Reynaud identifies as *bottom-bottom*. From a linguistic point of view, however, the BLT notices linguistic corruption in the digital audio file.

The BLT report makes the following conclusion, without analysis of the related phenomena: "The foreigner tries with much difficulty to look like a south Somalian through the way he mingles in his speech. Apparently he is acquainted with a lot of Southern Somalia features but Southern Somali is undoubtedly not his mother language; the use of southern Somalia element does not sound natural and is hereby not consistent. It is not possible to determine immediately the ethnicity of the foreigner based on his speech."

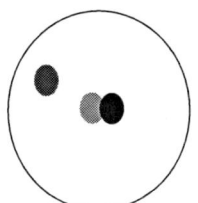

FIGURE 4A: Bottom-Bottom

Bottom → Up and Top → Down

In this second example, I start with the same previous case wherein the lineage of the interpreter is still under the protection of religious leaders *Wadaad*, but current Islamic Salafists, while the lineage of the applicant remains under the same traditional protection *Wadaad*, which has lost some of its power. In Somalia, when a tribe loses its power to dominate another tribe, it takes all measures to reclaim it, including an ideological war, which translates into an internal struggle that occurs during recording. Applicants will seek either emancipation or submission.

Emancipation is illustrated thus. At the beginning of the conversation, the applicant answers all the questions with "*I do not know, yes and no*" to make it clear to the interpreter that he is not lesser.

Interpreter:	ma muslim baa tahay? – You're a Muslim?
Answers in a low voice:	Haa – Yes.
Interpreter:	maxay sameyan muslinku? – What does a true Muslim do?
Answers in a low voice:	ma garanayo – ahhh I do not know.
Interpreter:	Waxaad tiri waxaan dhigan Jaray malmaacaad, malcaamaddiina xaggay ku taallay? – You said I had studied in Madrassa, where is it in Madrassa that I was?
Answers in a low voice:	ma garanayo – ahhh I do not know.

As the interpreter questions the applicant, he makes him betray himself. In fact, Salafist envoys often try to recruit around mosques on Fridays. They always start the dialogue by asking a practising person met in a mosque if he is a Muslim. In addition, he uses the North Somalian word *malcaamad* to refer "the Koranic school." The applicant's answers are evasive because he aims to combat this domination. From this interaction, BLT concludes that "*the foreigner refuses sometimes to speak or speaks slowly when he is confronted with the imitation of the southern Somalia dialect.*"

Once the immigration officer observes there to be a problem and asks a follow-up question, the two protagonists answer that there is no problem. In this way, the interpreter acknowledges having lost his position of strength by adapting to the language of the applicant. He begins to speak in a manner consistent with his lineage, and resumes the process of construction of the applicant.

| Applicant: | Marka goorma ayaad tagi jirtay madrasa? – When did you go to the Madresa? |

Interpreter: Ka soo qaad dugsigii baad aadday, maxaa laga soo qabanayaa? –
              When you were at the Madresa, what did they do?
Applicant: Carabigaa lagu dhigaa quraanka, iyo xoogaa Ingiiris ah. – We
              studied Quran and some English.
Interpreter: Marka magacooda guud midgaan weeye? – The common name
              is Midgaan?
Applicant: Magacooda guud midgaan waaye – The common name is
              Midgaan.
Interpreter: Afka ilaa hadda aad ku hadahay afkee waaye? – What language
              do you speak at this moment?
Applicant: Af Soomaali waaye – It is Somali.

The applicant uses the South Somalian term *madrassa* (the Koranic school). The interpreter responds by again testing his dominion in asking the question with *dugsi* (the Koranic school), also used in South Somalia. Once the applicant ignores *dugsi* in his reply, he frees himself. From this moment, it is the interpreter who follows the applicant in the linguistic expressions South (*waaye*) and North (*weeye*) of Somalia until the end of the interview. This is an example of autonomous regulation of the type Reynaud calls *bottom-up* because the applicant resists a preexisting power. This process leads to corruption in the linguistic schematic in Figure 4b, depending on the degree of involvement of the actors.

The BLT report makes another conclusion, again without requisite analysis of the emancipatory phenomena: "The foreigner may have learnt some of the southern Somalia language during a short stay in southern Somalia. Another possibility is that the southern Somalia elements noticed in the speech of the foreigner may have resulted from his efforts to imitate the southern Somalia. It is not possible to determine immediately the ethnicity of the foreigner based on his speech."

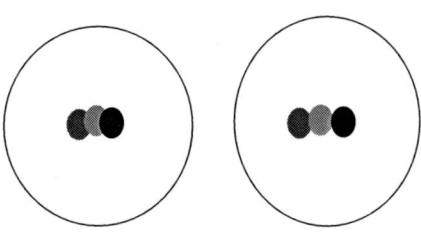

FIGURE 4B: Bottom-Up

The alternative to emancipation is submission. This form of regulation occurs among applicants throughout their socialization, particularly among those who have consistently lived in oppressive environments and never protested against a decision.

Interpreter:	ma taqaanaa magaalada? – You know the city?
Applicant:	Haa taqaanaa magaalada – Yes I know the city.
Interpreter:	suuq ma leedahay? – The market is there?
Applicant:	Haa way leedahay – Yes, the market is there.
Interpreter:	maxaad ka qaban jrtay magaalada? – What were you doing in town?
Applicant:	waan ka shaqayn jiray – What was I doing in town? – Working.
Interpreter:	ma birtaan ka shaqayn jiraytay? You worked in the metal?
Applicant:	haa birtaan ka shaqayn jiray – Yes, I worked in the metal.

Repeating the same intonations, words, or grammatical constructions that the interpreter used, the applicant follows the rules that are dictated by protocol (definition of the problem) and socialization. Using expressions used by the interpreter, he speaks naturally as he does in his country and throughout his socialization. As all rules are being respected, it is a matter of autonomous regulation of the type Reynaud calls *Top-Down*. This control produced the linguistic corruption displayed in Figure 4c.

The BLT report concluded, again without analysis of the submission phenomena, that "the language analyst suspects that North Somalia language is the real dialect of the foreigner. The foreigner tries with much difficulty to look like a south Somalian through the way he mingles in his speech. He imitates the interpreter. It is clear the foreigner did not live or did not socialize in southern Somalia. It is not possible to determine immediately the ethnicity of the foreigner based on his speech."

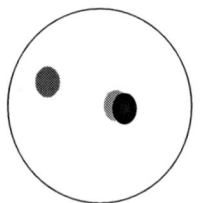

FIGURE 4C: Top-Down

These dialogues point to the argument that social exchange provides a basis for initiative in the interviewing context. Asymmetry of power is not the sole cause of imbalance; equally important are localizations embedded in the interrogative initiative as the interview unfolds. More precisely, the cognitive and normative regulation initiative is a major expression of power (Reynaud 2003, p. 107). Informed by this perspective, certain other elements of the interview may be subjected to renewed scrutiny. For example, the applicant takes the initiative when ordered to give details of his clan and his genealogy. He stated, "*Waxaa lay dhahaa Ashia Cabdulaahi Alimoge Hassan Cali. Waxaan ahay tumaal oo ka ahay Naaleeye, waxaan ka ahay Samade, Digifle, Ismaaciil, Saciid.*"[11] An anthropologist who worked on this case with the linguist, interprets this information as follows: "In Somalia, the genealogy of a person builds, as does his name, his fathers and his grandfathers, back great-grandfathers, etc.[12]

Applicant name:	Ashia
His father:	Abdullaahi
His grandfather:	Alimoge
His great-grandfather:	Hassan
His back great-grandfather:	Ali

The applicant then says she is of the sub-clan Naleeye, sub-clan Samade branch below Digifle, subgroup Cuntow finally Sicid Isma'il. That is extremely accurate information. As there is only a few Tumaal under this branch, it would be very easy to identify her. She's called Ashia Abdullaahi Alimoge. In addition, with the names Hassan and Ali, I can get all the information about this family, following the family tree."

This anthropological analysis, ostensibly to establish the true identity of an applicant, supports my early assertion that the social regulation theory is a social system that feeds power relations, crisis of authority, and legitimacy crisis. In view of this, only a psychological model can help maintain order in this schema.

---

[11] This is a pseudonym.

[12] Mohamed Abdi Mohamed was a professor at the University of Besançon when he developed this expertise for Makano International. More recently, he was Minister of Defense and president of the autonomous region of Jubaland in Somalia.

Framework Three: The Decision-Making Theory of Psychologist
Daniel Kahneman

Kahneman (2011) allows us to understand how applicants make decisions during the recording and how experts make decisions during the analysis of the digital audio file. Decisions are related to the respective socialization of the applicant and decision maker, and the focus of the task becomes precisely how and under what conditions an individual's brain is "programmed." Kahneman tells us that our memory often plays tricks on us and can lead us to make poor decisions. Kahneman (2011, pp. 20–50) describes this as "System One and Two thinking."

Kahneman argues that a person using System One "fast thinking" is always sure of himself, does not hesitate and is always ready to give answers when a question arises. He does not consider the possibility of a different interpretation and when faced with uncertainty, he uses his own intuition, past experiences or makes bets. Once an expert listens to the digital audio file, his memory is mentally programmed to analyze the language of the applicant and is unable to hear anything else (Chabris and Simons 2010). He thinks that he is listening to the language of the asylum seeker, whereas this is not always true. In fact, even before starting the analysis, his System One thinking had already constructed an analytical framework, which Kahneman calls *"the associative machine."* For this expert, System One "constructed a story" and System Two ("slow thinking") "believed it" (2011, pp. 50–58).

It is thus important to become familiar with the system used by the applicant. He may already be happy having arrived in a country without war and where he can eat, sleep, and see a doctor (Kam 2009, p. 76). In addition, during the interview he has neither the time nor sometimes the ability, to make in-depth decisions. As Kahneman (2011, p. 59) states, "the assessments are carried out automatically" by System One. I can therefore conclude that the language of the applicant is recorded by System One. Consequently, the digital audio file is created in the context of System One. But what about the experts? Just like asylum applicants, native speakers use their intuition (Davies 2004, p. 433). Thus BLT uses System One to produce their reports. Second opinion experts use scientific knowledge and consult several sources such as libraries, before establishing their report, which is consistent with System Two or "slow thinking," namely, rational thought, mental effort, and conscious doubt. The problem therefore established by using different systems for the reports is presented on the schematic diagram in Figure 5.

As a result of this analysis, it may be argued that disagreement is caused by difference of perspectives – whereas the BLT is using System One,

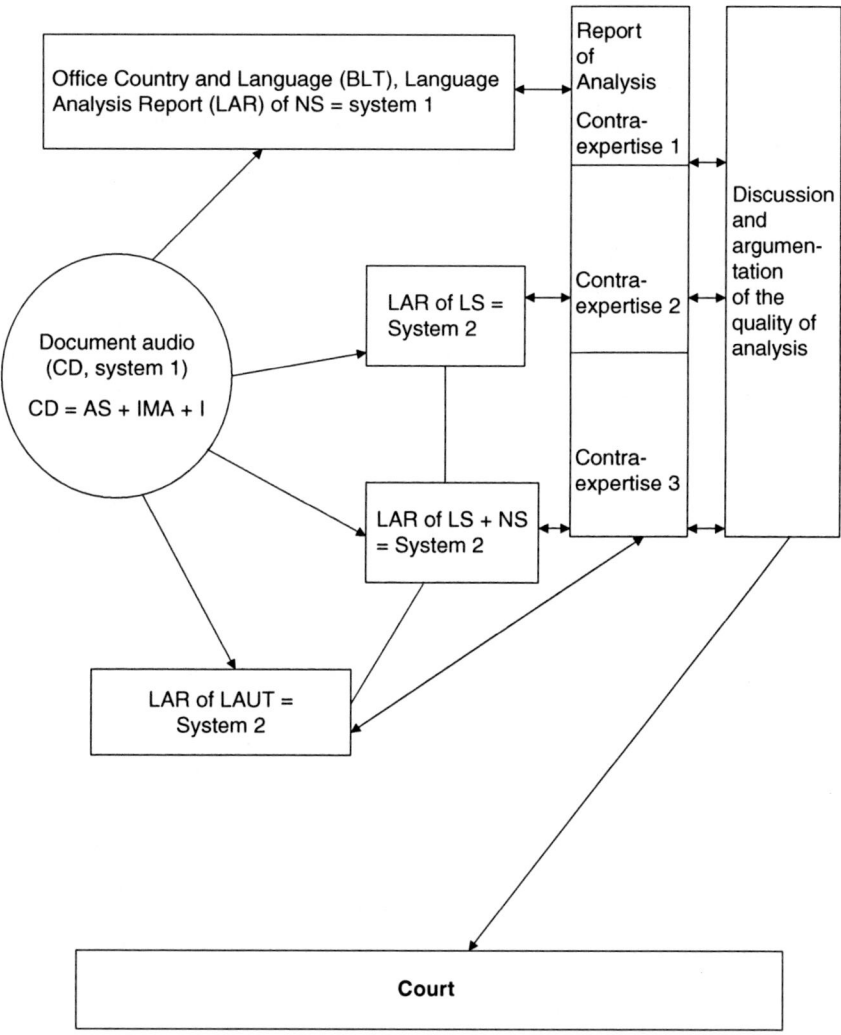

FIGURE 5: Production System of Language Analysis Report

jurisprudence requires second opinion experts to use System Two. This divergence also affects the content of reports because although second opinion experts argue with scientific knowledge, BLT uses intuition as the basis of its reports. In conclusion, drawing all the examples above together, it is worthwhile noting that the adjudicator received two reports upon which he had to make his decision: one report referred to sweet potatoes and the second spoke of potatoes.

CONCLUSION

The global desire to help persecuted people resides at the core of the search for sociological identity. By focusing on linguistic identity, certain "developed" countries, particularly in the European Union, have chosen to adopt LADO However, it has been revealed to be unreliable and controversial for many reasons. Here I have employed three theoretical frameworks to argue that the very production of the audio document is the productive site of many of the methodological problems associated with LADO

Ferdinand de Saussure demonstrated first that the recording of the audio document is done with the help of three actors who are limited by their own *language, and second* that *language* is active and individual, on the one hand, and social, on the other. Too often, so-called language "experts" do not distinguish between these two components of *language* in their analysis; they do not adhere to prevailing and established practices in language science. In fact, linguistic study of the active and individual part (*speech*) does not yet exist as a subfield of the discipline of language science. Thus, the scientific legitimacy of LADO analysis is inherently in question due to the bias embedded in the assumptions informing the methodology. By contrast, however, Dutch jurisprudence does not recognize the analyses of sociologists, anthropologists, psychologists, and others, and so such reports have no legal legitimacy. At least in The Netherlands, LADO has established itself as a methodological isolate, yet clings to the legitimacy of linguistic disciplinary heritage.

Reynaud permits us to look at the nonlinguistics, or the social part, of *language: the language*. I have demonstrated that *the language* used in the digital audio file may be revealed to be a power struggle based on negotiations and cultural types. The outcome of these negotiations determines how the applicant has to use *language* (*the language* and *speech*) during bargaining. The "experts" use only the bargain in their analysis. As such, the reports belie the fact that the language the applicant is using, regardless of the wishes of the applicant, may very likely not be his language. This is where the consideration of Daniel Kahneman's theories also becomes essential.

According to Kahneman, before listening to the digital audio file, an expert's memory (System One) had already constructed a story. The expert is sure and confident that he is listening to the language of the applicant. This analytical framework that is imposed by System One prevents the other part of his memory (System Two) to listen to the hidden transcript embedded in the digital audio file. Kahneman's theory thus explains why the language of the applicant may in fact not be his language. In addition, Kahneman theories help us appreciate how the digital audio file is registered in System One. BLT reports are analyzed in System One, whereas those of second opinion experts operate under System Two. Thus, adjudicators must make decisions based on effectively oppositional reports.

Pursuing the logic of De Terssac (2003, pp. 19–21), I observe that norms and values sometimes do not determine the behavior. Society considers the existing social system to be more important than individuals. On the contrary, theories of language, the rationality of judgment, decision making, and social regulations are part of an antithetical epistemological process because they are the actors who produce the system and not the reverse. Actors pose decisions even when these decisions are made in a structured context and pressures are not equal to determinism. That is why, in De Terssac's words, "society appears as a collective bricolage, whose effectiveness and legitimacy remains to be unexplained."

A careful scrutiny of the productive context of the digital audio file reveals how the search for the socialization of every applicant is a Kafkaesque episode for lawyers and adjudicators alike. Only further research will demonstrate whether a method of socialization may provide a solution to the methodological problems associated with LADO (Kam 2012a).

REFERENCES

Alter, Norbert. 2003. "Régulation Sociale et Déficit de Régulation." In Gilbert De Terssac, ed., *La Théorie de Régulation Sociale de Jean-Daniel Reynaud*. Paris: La Découverte.

Bronsdijk, Myrthe. 2006. "Interpreter in the Language Analysis Interview: Translation Machine or Second Interviewer?" Masterscriptie Faculteit der Letteren, Utrecht Universiteit.

Blommaert, Jan. 2008. *Grassroots Literacy: Writing, Identity and Voice in Central Africa*. London: Routledge.

Blommaert, Jan. 2009. "Language, Asylum and the National order." *Current Anthropology* 50(4): 415–41.

Blommaert, Jan. 2010. *The Sociolinguistics of Globalization*: Cambridge University Press.

Chabris, Christopher and Daniel Simons. 2010. *The Invisible Gorilla: And Other Ways Our Intuitions Deceive Us*. New York: Crown.

Cook, Vivian. 1999. "Going Beyond the Native Speaker in Language Teaching." *TESOL Quarterly* 33(2): 185–209.

Coppieters, René. 1987. "Competence Differences Between Native and Near Native." *Language* 63: 544–73.

Davies, Alan. 1991. *The Native Speaker in Applied Linguistics*. Edinburgh: Edinburgh University Press.

Davies, Alan. 2003. *The Native Speaker: Myth and Reality*. Clevedon: Multilingual Matters.

Davies, Alan and Catherine Elder. 2004. *The Handbook of Applied Linguistics*. Oxford: Blackwell.

Delvaux, Véronique et al. 2010. "Interactions mimétiques entre locuteurs: une étude expérimentale." Université de Mons.

De Mauro, Tullio. 1984. *Ferdinand de Saussure: Cours de Linguistique Générale*. Paris: Payot.

Department of Immigration. 2007. "BLT Language Analysis work Document (vakbijlage Taalanalyse)." Den Haag: BLT

Detailleur, Joachim N. 2010. "Shibboleth aan de poort: de theorie van de taalanalyse als middel kerkomstbepaling in de Nederlandse asielprocedure versus de praktijk van een Soedanese Arabisch-sprekende asielzoeker met vermeende Nuba-achtergrond." Doctoral thesis, Dept. of Middle East Studies, University of Leiden.

De Terssac, Gilbert. 2003. *La Théorie de Régulation Sociale de Jean-Daniel Reynaud*. Paris: La Découverte.

De Terssac, Gilbert. 2003. "La Théorie de Régulation Sociale: Repères Pour un Débat." In Gilbert De Terssac, ed., *La Théorie de Régulation Sociale de Jean-Daniel Reynaud*. Paris: La Découverte.

De Terssac, Gilbert. 2003. "Introduction." In Gilbert De Terssac, ed., *La Théorie de Régulation Sociale de Jean-Daniel Reynaud*. Paris: La Découverte.

Dressen, Marnix. 2003. "Autonomie et Controle, Terminologie et Relation." In Gilbert De Terssac, ed., *La Théorie de Régulation Sociale de Jean-Daniel Reynaud*. Paris: La Découverte.

Dubet, Francois and Danilo Martuccelli. 1996. "Théories de la Socialization et Définitions Sociologiques de l'École." *Revue de sociologique française* 37(4): 511–35.

Dumonteil-Kremer, Catherine. 2003. *Élever son Enfant Autrement*. Paris: La Plage.

Eades, Diana. 2009. "Testing the Claims of Asylum Seekers: The role of Language Analysis." *Language Assessment Quarterly* 6: 30–40.

Erard, Michael. 2003. "Immigration by Shibboleth: Should a Refugee Be Judged by What He Says or How He Says It?" *Legal Affairs: The Magazine at the Intersection of Law and Life*. Accessed April 2, 2013. http://www.legalaffairs.org.

Hedebris, Hélène. 2010. "The Need for Language Analysis in Swedish Asylum Cases and the Problems Regarding Language Analysis in Swedish Court Practice". Presented at G.W.L.A., Gothenburg.

Irigaray, Luce. 1974. "Le Schizophène et la Question du Signe." In *Les Deux Saussure*. Fontenay-Sous-Bois: CERFI.

Kam, Noé M. 2009. "Recours à la Demande d'Asile par Analyse Linguistique: l'Exemple des Pays-Bas: l'Identité linguistique et Psychoculturelle." Master's thesis. UCL-Louvain.

Kam, Noé M. 2010. "Language Test and Interview by Author." Tape recording. Stadskanaal, ME, 10 January–16 February.

Kam, Noé M. 2012a. "Language Analysis for Determining the Origin (LADO) of Asylum Seekers: A Socialization Method." Presented at the 2012 Conable Conference in International Studies. R.I.T., Rochester.

Kam, Noé M. 2012b. "African Projects for Asylum Seekers' Language Analysis: The Case of Ifo Refugee Camp." Presented at Workshop Researching and Writing About Africa. University of Lancaster.

Kahneman, Daniel. 2011. *Thinking, Fast and Slow*. London: Penguin Books.
Komatsu, Eisuke and Roy Harris. 1993. *Saussure's Third Course of Lectures on General Linguistics 1910–1911*. Oxford: Pergamon Press.
Krauss, Robert M. and Jennifer S. Pardo. 2006. *Speaker Perception and Social Behavior: Bridging Social Psychology and Speech Science*. Columbia University.
Leseman, Paul. 2010. "Taal is macht – De Macht van de Taal." Presented at FSW. University Utrecht.
Ly, Boubakar. 1985. "La Socialization des Jeunes dans les Villes du Tiers-Monde: le cas de l'Afrique." *International Review of Education* XXXI, 4: 413–27.
Malmberg, Bertil. 1991. *Histoire de la Linguistique de Sumer à Saussure*. Paris: PUF.
Martuccelli, Danilo. 2005. "Les trois Voies de l'Individu Sociologique." EspacesTemps.net, http://espacestemps.net, Last accessed March 20, 2009.
Maurer, Willi. 2004. *Mère et Bébé l'un Contre l'Autre: du Processus d'Attachement à l'Appartenance Sociale*. Barret-sur-Méouge: le Souffle d'Or.
Maxamed, Cabdi M. 1986. *Eraybixin Soomaali-Faransiis/Lexique*. Paris: Maxamed Cabdi M.
Médina, José. 1978. "Les Difficultés Théoriques de la Constitution d'une Linguistique Comme Science Autonome." In *Claudine Normand: Langages, Saussure et la Linguistique pré-Saussurienne*. Paris: Didier Larousse.
Mejía, Claudia. 1998. *La linguistique diachronique*. Geneva: Droz.
Mohamed Abdi, Mohamed. 2000. "Les Bouleversements Induits par la Guerre Civile en Somalie: Castes Marginales et Minorités." *Autrepart* 15: 131–147.
Mohamed Abdi, Mohamed. 2003. "Retour Vers les 'Dugsi'." *Écoles Coraniques en Somalie* 43(CEA 169/170): 351–69.
Normand, Claudine. 1978. *Langue/Parole: Constitution et Enjeu d'une Opposition*. In *Claudine Normand: Langages, saussure et la Linguistique Pré-Saussurienne*. Paris: Didier Larosse.
Pardo, Jennifer. S. et al. 2010. "Conversational Role Influences Speech Imitation." *Attention, Perception, and Psychophysics* 72(8): 2254–64.
Ramadan, Tariq. 2009. "Mission d'Information sur la Pratique du Port du Voile Intégral sur le Territoire National." LCP Television, December 2.
Rocher, Guy. 1968. *Introduction à la Sociologie Générale*. Vol. 1. Paris: L'Harmattan.
Reynaud, Jean-Daniel. 2003. "Régulation de Contrôle, Régulation Autonome, Régulation Conjointe." In Gilbert De Terssac, ed., *La Théorie de Régulation Sociale de Jean-Daniel Reynaud*. Paris: La Découverte.
Teubert, Wolfgang. 2010. "La linguistique de corpus: une alternative," *Semen* 27 [on line], 2009. http://semen.revues.org [last accessed November 12, 2011].
UNHCR 2000. *The 1951 Convention Relating to the Status of Refugees and Its 1967 Protocol*. Oxford: Oxford University Press.
Vilkou-Pustovaïa, Irina. 2002. "Cahiers Ferdinand de Saussure." *Librairie Droz* 55: 115–36.
Wasow, Thomas and Jennifer Arnold. 2005. "Intuitions in Linguistic Argumentation." *Lingua* 115: 1481–96.
Winch, Peter. 1958. *The idea of a Social Science and its Relations to Philosophy*. London: Routledge & Kegan.

3

Research and Testimony in the "Rape Capital of the World": Experts and Evidence in Congolese Asylum Claims

Galya Ruffer

As I prepared for my first field research trip in March 2010 to the eastern Democratic Republic of Congo (DRC) to study the introduction of criminal justice and rule of law programs to combat sexual and gender-based violence in the war-torn country, I collected human rights reports and read up on the past ten years of instability and conflict that has led to the official understanding of the DRC as the "rape capital of the world."[1] Well versed in the human rights reports detailing the mass rapes of women in villages and the rough condition of fieldwork in the worst country in the world according to the international development index, I was quite unsettled to find myself seated on the floral hillside terrace of L'Orchid hotel with its honeymoon view of Lake Kivu, watching the fishermen, sipping red wine, and listening to Jonathan, a fortyish man who, seated alone, had invited me to dine with him, tell me his view about rape in the DRC. He had been a South African soldier stationed in Zaire in 1994 and was now working to set up an artisanal mine. He told me up front that he was not in it for humanitarian purposes. It was business, but at least, unlike the humanitarians, he was honest about it. What he wanted me to know is not to believe everything I hear, that Western researchers come and take away the wrong lessons. He emphasized that people here are clever and that rape had become a lucrative NGO business for locals and internationals alike.

.

---

[1] *U.N. Official Calls D.R. Congo 'Rape Capital of the World,'* B.B.C. News (April 28, 2010), http://news.bbc.co.uk/2/hi/8650112.stm; Flynn Lloyd-Davis, *Why Eastern D.R. Congo Is 'Rape Capital of the World,'* CNN (November 25, 2011), http://www.cnn.com%20/2011/11/24/world/africa/democratic-congo-rape; Lauren Wolfe, *End Culture of Rape in 2013,* CNN (Jan. 3, 2013), http://www.cnn.com/2013/01/01/opinion/wolfe-end-rape-in-2013/index.html.

During my field visits over the course of two years, I interviewed people such as Christof, who had been working with Malteser International for twenty years in eastern DRC who agreed with Jonathan that by the time the West came in with its moral authority to do justice and reconstruct rule of law, the kind of military operation rape they came to combat had ended. According to him, the main trouble areas remain the ones with severely limited access that no one can do anything about, whereas accessible villages and centers are no longer the problem they had been during the peak years of instability and war. Descartes Mponge Malasi, the countrywide coordinator for the Action of Christian Activists for Human Rights in Shabunda territory, a local partner receiving funds to provide support for rape victims to bring their cases and community educational programs on sexual and gender-based violence, wanted me to understand that military rape is just a small aspect of the problem and that the larger problem, that internationals do not want to fund, is the underlying cultural aspect of rape that supports underage sex or cohabitation. What emerged from my many conversations and testimony collection was that even if rape did not exist as framed by Western advocacy efforts, women were severely marginalized and rape, as domestic abuse, incest, child abuse, underage marriage, or a way for a girl to pay her school fees seem to be part of daily life in the DRC. There is, therefore, a deep injustice of rape against women that, I would argue, rises to the level of persecution.

Studying the political and historic situation for months, speaking with academic and human rights experts and, now, having spent months on the ground, I felt I could speak with some authority to what I saw and heard. I knew many of my colleagues had served as expert witnesses in asylum cases. As I hold both a law degree and doctorate in political science and was a pro-bono asylum lawyer myself, I thought that I might be able to contribute my expertise in Congolese cases. But, as I began to read through the descriptions of cases in need of pro-bono assistance coming out of the DRC, I was struck by how the expertise wanted of me bore little resemblance to the narratives people shared with me and situations I encountered while conducting my field research. Whereas I felt best able to share my expertise of everyday, indiscriminate rape as an insidious form of social control and persecution, almost all of the cases framed the rape as politically motivated. Given this gap, the question is how can field researchers best contribute as experts, given the ethical tensions between narrating what the researcher sees on the ground and the need to engage with the questions formulated by an adjudicator?

THE NEED FOR EVIDENCE AND THE REALITIES OF FIELD
RESEARCHER EXPERIENCE

After decades of human rights advocacy, rape and sexual violence are recognized as a war crime and an atrocity crime in the International Tribunals and the Rome Statute of the International Criminal Court and, for purposes of seeking asylum, as a form of persecutory harm. In the United States, women's rights activists litigated hard to have rape, sexual violence, and gender-based crimes and discrimination recognized as persecution, to have women understood as a particular social group targeted for persecution, and to expand understandings of political opinion such that the rape of a woman whose husband belongs to a political party, tribe, or ethnic clan in a country where women are locked out of politics is understood as persecution on account of an imputed political opinion. A major limitation in these legal advocacy efforts has been the lack of evidence and the complexity of credibility determinations.

In a section on evidentiary matters, the United Nations High Commissioner for Refugee (UNHCR) Guidelines on Gender-Related Persecution state, "It is important to recognize that in relation to gender-related claims, the usual types of evidence used in other refugee claims may not be as readily available. Statistical data or reports on the incidence of sexual violence may not be available, due to under-reporting of cases, or lack of prosecution. Alternative forms of information might assist, such as testimonies of other women similarly situated in written reports or oral testimony, of non-governmental or international organizations or other independent research."[2] These guidelines ring true for cases of sexual and gender-based violence in the DRC where the main form of evidence is testimony collected by internationally NGOs and their local partners. Although women do often receive medical exams in places such as the DRC after a reported rape, these are not usually available for use in legal proceedings.

There is, of course, no shortage of country information documenting human rights abuses, massive rapes, and ongoing instability and conflict the DRC. But, even with over three thousand country information documents in the *Refworld* database of the United Nations High Commissioner for Refugees and thirty-nine focusing specifically on rape confirming the "deprivations endured by thousands of victims of sexual violence in the DRC, including

---

[2]   UN High Commissioner for Refugees (UNHCR), Guidelines on International Protection No. 1: Gender-Related Persecution Within the Context of Article 1A(2) of the 1951 Convention and/or its 1967 Protocol Relating to the Status of Refugees, 7 May 2002, HCR/GIP/02/01, available at: http://www.refworld.org/docid/3d36f1c64.html [Retrieved February 23, 2014], paragraph 37.

poverty, denial of justice and lack of access to medical and psychological treatment, and recommends the establishment of a reparations fund," establishing that an asylum applicant from the DRC has a credible claim as a victim of sexual and gender-based violence based on one of the protected grounds is more complicated.[3] Indeed, in the United Kingdom, the applications of Congolese women are regularly denied.[4] Lindsey Harris's study of asylum claims in South Africa highlights that although South Africa has signed a number of international agreements and treaties recognizing rape as a form of torture, including the Convention on the Elimination of Discrimination Against Women, the Convention Against Torture, the recognition of rape as a form of persecution is inconsistent within the South African refugee system (Harris 2009).

In the United States, rape and sexual violence have been recognized forms of persecutory harm for over 15 years (Anker 2013, §4:15). Yet, although rape is "one of the least controversial forms of serious harm" and has been recognized as an instrument of repression and domination that qualifies as persecutory harm under the Convention, for the individual woman or girl seeking protection in her own country or a country of refuge or justice in a court of law or international tribunal, the reality is that ambiguities in societal understanding of rape and cross-cultural understandings continue to inhibit her protection and legal forms of relief (Anker 2013, §4:15). The main problem is that the refugee determination requires both that the applicant suffered persecutory harm and that the harm was "on account of" one of the five protected grounds under the refugee Convention. Sexual violence experienced by women "is often considered to be irrelevant within the normative framework of asylum determination: sexual violence is viewed as something inherently private, and it is this conceptualization that is reproduced in refugee law" (Crawley 2000, p. 95). The result is that adjudicators have interpreted rape as a private or personal act distinct from the political motivation on which the claim might otherwise be based. The logic is that whereas the torture and execution of family members is a political act, a rape that occurs in the course of such events is "derailed sexuality" (Crawley 2000, p. 96).

Although there have been significant advancements in terms of both the UNHCR and states stipulation of gender guidelines for the determination of asylum claims, there is still a significant inability on the part of adjudicators to

---

3   U.N. News Service, "Democratic Republic of the Congo: U.N. report details suffering of rape victims, recommends reparations." March 3, 2011. http://www.refworld.org/docid/4d7089ed1a .html [Retrieved June 27, 2013].

4   Kamena Dorling, Marchu Girma and Natasha Walter, "Refused: The experiences of women denied asylum in the UK," http://wssagwales.files.wordpress.com/2012/10/refused.pdf

"bear witness" to the complexity of rape as persecution comprised of state inaction, the role and status of women in a culture or society, nature of family relationships, and attitudes toward sexual relations. In addition, even though the UNHCR guidelines state that adjudicators should consider a number of issues – including the position of women before the law, the political rights of women, the social and economic rights of women, consequences for women who refuse to abide by or who challenge social, religious, or cultural norms regarding their behavior, incidence and form of violence against women, efficacy of protection available to women, and the consequences that may befall a woman on her return – there are often little or no facts concerning these issues (Crawley 2001, p. 216).

The ambiguity surrounding what constitutes persecutory rape has pushed human rights advocates to try to present in as clear terms as possible the connection of rape (so that it's not misunderstood as a general criminal act or private gratification, but rather as having a state connection or nonstate agents that the state is unwilling or unable to control) to ethnic cleansing, conflict minerals, rebel war lords and failed states, omitting, as beyond public comprehension, the complexity and commonness of rape in all societies. "Rape as a weapon of war" has emerged as a forceful legal argument, although much more difficult has been proving the chain of command necessary for purposes of conviction. Rape and sexual violence by members of the armed forces or rebel groups have been recognized as a solid ground for refugee status. Therefore, NGO reports and testimonies are strategically collected to present a singular argument, a "rape script" (Buss 2009). This mass data, however, ends up silencing, rejecting, and ignoring the testimony of an individual woman in need of protection and justice from the men and boys in her village or the one nearby who sometimes wear military uniforms and other times do not (Ruffer 2013). The images of military or rebel rape mask that these "official rape scripts" are often men and boys who, on another day, might be the schoolteacher, businessman, neighbor, unemployed bandit, or school-boy in love with the girl in the field who have raped these same women throughout the course of their lives. In the Republic of Congo (also known as Congo Brazzaville), I met with a physician who has been working with Congolese refugees who fled the violence in Equiteur province across the river for the past fifteen years. He came with his family as a missionary and, in his introduction to me about his work, said, "I am here because I love the Congolese (pause), let me rephrase that, I am here because, through God, I have love for the Congolese. I do not love them, they are difficult to love." He said that I need to understand that these Congolese girls do not see their bodies as their own in the Western sense of being the decision maker of what one does with ones body. Instead, when he tries to give a girl the standard talk about "you have a choice whether or not to have sex," they giggle with incomprehension as such a foreign idea that she would have control over what happens to her body.

The "rape script" documented in human rights reports stands in tension with field researchers, such as myself, who have examined the underlying context of rape. Although the "rape script" is an accurate documentation of events that have occurred, the problem of rape in the DRC cannot be understood or, for that matter, "combatted" through the lens of the rape script. Take, for example, the case of the two girls, ages sixteen and thirteen, who were assisted by a local partner NGO in the village of Katana that has assisted over two hundred victims of sexual violence. Given the 2006 rape law in the DRC, sex with anyone under the age of eighteen is a crime. The director I interviewed played a video recording of his interview with the two girls at the police station. As was translated to me, the girls were taken by military men who caught them and took them to their post to have sex with them. Men from the village saw that the girls were being abducted, followed them into the forest and were able to take them back. They brought them to the police so that they may explain what happened. At the end of the interview the director put the question to the girls, don't you want that these men be put to justice? The girls said, no why do you want to put him in jail, he's innocent. After the interview at the police station, the police went to the family and, as was stated to me, "received some corruption" and released the girls. The joke, as was explained to me, is that two months later the director met that thirteen-year-old girl in the village and she told him, you know you were stopping me from going to the military, I'm married with him and let me give you money. As the director explained to me, as long as people need money, the girls will go and, because of the 2006 rape law that criminalizes underage marriage, there will be arrests to extract corruption that brings in money.[5]

The problem is that the "rape script" derives from a conflict and security lens and that, beyond that, it is written with a Western understanding of rape that ends up undermining efforts to address the injustice of rape and sexual violence in eastern DRC. In eastern DRC, one must take into account that community interests are more important than individual rights, marriage is a common ritual but not an institution in Western understandings, there is great value placed on fertility and having many children is important given concepts of wealth and/or the need to cultivate land, depriving a man of the ability to work by putting him in jail is frowned upon, the person who brings a crime to

---

[5]   Field Research notes September 13, 2010.

the attention of the authorities has the responsibility to decide what to do with the perpetrator (there is no state obligation to prosecute crimes), and, often-times, the local authority will lock up the rape victim preventing her from seeking medical aid as a way to protect her. During my interviews I learned that many of the cases of rape originated in land disputes and that women, who had been raped, and bystanders attributed most rapes to witchcraft (i.e., drugs) having overtaken the man or the woman.

As a field researcher called on to evaluate the merits of an applicant's claim and assess her credibility by speaking about the political and social conditions, likelihood of persecution, the applicant's community, the circumstances of her claim, or to clarify her testimony, the personal narratives I encountered can easily support the harm inflicted, culture of impunity, and the deeply rooted injustices against women in the Congo. Given the personal narratives I heard during my research, I cannot as easily support a legal argument based on commandos executing rape as a direct military order in a war over minerals or as part of a systematic attack on the political opposition. It's not that such arguments cannot be constructed based on rapes that occurred by men in uniforms or men who belong to political parties; it's that rape and unwanted sexual encounters are so widespread that, for the victims and investigators attempting to document the rapes, it is often unclear who are the perpetrators and who is in charge. And, given the lack of military training, shortage of uniforms, inadequate pay, integration of rebel forces into the national mili-tary, the Armed Forced of the Democratic Republic of Congo (FARDC), and years of instability, most of the so-called soldiers are more accurately "bandits," that is, boys and young men without a job. For example, although almost all of the women I interviewed used the term "FDLR," in speaking about the rapists, when I asked them if they meant that the men were the Democratic Forces for the Liberation of Rwanda (FDLR) rebels, would tell me they did not know and that, by FDLR they meant "bandits". In all the interviews from my three site visits, only two of the women that I interviewed said that they had been raped by FDLR during looting raids or other attacks on villages. In particular, the rapes by the FDLR who, in the international press, are the main perpetrators of the massive rape in the DRC, have never been prosecuted as none of the FDLR have ever been caught. Just about all were raped throughout their lives by neighbors, family members, or soldiers stationed in the village to protect them and, when I asked the women to tell me more about where they had come from and if they owned land, many of the rapes were on account of land disputes.

In February 2011, I attended the mobile gender court trial of Lt. Colonel Kibibi in the remote village of Baraka in the southern part of South Kivu. According to the charges and testimony that I witnessed, the rapes were precipitated by a bar brawl over the girlfriend of a local villager with whom an off-duty soldier had made an advance and was then attacked by the local villager and killed. Upon hearing that their fellow soldier had been killed, members of the battalion raided and looted the village raping women in the process. The 2011 U.S. State Department report, however, documents the case as follows:

> In February a military tribunal sentenced 10 FARDC officers to 10–20 years in prison for a mass rape committed in Fizi on January 1 that victimized at least 35 women. Lieutenant Colonel Kibibi Mutware, a former National Congress for the Defence of the People (CNDP) rebel integrated and promoted within the FARDC and the main defendant, received a 20-year sentence.[6]
>
> According to MONSCO, that same night in the town of Fizi, South Kivu, FARDC Colonel Kibibi and his men raped at least 35 women in retaliation for the killing of a FARDC soldier by civilians. As discussed in section 1.d., authorities arrested Lieutenant Colonel Kibibi and 10 of his men and tried them for the rapes. The military tribunal sentenced Kibibi and three other officers to 20 years in prison, two soldiers to 15 years, and three soldiers to 10 years in prison for human rights violations, including mass rapes. In addition, one soldier was acquitted while a minor who was among the accused was transferred to a juvenile court. At year's end, Kibibi was reportedly serving his sentence.[7]

A U.N. News Service report documenting U.N. provision of logistical support for rape trials states:

> Last month, a military court sentenced several army officers and soldiers for rape and other human rights abuses, marking the first time that a high-ranking commander and several other personnel serving with the Congolese national armed forces were arrested, tried and sentenced for conflict-related sexual violence.
>
> Lt. Col. Kibibi Mutware was reportedly sentenced to 20 years in jail after being found guilty of crimes against humanity for sending his troops to rape, beat and loot from the population of Fizi, in eastern DRC, during the night of 1 to 2 January 2011. Judges also sentenced three officers serving under the commander to 20 years in jail and five soldiers to between 10 and 15 years.[8]

The mobile court trial, a collaboration of international NGOs costing tens of thousands of dollars, was organized by the American Bar Association Rule of

---

[6] State Department Human Rights Report, 2011, section 1.d.
[7] State Department Human Rights Report, 2011, section 1.g.
[8] U.N. News Service, "Democratic Republic of Congo: U.N. provides logistical support for rape trial of army general." March 30, 2011. http://www.refworld.org/docid/4d957302c.html [Retrieved June 27, 2013].

Law Initiative. Local villagers understood it as an international performance because, as they noted, none of the perpetrators will stay in jail and there will be no change in the military that has been preying on villagers for years. To date, the victims have been forgotten having received no reparations. In their publication "Our Voices Matter," the Women's Initiatives for Gender Justice interviewed one of the victims who was among the sixty-three women who were raped by Kibibi's FARDC soldiers during the Fizi New Year's mass rape. As they document, following the sentence, the Congolese Government declared that it would compensate each victim with U.S. $10,000. However, no action has been taken to compensate victims of this case. They then quote the interviewee as saying, "We won the trial in Baraka but until now we haven't even received copies of the judgement [*sic*]. The government told us that it would compensate us, but since then we haven't seen anyone come to us, neither the authorities nor the judges" (Ruffer 2013, pp. 141–2).

Although some of the rapes being prosecuted were military, such as this one by Kibibi, most were civilian. Most remarkable to me was that no one I had interviewed had benefited from the process of justice, all of their lives had been made worse. If they were schoolaged girls, they were no longer allowed back in school having been stigmatized and bullied by teachers and children. Women were shunned by neighbors for having been the cause of a male provider being put in prison. Or, because the prison system is so ineffective, often the perpetrator was back living in the village and the woman was being harassed and chased off her land, if she had some. Having never received any reparations, they were destitute. After the fact, most would have preferred mediation that would have afforded them a bit of money and reintegration into community life. Although there were a few who were engaged in internationally funded social and economic programs, the reality is that most women cannot benefit from these programs given the vast numbers of women in need.

These "messy realities" rarely appear in international press reports that, focused on the formal legal process, provide statistics on the number of convictions or sexual and gender-based violence (SGBV) educational trainings. International and NGOs working in the DRC who are the main providers of information have particular agendas and policy objectives. Data they collect, therefore, is targeted to respond to donor questions. This is not unknown and even the State Department in its 2012 report states:

> Statistical information on rape remained fragmented and incomplete. Statistics often came from international and local NGO service providers and therefore were skewed towards priority implementation areas. For

example, the Ministry of Gender was unable to supply information for Equateur, Kasai Occidental, Kasai Oriental, and Maniema provinces.[9]

The point is that "official" narratives of rape in the DRC have always fulfilled particular objectives be they humanitarian, security or foreign policy. Conducting a genealogy of rape in the DRC, it turns out the region has a long history of concerns of rape having reached crisis proportion, but that the official narratives regarding rape in the Congo have shifted over time.

Whereas one can tell the story of rape in the DRC as a part of the regional conflict over land rights and minerals, the view that emerges from a study of the scholarship and journalistic accounts of the DRC since the late 1880s suggests that rape in the DRC has been, at different times, part of the international narrative of the conquest, Belgian rule, struggle for independence, secession of Katanga, character of the undisciplined military, Mobutuism administration, and, now, Rwandan and Ugandan influence in the conflict over minerals, ever since the first Western colonizers arrived (Ruffer 2013).

The genealogy of rape highlights the particularity of the official narratives of rape in the DRC today as captured by a 2009 Congressional Report:

> The prevalence of sexual violence has been attributed to the eroded status of women over years of conflict, weak state authority, a weak justice system, and a breakdown in community protection mechanisms. Sexual violence by the military has also been linked to waves of integration of rebel organizations into the military through successive peace accords, with little accompanying attention to military discipline or the chain of command. Military troops are poorly paid, and troops deployed in conflict areas are not provided adequate food or supplies, which some observers believe encourages looting and other abuses. Reports suggest that while most sexual crimes are carried out by members of armed groups in conflict zones, incidents or rape by civilians are also increasing. One report expressed concern that rape may have "become trivialized and has been increasingly perpetrated in zones of relative stability" (Arieff 2009, p. 18).

The report mentions that there are few reliable statistics on sexual violence in most African countries and that data collection is not a component of most U.S. programs. Furthermore, little is known about the effectiveness of individual programs in reducing the scale of violence" (Arieff 2009, p. 23). The governing narrative sees rape as part of ongoing conflict in the DRC and, as such, some have "questioned whether responding to sexual violence deserves prioritization over broader conflict resolution efforts and programs aimed at improving women's status and economic power in African societies" (Arieff

---

[9]   State Department Human Rights Country Report, DRC, 2012.

2009, p. 23). Others have argued that "policies are, at times, designed with little input from local communities, and may emphasize, for example, technologically advanced solutions that may not be feasible in impoverished, conflict-affected regions of Africa" (Arieff 2009, p. 23–24). Because of the particular narrative of rape that has emerged in the DRC, policy responses lack continuity and long-term focus. Instead, sexual and gender-based violence programs are generally funded, in the United States, for example, "through accounts such as Economic Support Funds, Peacekeeping Operations, International Narcotics Control and Law Enforcement, which inhibit long-term planning (Arieff 2009, p. 24).

What the "official" narrative silences are the problems and issues associated with, what I have termed, the "injustice of rape" (Ruffer 2013). In this chapter, I turn to the question of expert testimony of rape as persecution. International law does not recognize the injustice of rape of the kind narrated by the many women I met in the DRC as "persecution" for the purposes of receiving asylum. Nor does it recognize endemic rape in a society as an atrocity crime of the kind that is prosecuted in the International Criminal Court (ICC). Therefore, charges of rape in the DRC have been dropped from ICC prosecutions. The question for this study of sexual and gender-based asylum claims coming from the DRC is how can field researchers best contribute as experts given the ethical tensions between narrating what the researcher sees on the ground and the need to engage with the questions formulated by an adjudicator?

CREDIBILITY ASSESSMENTS AND THE RESEARCHER AS EXPERT

Considering the international attention on rape in the DRC, one might expect that many Congolese women are seeking refuge in the same Western states that are contributing to combating rape in the country. It is striking, therefore, that much fewer women actually receive asylum based on rape in the DRC. The main limitation is that while gender-specific persecution can be inflicted on women for political reasons, it does not necessarily constitute persecution because of gender as opposed to a criminal act committed by individuals.

Because the well-founded fear of persecution standard requires an individualized determination, country reports, while being able to establish a generalized possibility of persecution, cannot establish that the individual applicant is at particular risk. In order to establish a well-founded fear of future persecution, the applicant must present "credible, direct, and specific evidence" that she has a reasonable fear of persecution. In other words, that she "faces an objectively reasonable risk of persecution, as well as a genuine, subjective fear or 'an apprehension or awareness of danger'" (Anker 2013: § 2:5). Given the number and content of reports documenting rape in the DRC, it would seem fairly straightforward for a woman or girl from the DRC to corroborate the elements of subjective and objective fear as these reports clearly show that there are country-specific conditions. The applicant, however, still has to show that she has either been the victim of SGBV in the past, was targeted and harmed, or that others associated to her were targeted or persecuted, or that there is a "pattern or practice" of persecution of persons similarly situated to her (Anker 2013: § 2:5).

The UNHCR Guidelines on Gender-Related Persecution emphasize that it is important to approach the assessment "holistically" and that it is "essential to have both a full picture of the asylum-seeker's personality, background and personal experiences, as well as an analysis and up-to-date knowledge of historically, geographically and culturally specific circumstances in the country of origin."[10] Recognizing that women are often excluded from politics, the section on Procedural Issues the Guidelines council adjudicators that "[w]omen who have been involved in indirect political activity or to whom political opinion has been attributed, for example, often do not provide relevant information in interviews due to the male-oriented nature of the questioning. Female claimants may also fail to relate questions that are about 'torture' to the types of harms which they fear (such as rape, sexual abuse, female genital mutilation, 'honour killings'or forced marriage)."[11]

Given the clear documentation of pervasive rape in the DRC, lack of or failed state authority, culture of impunity for perpetrators, and political unrest and instability, it was surprising to me to learn that there is only one published case of a woman receiving refugee status in the United States for rape in the DRC or, for that matter, sexual violence from any country. The case, *Vumi*, concerns a woman who fled the DRC in 2001 alleging that she had been twice arrested, interrogated and mistreated by the Congolese military, which suspected her ex-husband of involvement in the January 2001 assassination of former President Laurent Kabila. On December 10, 2004, the Immigration Judge granted Vumi's claim for relief under the Convention Against Torture but denied her application for asylum finding that she had failed to demonstrate that the harm she suffered was on account of a protected ground. The

[10] IIA(7), Guidelines on International Protection No. 1: *Gender-Related Persecution within the Context of Article 1A(2) of the 1951 Convention and/or Its 1967 Protocol Relating to the Status of Refugees*, H.C.R./G.I.P./02/01 (May 7, 2002).

[11] III 36 (vii) Guidelines on International Protection No. 1: *Gender-Related Persecution within the Context of Article 1A(2) of the 1951 Convention and/or Its 1967 Protocol Relating to the Status of Refugees*, H.C.R./G.I.P./02/01 (May 7, 2002).

Board of Immigration Appeals (BIA) affirmed this determination, but the Second Circuit overturned the BIA on August 31st, 2007.[12] The issue on appeal was whether Vumi's persecution was on account of her membership in a particular social group or her political opinion.

The *Vumi* case illustrates the hurdles an applicant faces in submitting a claim based on sexual and gender-based violence. The two essential elements for a grant of asylum for rape in the DRC tend to include harm, that is, rape ordered by the military or a rebel group that was "on account of" her membership in a political party, ethnic group, or nationality, that such an affiliation was imputed to her, or that she was targeted based on her membership as a family member or some other visible and immutable group. Even though there is no objective evidence that exists, anywhere, of a commander ordering rapes (even at the International Criminal Court this was the main problem that has led to rape charges being dropped), she must offer credible testimony that there was an order by a commander in order to distinguish her rape from that of a victim of a random crime and that the order was made because of her political activity or that of a family member.

It is no wonder that most of the Congolese asylum cases based on SGBV are framed in political and activist terms. The personal backgrounds of the women in these cases tend to be educated, activists, or the daughters of fathers and uncles who hold political office or have worked as security guards or in the military. Each month, for example, I receive the National Immigrant Justice Center pro-bono case list. During the period of my field research, I recorded the cases in need of legal assistance. One concerned a woman who had been married to a district treasurer for the Movement for the Liberation of Congo (MLC), an opposition party that had protested Kabila and his government. The applicant in the case was kidnapped and brought to a military camp by soldiers looking for her husband where she was raped by a guard. After traveling to the United States in 2010 on a tourist visa to attend her brother-in-law's graduation, she was contacted by government security officers and then raped again when five armed met invaded her house in the middle of the night. Another case concerned a commercial flight attendant who joined the MLC and became the leader's personal flight attendant. After the MLC leader fled the DRC, she returned to her job as a commercial flight attendant but military men appeared at her house, took her for interrogation and threatened to rape her. When she heard that they had come again to look for her, she fled. A third case concerned a businesswoman in Katanga who was a board member of a very large evangelical Christian church. The pastor of the church had a

---

[12] *Vumi v. Gonzales* 502 F.3d 150 (2007).

history of political opposition and owned a radio station through which he publicly stated his opinions regarding the Congolese government. In July 2004, the National Intelligence Agency (ANR) arrested and imprisoned him after he gave a sermon criticizing the government and demanding social reform and the sermon was broadcast on the radio station. The pastor eventually died from medical problems related to the torture and harsh conditions in the prison. In March 2008, the applicant received a warning that she was in danger having given a speech to church members that the government was trying to take over the church. She fled to another city, learned that the ANR had imprisoned, tortured, and interrogated her husband for three days regarding her whereabouts, returned to Katanga in September 2008, but was warned again that the ANR was looking for her and fled to Kinshasa. On the day she left, the ANR arrested her husband and tortured and interrogated him for two weeks. She tried coming back to Katanga in October 2008 to find her family, but was detained by the ANR and brutally tortured, raped, and interrogated regarding her political connections and motivations. A fourth case concerned a twenty-two-year-old woman who studied law and worked as an independent journalist writing about politics, human rights abuses, economics and the current situation in the DRC. In mid-October 2008, she attended the live broadcast of a speech given by Roger Lumbala, a Parliament member and leader of a political opposition party in which he explicitly accused the president of winning the 2006 elections through fraudulent means. After learning that the secret police arrested and imprisoned some of the other journalists who had attended the broadcast, she hid in a friend's home and fled to the United States. After arriving in the United States, she learned that the government had imprisoned the other two journalists present at the broadcast, none of whom have received a trial and remain in prison. She learned from neighbors that the secret police interrogated others living in her apartment building regarding her whereabouts. The fifth case concerned a twenty-one-year-old woman who is part of the Nande tribe in northeast DRC. Her father died when she was young. In 2006, after graduating from vocational school in Gandalungwa, she went to live with her mother and brothers in Kiwanja. In June 2008, her mother heard rumors that the rebel group National Congress for the Defense of the People (CNDP) was planning a massacre of Nande people, and she sent the applicant to Goma to find refuge with a Christian organization known to help refugees. While en route to Goma, a rebel group kidnapped and imprisoned her in a house with other Nande women. The rebels frequently raped and beat her and threatened to kill her because she was Nande. She eventually escaped the rebels and fled to Goma where she took shelter with the Christian organization she had been trying to reach in June.

While there, she heard that her home in Kiwanja had been burned down and her mother killed. The Christian organization helped her escape to Kenya, France, and then the United States.

Although it might seem that the best expert to corroborate testimony of political membership or military affiliations is someone, such as me, who has read extensively on the history, recent wars, and current situation in the DRC, conducted research in the field on sexual violence and has knowledge of rebel factions and political affiliations (I monitored the 2011 national elections), my personal experiences did not enable me to feel I could serve as an expert witness in any but, perhaps, the fifth of these cases. As African scholar colleagues with decades of field research under their belt have warned me, engaging with asylum adjudicators is difficult in that their line of questioning rarely corresponds to field knowledge and, if you are not careful, you can end up undermining an applicant's case during cross-examination. I have, therefore, generally avoided offering my services as an expert since so few of the cases correspond with what I heard and learned in the field.

The DRC cases for which I have been asked to serve as an expert witness and the unpublished opinions and briefs that I have researched have almost all been on account of political opinion.[13] The lawyers I have worked with have found it particularly hard when the client is credible in terms of her testimony of rape, but cannot articulate who raped her, in terms of an identified rebel group, why she would have been targeted and whether she is part of a visible ethnic group. Even though the victim might not be able to articulate these indicators of persecution on account of political opinion or ethnic group, as an expert, I can help clarify that raising cattle or paying school fees can identify someone as from a particular tribal or ethnic group and that a particular town or region is a stronghold of a rebel group even if the victim is young or uneducated and, therefore, not well informed. I can also explain that girls, and young women, are often taken by rebel groups to cook, clean and perform other chores. Unfortunately, the way that the grounds of asylum are established, these insights do not easily come together to explain the victim was persecuted on account of being part of a particular social group. At least not in the clear-cut way that political opinion frames a case for asylum. That is why, to the extent possible, most of the cases are cast as political opinion.

Whereas while I was in the DRC no one expressed their identity or violence in terms of their political affiliations, I am regularly asked to provide an expert affidavit concerning persecution suffered by members of various opposition

[13] I want to thank the Center for Gender and Refugee Studies at U.C. Hastings College of Law for conducting a search for my research of their database for Congo asylum cases based on sexual violence.

parties. For example, retaliation for mobilizing citizens to join the party, witnessing police killings as a result of party activism and government targeting of the political opposition during and after the 2011 elections. I was also asked to provide an expert affidavit in a case concerning a young woman who turned to prostitution in Kinshasa and became a victim of trafficking being flown to Brussels and locked in a house until she escaped to Paris and, through the help of Congolese man she met in a train station, made it to the United States under false identity papers. In my expert affidavit I provided information concerning the situation of young women without familial support. I was able to confirm that orphaned children are commonly taken in by relatives but are used as help in the house and, if they want to attend school, must earn their own money to pay for school fees that could often means selling sex. I also confirmed that women who have been raped are social outcasts and that sex-trafficking is a problem in Kinshasa. Finally, I confirmed that a single woman without an education or family has no means of support and that a single woman cannot relocate to a village or other part of the country. She was granted asylum.

There are actually very few Congolese asylum cases adjudicated in immigration court in the United States. The U.S. Statistical Yearbook of the Executive Office for Immigration Review has the following number of Congo cases recorded per year:

FY	Received	Granted	Denied	Abandoned	Withdrawn	Other
2011	36	12	14	3	2	10
2010	37	12	22	3	4	14
2009	50	10	12	2	0	8
2008	46	24	14	1	6	3
2007	45	23	13	5	9	6

There are additional cases from the DRC that do not end up in Immigration Court having been filed affirmatively through the United States Citizenship and Immigration Services (USCIS) Asylum Division and granted at that stage in the process. According to the USCIS Asylum Statistics for the "Refugees, Asylum and Parole System: Female principal applicants filing by Nationality (Citizenship), there were 37 Congolese applicants in FY2011 and 45 in FY2012 (out of a total female applicant pool across all countries of 15,807 FY2011 and 14,277 FY2012).[14] According to the Department of Homeland Security Annual

[14] R.A.C.L. 1255 (7/24/2012) A.I.L.A. InfoNet Doc. No. 12073140. (Posted July 31, 2012).

Flow Reports for 2011 and 2012, refugees arriving from the DRC were among the leading countries of refugee admissions comprising 3–4% of total admissions [in fiscal years 2008 to 2010 the refugee arrivals from the DRC were: 1,863 (2012), 977 (2011), 3,174 (2010), 1,135 (2009), 727 (2008)]. Some of these refugee admissions were part of a new U.S. program to admit victims of sexual and gender-based violence. In other words, women from the DRC are being granted admission to the United States, but not through the asylum adjudication. The cases that are brought before adjudicators still remain focused on the need to show that the rape was "on account of" political persecution.

The gap between the reality of indiscriminate wide spread sexual and gender-based violence in the DRC committed by government military men, rebel men, criminal gangs, out of work boys and men, friends, neighbors, and husbands as document by hundreds of reports stands in stark contrast to the adjudication of Congolese rape cases in the asylum system where rape is consistently framed as a political retaliation for membership in an opposition party or human rights advocacy. Although the rapes can be framed as political, they are more accurately on account of women being part of a marginalized social group. The need to frame the rapes as political persecution, ultimately, undermines efforts to combat rape in the DRC that is, more fundamentally, on account of women being a marginalized social group.

The need in the asylum process to oversimplify and cast the context of rape in political terms ends up enlisting country conditions experts in the framing of rape in ways that might be more comprehensible to Western audiences, but creates a narrative of the DRC that does not exist in reality. What I learned in my time in the DRC is that there are hundreds of political parties that rarely correspond to any consistent platform or ideology. Membership in political parties is not particularly meaningful, beyond the payment one might receive around election time. The military and rebel forces are comprised of local men and boys who are mainly looking for a source of income and membership is more opportunistic (or a necessity) than ideological. The political and conflict narrative of rape in the DRC has generated a business in sexual violence in the form of mobile courts, proliferation of local NGOs, sensitization and education programs – which is not a bad thing in a poor country such as the DRC – but, for the broader purposes of reducing the incidence of rape and providing greater access to justice, not that productive. However, asylum lawyers and judges who are far removed from events in the DRC should be more aware of the effect that channeling expert testimony into narratives of rape as political ultimately has on our ability to acknowledge that, fundamentally, rape is on account of the marginalization of women in Congolese society.

It would be better if experts who were called in to corroborate and clarify the country conditions in cases of rape in the DRC were being asked to offer their testimonies in validation of the experience of women as a marginalized social group. Instead of confirming a narrow understanding of rape as politically motivated, expert testimony should broaden the ability to bear witness not just to rape as a weapon of war or rape as politically motivated, but rather the much more pervasive persecution and insidious form of social control women face by being raped on account of being a woman.

REFERENCES

Anker, Deborah E. 2013. *Law of Asylum in the United States: 2013 Edition*. Eagan, MN: Thomson Reuters.

Arieff, A. 2009. *Sexual Violence in African Conflicts*. Washington, DC: Congressional Research Service.

Autesserre, Séverine. 2012. *African Affairs*: 202–222.

Bartels, S. 2010. *'Now, the World Is Without Me': An Investigation of Sexual Violence in Eastern Democratic Republic of Congo*. Boston: Harvard Humanitarian Initiative.

Breton-LeGoff, G. 2010. Ending Sexual Violence in the Democratic Republic of the Congo. *Fletcher Forum of World Affairs* 34: 13–34.

Buss, Doris E. 2009. "Rethinking 'Rape as a Weapon of War'." *Feminist Legal Studies* 17: 145–63.

Crawley, H. 2000. "Engendering the State in Refugee Women's Claims for Asylum." In S. Jacobs, R. Jacobson and J. Marchbank, eds., *States of Conflict: Gender, Violence and Resistance*. London: Zed Books Ltd.

Crawley, H. 2001. *Refugees and Gender: Law and Process*. Bristol, UK: Jordan Publishing.

Harris, L. M. 2009. "Untold Stories: Gender-Related Persecution and Asylum in South Africa." *Michigan Journal of Gender & Law* 15: 291–347.

Lemarchand, R. 2009. *The Dynamics of Violence in Central Africa*. Philadelphia: University of Pennsylvania Press.

Lincoln, R. S. 2011. "Recent Development: Rule of Law for Whom? Strengthening the Rule of Law as a Solution to Sexual Violence in the Democratic Republic of the Congo." *Berkeley Journal of Gender Law & Justice* 26: 139–67.

MacKinnon, C. A. 1993. "Rape Genocide and Women's Human Rights." *Harvard Women's Law Journal* 17: 5–16.

Special Rapporteur on Violence Against Women, Its Causes and Consequences, Mission to the Democratic Republic of the Congo, Addendum. Vol. P 2, 8. (Feb. 28, 2008). United Nations.

Reyntjens, F. 2009. *The Great African War: Congo and Regional Geopolitics, 1996–2006*. Cambridge: Cambridge University Press.

Ruffer, Galya. 2013. "Testimony of Sexual Violence in the Democratic Republic of Congo and the Injustice of Rape: Moral Outrage, Epistemic Injustice, and the Failures of Bearing Witness." *Oregon Review of International Law* 15: 101–47.

4

Beyond Expert Witnessing: Interdisciplinary Practice in Representing Rape Survivors in Asylum Cases

Miriam H. Marton

"Sometimes stories can only be told when there is safety, the possibility of a future, when one is drawn back from the 'abyss'; when the shame, guilt, and anger can be faced in circumstances of trust; when 'perennial' losses can be accommodated; when needs for human rights and justice can be expressed; when therapists and others can bear to hear; and when compassion abides."

(Raphael, in Wilson and Drozdek 2004)

INTRODUCTION

Before going to law school, I spent fourteen years as a social worker working with survivors of gender-based violence. As a lawyer representing clients seeking asylum based on rape, I often draw on my social work skills. But as a lawyer, the client has engaged me to obtain legal relief, for example, asylum, and not as a social worker. To maximize the chances of obtaining asylum, the lawyer must press the client for graphic details of a painful and traumatic experience that the client would rather leave buried. To do anything less, the lawyer would be failing miserably at her obligation as lawyer. Strict adherence to legal obligations, however, does not detract from the inevitably brutal legal process in which both the client and the lawyer must operate in order for the client to obtain asylum.

The question of what the lawyer's role is in cases involving human trauma is a common problem for lawyers in refugee law. Regardless of prior mental health training, many lawyers and law student representatives struggle with the tension between what is necessary to prepare a successful legal case and the additional trauma that they are inflicting on the client by forcing the client to revisit the incidents of the underlying persecution.[1] Lawyers may also be woefully

[1] In many law schools, students may enroll in clinics in which the students represent real clients with real legal problems. There are numerous asylum and immigration law school clinics in the United States. At the University of Connecticut School of Law, our students work in teams

unprepared to recognize or address this tension, tension that is exacerbated because there is rarely a structured interdisciplinary team in place in which the legal representatives and the clients have guidance and support with respect to the client's (and their own) mental health. In rape cases in particular, there are powerful nonlegal issues at play that can negatively impact the success of the advocacy. I was, for example, part of a legal team representing Naomi, a survivor of brutal gang rape seeking asylum. There was one part of the story so heinous Naomi could not recount it. It is often uncomfortably true in the law that the greater the client's suffering, the greater the chance of obtaining relief. Thus, Naomi's legal team made a decision that the missing part of her story was essential and decided to try one more time to elicit the information from her. Because of my background, it was decided that I would interview Naomi for purposes of this particular information. Viewed through a legal lens, the interview was a success. Naomi provided details about the missing piece and the immigration judge granted Naomi a specific form of asylum under U.S. law based exactly on the severity of the persecution that she had suffered.[2]

For Naomi and for me, however, disclosure of the hardest piece of her narrative was not one of unqualified success. Bound by an obligation to zealously advocate on Naomi's behalf, my decision to question her was governed by an understanding of the evidentiary requirements in the U.S. immigration system to obtain asylum.[3] These requirements necessitated that Naomi disclosed each piece of the brutality she had endured. But disclosing for survivors like Naomi is akin to emotional torture. The decision to push her to disclose stood in sharp contrast to my mental health training in which the goal was the client's mental health; what governed was the client's choice as to if, what and when she disclosed.[4] Naomi's case exemplified the conflict

---

of two representing a client seeking asylum in the United States. Students take the lead on these representations, supervised by a licensed faculty member.

[2] In contrast to the Refugee Convention, U.S. law allows for an asylum grant based solely on past persecution. Commonly known as "humanitarian asylum," an applicant is eligible for this form of relief if the applicant meets one of two conditions, p. either "the applicant has demonstrated compelling reasons for being unwilling or unable to return to the country arising out of the severity of the past persecution; or the applicant has established that there is a reasonable possibility that he or she may suffer other serious harm upon removal to that country." 8 C.F.R. § 1208.13 (b)(1)(iii).

[3] Lawyers are bound by Rules of Professional Conduct. While each licensing body can differ, some principles, like zealous advocacy, are a constant. *See, e.g.* American Bar Association Center for Professional Responsibility. "Model Rules of Professional Conduct, p. Preamble & Scope." American Bar Association. Retrieved November 27, 2013, from http://www.american bar.org/groups/professional_responsibility/publications/model_rules_of_professional_con duct/model_rules_of_professional_conduct_preamble_scope.html.

[4] In a recent interview with Naomi, she told me that, while she understood the importance of the brutality, she would still choose not to disclose the particularly heinous part of the persecution to me (Naomi 2012. Interview by author).

between what the legal system demands and what the asylum seeker can give without extraordinarily emotional damage.

In addition to issues of trauma, the legal representatives may run into silencing mechanisms that inflict dire consequences for disclosing rape that I call "disclosure taboos." Disclosure taboos are taboos that are put in place by victim-blaming familial, cultural or religious structures. Disclosure taboos are universal and arise from patriarchal beliefs that women are responsible for being raped, that the rape irreparably defiles a woman and that the structures themselves are dishonored through rape. The most palpable consequences for breaching the disclosure taboos are dire consequences like forced marriage or divorce, loss of custody of children, social ostracism, and severe economic deprivation or even death. Consequences for breaching the disclosure taboos can also be much more subtle, like the shame imposed on the victim for being raped. Here, the shame itself silences the survivor and can be severely debilitating.

Given these underlying complications in representations of rape survivors seeking asylum, I was looking for a solution that reconciled the tension between the client's mental health and the client's legal goals. The obvious choice was an interdisciplinary team in which mental health professionals and lawyers worked together, educating each other as to the roles and expertise of each profession and providing unqualified support for the clients.

This chapter examines the particular problems that arise in representing rape survivors seeking asylum. The chapter argues that representing rape survivors seeking asylum requires an interdisciplinary approach in which mental health professionals assist legal representatives in understanding the particular psychosocial, political and cultural dynamics that surround and arise out of rape. The goal of such an interdisciplinary approach is to minimize the risk that the consequences of rape – the very persecution for which the applicant was seeking relief – will sabotage the asylum claim by addressing the three areas in which rape as persecution in an asylum case can present the most challenges: the legal system's propensity to erroneously interpret the consequences of rape as evidence of fabrication; the legal representatives preconceived notions about rape and rape survivors; and the lack of a safe environment in which a rape survivor can disclose the details of her persecution necessary to satisfy evidentiary requirements of the courts and withstand questions from her own legal team about that persecution that can feel persecutory in and of themselves.

Before continuing the discussion, I want to clarify three points. First, many of the issues raised here arise in representing any asylum seeker. What distinguishes rape survivors is not a question of a hierarchy of pain but a

particular form of suffering that manifests during representations of rape
survivors that stems from the need to recount the intense shame and sense of
personal violation arising from rape. Compounding this suffering is that rape
survivors often go through the asylum process alone. Second, the chapter is not
meant to imply that the asylum system is just. This system is, however, often
the clients' only option for relief. Consequently, I am advocating for a way to
work within a hostile system such that the dynamics created by the very
persecution that forms the basis of the claim for asylum do not sabotage
that claim.

   Finally, I want to address the issue of the gendered system in which asylum
claims are adjudicated. Persecution deemed worthy of refuge has traditionally
been the persecution tyrannical governments inflict on male political dissidents (Freedman 2007). Defining persecution in this manner genders the
question of what constitutes persecution as well as potentially the framework
in which asylum cases are adjudicated. There has been significant progress in
the recognition of gender-based violence, including rape, as persecution.[5] It is
crucial, however, that lawyers and clients be aware that gendered notions can
still be at work in adjudicating rape cases. Thus it is not unusual to feel, in
framing the legal case, as if the proverbial square peg simply does not fit into
the round hole. Particularly with respect to credibility, judgments may
"penalize those who do not fit within normative male, heterosexual,
American cultural expectations for testimonial behavior" (Conroy 2009,
p. 13). This is another area in which mental health professionals can assist
the lawyer by explaining the gendered misconceptions that can accompany an
analysis of rape.

ISSUES INHERENT IN REPRESENTING RAPE SURVIVORS SEEKING ASYLUM

The Legal System

Asylum applicants have survived inconceivable brutality that forces them to
flee their homes, leaving behind families they may never see again or, in cases
of rape, families that have disowned the asylum seeker, or who even seek to
punish the survivor for the rape. In making their way to what they assume will be
a country of refuge because of the persecution they have survived, they have, as
Naomi observed, "a simple view of the asylum process: 'I will just tell them the

---

5   *Lopez-Galarza v. I.N.S.*, 99 F.3d 954, 959 (9th Cir 1996.); *Matter of D-V-*, 21 I&N Dec. 77,
    79–80 (B.I.A. 1993). For analysis of the gendering of the asylum process, *see* Kelly (1993);
    Musalo (2003, 2010); Podkul (2005); Freedman (2007); Frydman and Seelinger (2008).

truth and that should be enough."[6] Refuge from persecution, however, requires the asylum seeker to subject herself to a process during which all that she knows to be true is questioned by those with the authority to determine whether she has suffered to a satisfactory extent such that she "deserves" to stay in the receiving country. Many asylum applicants have never told anyone that they were raped, let alone the details of that rape, and are unprepared for the harsh reality of the legal system in which reciting the narrative once is never sufficient.

The narrative, for example, must be microscopically examined for the credibility problems discussed by Bruce Einhorn and Megan Berthold in this volume. This scrutiny requires the asylum seeker to recount the narrative numerous times in gruesome detail first to her legal representatives and later to the adjudicator in response to the cross-examination by a government attorney. Observers may rightly assert that litigants in any legal proceeding must provide credible evidence to succeed. The difficulties for rape survivors seeking asylum is that the legal system has preconceived notions of how credible victims "should" present. Thus, "credibility assessments ... 'ultimately privilege [immigration judges'] individual ideas of how refugees should psychologically respond to persecution'," (Conroy 2009, p. 45). One study, for example, revealed that asylum adjudicators assumed that all people respond in specific ways to trauma and "that traumatic material is always clearly remembered" (Herlihy 2010, p. 361). A judge interviewed in that study opined that rape "is not the type of event which I would expect a person to forget about or confuse." There is, however, no "normal" demeanor for rape survivors. What one survivor presents emotionlessly another will be unable to recite. One survivor may look defiantly at those questioning her account while another will stare paralyzed at her lap. Furthermore, survivors often do not recall key details of a rape and may powerfully suppress memories when they threaten to surface to consciousness.

In judging an applicant's credibility, moreover, adjudicators are not required to consider that the very persecution for which refuge is being sought may severely impact the factors used to make the credibility determinations. Instead, an adjudicator can rely on factors such as the applicant's demeanor or inconsistencies in the applicant's testimony.[7] But demeanor is extraordinarily relative and varies widely depending on a whole host of factors such as reaction to trauma or the shame that is at the heart of rape. A person's demeanor can also be greatly altered by the rape itself or appear very differently while

---

[6] Interview with the author, August 5, 2012.
[7] 8 U.S.C. § 1158(b)(1)(B)(iii).

discussing the rape. Naomi, for example, would come alive when speaking about her country's history and politics, using her hands to speak, speaking directly to her legal team, making consistent eye contact and infusing her speech with passion and sometimes sadness at the loss of her home. When speaking about the rape, however, she would lower her head almost to her knees and talk very softly, if at all. Naomi's two distinct demeanors were unrelated to her credibility but were instead indicative of the severe trauma and shame that accompanied the rape.

Likewise, what may appear to the adjudicator as "inconsistencies" in a rape narrative may only appear to be inconsistencies within a legal framework that continues to expect linearity and fails to account for survival mechanisms. For example, a skilled mental health clinician would expect a certain amount of fragmented memory – memory that comes in bits and pieces – with respect to a rape narrative. Like Naomi's different demeanors, this fragmentation is likely to be indicative of the level of trauma inflicted on the asylum applicant. Thus, it is likely not related to credibility at all.

Certainly there are adjudicators sophisticated enough such that there is an understanding of the consequences and impact of trauma on narrative. Too often, however, the biased expectation of linearity interferes with an adjudicator's ability to take mental health issues into account, putting the asylum seeker at risk for being sent back to her country of origin based on erroneous interpretation of the emotional consequences of the very persecution from which she is seeking relief. As Berthold and Einhorn argue, in such cases, there is a need for mental health professionals as expert witnesses who can educate adjudicators as to the dynamics and impact of trauma. Mental health professionals as expert witnesses, however, can only address the adjudicator's lack of understanding of mental health issues, leaving unaddressed the questions of what the lawyer brings to the table and what the client may need during the process of preparing for the case.

THE LAWYER

Isabelle's Story

Isabelle's experience trying to obtain refuge offers a case study in the problems in asylum representations that trace back to the lawyer. The case also offers a particularly insightful window into both the danger and the power of disclosure taboos. Isabelle's original lawyer was woefully oblivious to the possibility of rape as a basis for asylum and consequently failed to establish a safe environment in which Isabelle could help him make her case. As is the case with many female rape survivors, before Isabelle filed for asylum, she was listed as a derivative[8] on the application of her husband, Alex. Alex and his father, Samuel, both filed for asylum based on political persecution they had suffered for their political activism in their home country. The U.S. adjudicators regularly deny asylum cases based on political persecution from this particular country because the prior tyrannical regime is no longer in control of the national government. Unsurprisingly, then, the regional Asylum Office referred both men's cases to the immigration court.[9] Both men then retained lawyer, Larry. Given the slim chances of success of an asylum claim based on political persecution from this country, Larry should have been looking for possible alternative bases for an asylum claim, including, with respect to Alex, any persecution that Isabelle may have experienced in which Alex could become the derivative claim.

Larry was an experienced immigration lawyer in private practice. Yet Larry, like the system in which he practiced law, did not take his legal analysis beyond the gendered notions of what constitutes persecution. Consequently, Larry's focus was on the male heads of the household, their political activities and the resulting persecution that the men suffered. Larry thus failed to view Isabelle as anything more than his client's wife. He created neither the time nor the space for Isabelle to disclose the rape. For example, Larry met with the entire extended family together. In Isabelle's and Alex's patriarchal culture, a victim who disclosed rape may be subjected to forced divorce, social ostracism, severe economic deprivation and even murder. She will also likely lose her children to her husband's family. All of these punishments were consequences that Samuel, as the family patriarch, would indubitably enforce should he discover that his son's wife had been raped. Larry never asked Isabelle why she had fled her home country, apparently assuming, consistent with the gendered framework in which asylum cases are adjudicated, that Isabelle left because Alex was fleeing. By failing to establish a safe environment in which Isabelle, a rape survivor, could disclose, Larry all but ensured

[8] Asylum applicants may include spouses and minor, unmarried children on their asylum applications. This means that only the applicant must have a basis for asylum and, if granted, the spouse and children, the "derivatives," are also granted without having to put forth a case of persecution.

[9] Because neither Alex nor Samuel were detained or placed into removal proceedings, they could file an asylum application with the asylum office. The asylum officer may either grant the application or, if the asylum officer does not believe the applicant's story or concludes that it fails to satisfy the legal standards for asylum, may refer the application to the immigration court. Once a case is referred, the applicant is then in removal proceedings. The applicant has another opportunity to present her claim for asylum to the immigration judge as a defense to removability.

that the rape would remain sequestered behind the cement disclosure taboos that governed Isabelle and her family.

What Larry focused on was the details of an incident in which Alex and Isabelle were together when four men, armed with semi-automatic weapons, beat Alex, referencing both his family name and his political party. Had Larry been trained to go beyond a gendered framework, his client interviews would have included exploring any and all persecution to which the family had been subjected and that could form the basis of an asylum claim that went beyond the political persecution claims. Indeed, beyond the rigid gender constructions was Isabelle's own basis for asylum independent of that of Alex's doomed political persecution argument. The rampant political violence that was gripping Isabelle's and Alex's home country at this time included numerous incidents of rape of female members of politically active families.[10] Because Isabelle was with Alex when the armed men beat up Alex, a legal analysis outside of the gendered framework would have included questioning whether Alex's attackers had done anything to Isabelle that rose to the level of persecution. In addition, Isabelle herself was quite rebellious based on the standards in her country, stirring great controversy in her hometown because the country was governed by rigid gender mores. Rape was one method that the society used to punish women who dared to step outside these rigid gender mores.

Trained to employ a careful perspective on gender and violence, Larry might have wondered how to start a dialogue with Isabelle to explore whether Isabelle had her own history of persecution. Instead, Larry went to trial on the political persecution theory. The immigration judge predictably denied asylum to both Samuel and Alex. The story would have been over and the family deported except for Isabelle's acts of courage.

It turned out that one of the armed men had indeed raped Isabelle while his companions beat up Alex. During the rape, the rapist referenced Isabelle's rebellion, Alex's family name and their political party affiliation. At the time of the rape, Isabelle was a young bride. To avert the harsh disclosure taboos, Isabelle and Alex made a pact: they would never again speak about what happened, to each other or to anyone else. After the immigration judge denied Alex's asylum claim, however, Isabelle did her own research and discovered for herself that she may have her own basis for asylum because of the rape. Isabelle, despite the great risk disclosure posed, informed Alex that the pact

[10]   Isabelle's case is also the quintessential example of why refugee lawyers must also take the time to research country conditions in their client's home country. Without a doubt, an asylum case takes an enormous amount of research and time for the legal representatives. Lawyers who do not take the time to properly educate themselves run a high risk of missing crucial facts or, as in Isabelle's case, an entire basis for relief.

was off and retained an attorney of her own. Isabelle spent hundreds of hours with her new legal team, explaining why she did not come forward initially, and recounting the rape in great detail. Isabelle relived her memories of the rape, the rigid gender mores and the terror over and over again in order to comply with the evidentiary requirements of the asylum system. She did this notwithstanding the constant presence of the disclosure taboos, including the shame that gripped both her and Alex. After years of this process, an immigration judge granted Isabelle humanitarian asylum based on the severity of the rape and the long-lasting effects it inflicted on Isabelle. By this time, she had been separated from her oldest son for over six years and it would be another year before the U.S. government would allow him to immigrate to this country.

Identifying the Lawyer's Issues

In asylum cases in which rape is the persecution for which relief is sought, the dynamics of rape inevitably color the representation, beginning, as with Isabelle, with the client's terror of disclosing the event. An argument for addressing the issues with an interdisciplinary approach in asylum cases can begin with reviewing the lack of skills that lawyers like Larry bring to the representation, and that diminish the lawyer's competency as legal representative. Larry, for example, did not comprehend the extent to which the physical environment in his office was counterproductive to disclosure. Larry also failed to understand that interviewing a rape survivor requires a specific skill set. In addition to Larry's shortcomings, lawyers sometimes may themselves measure their clients' narratives against expectations of linearity that arise out of a legal framework but that are not always present in recounting narratives of trauma. Larry, for example, may have had flawed expectations of Isabelle and may not have understood the "irrationality" of a refusal to disclose events necessary to obtain asylum. Lawyers themselves may be operating in a framework in which the client's narrative is constantly measured against unreasonable expectations of linearity. Ultimately, a lawyer like Larry, himself wed to the gendered legal framework, cannot imagine the possibility that his client's spouse may be a rape survivor with a good basis for an asylum claim.[11]

Importantly, the lawyer may have little or no training in recognizing or responding to indicators that the process of preparing for the asylum proceeding

---

[11]   As some commentators point out, "[w]omen are often granted asylum or refugee status based on their husband's claim and may not realize they can claim asylum in their own right" (Mezey and Thachil 2010, p. 247). With the law students I supervise, one of the issues we regularly address is whether any other family members have basis for relief and how to go about exploring that basis.

is re-traumatizing the client. Even if Larry had understood the potential for Isabelle's own basis for asylum, it is unlikely that he had training on how to move his and Isabelle's relationship passed the powerful disclosure taboos to which Isabelle could be subjected. Moreover, how far the lawyer may push the client to recall details of the rape raises ethical issues in terms of the lawyer's lack of clinical training. The lawyer may have the most admirable of goals – obtaining refuge. The client's psyche, however, may be hard at work at its own admirable goal of protecting the self from the overwhelming memory of the trauma. Removing this deep-seated protective layer during the legal process by inter-rogating the client about her memory raises grave concerns of retraumatizing the client without plans or resources to help the client deal with the resurfacing of post-traumatic stress symptoms.

At the other end of the spectrum and equally destructive, lawyers may be "hyper" sensitive to issues of sexual assault or cultural difference and resist having to ask the client questions the lawyer considers too personal, too embarrassing, or too indicative of judgment or cultural insensitivity. Shying away from those difficult conversations carries significant risks. First, a lawyer's own hypersensitiv-ity comes dangerously close to the "narcissism of pity" (Hesford 2011) as opposed to a constructive partnership. Relating to the client from a place of pity dehumanizes the client and may jeopardize the lawyer's ability to gain the client's trust or establish a safe place in which the client can confront disclosure taboos.

Second, to skip over the hard questions runs the risk that the first time the client is asked such questions will be by the adjudicator or the government. When a lawyer does not know the answer to these questions, neither the lawyer nor the client can be adequately prepared to respond. Finally, skipping over the hard questions means that the lawyer misses out on a chance to understand the complexities of her client's persecution, risking that she will not be able to explain such complexities to the adjudicator. In more cases than not, when I have asked the hard questions – the very questions that make me cringe at their insensitivity – it is my client who rises to the occasion, who shows much more courage than me, and who gives me compelling answers key to her successful asylum claim. This can happen for a multitude of reasons. There is so much that a lawyer may not know, about her client, the client's culture, history, or life, that what appear to be holes in the client's story may actually be holes in the lawyer's knowledge and understanding. Additionally, there may be an explanation for conduct that we cannot imagine from our place of relative privilege.[12] This is a common problem that presents with asylum seekers who have left children in

---

[12]   In their article on the Five Habits for Cross-Cultural Lawyering, Bryant and Koh Peters describe a multitude of reasons why our assumptions about a client's behavior or narrative may be incorrect. Bryant and Koh Peters encourage lawyers to engage in "parallel universe"

their country of origin. It is common for American lawyers to be particularly shocked, for example, that a mother could flee from danger and leave her children in the place of danger. This judgment, however, fails to take into consideration the expense and danger of the flight itself and the impossible choice in which the woman finds herself. Female rape survivors may come from patriarchal cultures in which it is normally the men who have access to or control of resources. Thus it is common for women to arrive here only from the charity of a sympathetic relative, who may not have much more than the cost of getting one person out of the country. Moreover, asylum seekers are also fearful of requesting visas for an entire family as doing so may alert authorities in either their home country or the receiving country of the intent to permanently flee. Whatever the explanation, the lawyer's avoidance of sensitive issues can significantly impair her ability to successfully advocate for her client.

Complicating any issues that the system raises or that either the lawyer or the client brings to the table are the issues of language and culture. Much has been written about cross-cultural lawyering. Lawyers must often be mindful of judgments and assumptions that are based on the lawyer's own cultural framework and that fail to account for cross-cultural differences (Bryant and Koh Peters 2005, p. 57). What often surprises new lawyers, or lawyers new to refugee law, is that language itself can greatly interfere with the lawyer's ability to understand the nuances, pain and terror of the brutality inflicted on the client. Translations from one language to another are fragile and influenced by factors such as dialect and the capability of an interpreter (specifically, interpreters find it difficult to translate legal concepts). In order for the lawyer to understand the enormity of what her client has experienced, and, in turn, in order for the lawyer to put that experience into an advocacy narrative, the client's full experience must be translated. Some languages, however, do not contain words for certain actions or even body parts. This of course increases the risk that the lawyer will not understand the persecution her client experienced.

There is another mental health implication in this situation, however. One asylum seeker's language, for example, contained no words for what her rapists had done to her. In order to explain the rape to her lawyers, this woman was reduced to pointing and gesturing to parts of her body, like a tragic game of charades, and to using phrases like "down there." This survivor was a competent adult explaining an extremely humiliating and painful rape to a room

thinking, in which the lawyer imagines all of the reasons beyond her own assumptions for a client's conduct (Bryant and Koh Peters 2005, p. 56–57). The purpose is not to reach yet another unsupported conclusion, but to "remind ourselves that we lack the facts to make the interpretation, and we identify the assumptions we are making" (Bryant and Koh Peters 2005, p. 56).

full of strangers. The lack of words and the necessity of pointing inflicted the added humiliation of appearing inarticulate and childlike. Within the current legal framework, a lawyer cannot avoid exploring every piece of the persecution with her client. Language problems may necessitate nonverbal explanations. If the lawyer is properly trained in an interdisciplinary approach, however, the lawyer can anticipate these issues and work in partnership with the client and mental health professionals to minimize the damage and humiliation on the client.

The Client

Like the legal system and the lawyer, the client will also bring her own issues to the representation. Chief among these issues are the disclosure taboos that forbid disclosing the rape at all. Unquestionably, survivors of other forms of torture, political torture, for example, may struggle to recount the atrocities they endured. Yet it is also common for political dissidents to feel proud that they are part of a struggle against tyranny in their country – pride that may be shared by family and community. This pride and support stand in sharp contrast to what I am referring to as disclosure taboos, silencing mechanisms that inflict dire consequences for disclosing rape. In preparing an asylum case, lawyers may thus see clients unable to provide the lawyer with the facts necessary to make the asylum claim. These circumstances are foreign to the lawyer, who believes she is operating within a rational system in which those who want relief naturally and willingly share the facts that entitle them to that relief.

The asylum seeker, by contrast, may feel as if she is "in a state of 'speechless terror' in which . . . she lacks words to describe what has happened." (van der Kolk and Fissler 1995, p. 6) Naomi talked about trying to describe the brutal rape inflicted on her:

> For gender-based violence victims, there is no excitement, you want to keep it to yourself. Talking about sexual abuse is very hard. When someone is beaten, they can give so many details, like, "they punched me in the eye" or "then a car came by." But how do you explain sexual abuse? And there is a pride in traditional political protesting but people don't talk about rape and pride. (Naomi. 2012. Interview by author).

Unfortunately, explaining the sexual abuse is exactly what is required in an asylum case.

A story about a women's therapy group that I ran when I was a clinical social worker illustrates the enormity of the task for the survivor. The group consisted of Western women, each a survivor of some form of sexual assault, who I also saw individually. Few of the women had shared their history of sexual assault with family, friends or community. One woman tried, but her family disowned her, choosing instead to believe the denials of the rapist, the survivor's uncle. Another woman's rapist was a "pillar of the community," and she was terrified of the social consequences she would pay for disclosure.

One therapeutic model intended to combat the internalization of disclosure taboos and empower the survivor is to give voice to a silenced part of the survivor (Courtois and Ford 2013, p. 121, 160). This model is particularly effective with memories of shameful trauma as it gives the survivor an opportunity to be supported, rather than blamed or shamed for the abuse she experienced (Courtois and Ford 2013, p. 121). When I proposed engaging in a form of group narrative therapy, the women vehemently resisted, making it clear to me the enormity of what I was asking them to do. In contrast to the asylum process, the purpose of this exercise was therapeutic. It was neither to scrutinize the women's narratives of rape nor to subject any part of those narratives to interrogative cross-examination. Thus, no one was to be exhaustively questioned about the details of their sexual assault. No one would be asked, for example, what time of day the rape occurred; or what color shirt the rapists were wearing; or what the rapists exactly did or said before, during, and after the rape.

This lack of examination stands in sharp contrast to the legal process to obtain asylum, in which the survivor will be expected to recount all such exhaustive details. And while the women in the group all eventually agreed to share their narratives in the group setting, that agreement was reached only after months of intensive individual and group work in a safe therapeutic atmosphere. Disclosure taboos, hard at work within the safe context of a therapeutic container, are likely to be working overtime in a legal environment that is notably less safe and can even appear hostile or authoritarian. Isabelle's story is a story of the impact such a hostile environment can have. Among other parts of her experience with Larry, Isabelle described him as loud, abrasive, and male. As detailed earlier, there was little in the environment of Larry's office that would have created a safe place in which Isabelle could disclose the rape.

Another issue that a rape survivor seeking asylum may encounter is that the adjudicator may base a credibility finding on the adjudicator's expectation that the asylum seeker's narrative will be a sequential recitation of the persecution. The human psyche, however, will not necessarily allow memory of trauma to be recorded in this manner because the pain of the trauma may be intolerable. The psyche may edit or even delete memories of the rape to protect itself from irreparable damage, creating a narrative that is equally edited or missing (Halligan 2003). Although this self-editing can play a positive role in the survivor's psychological healing, clients and lawyers are likely to find it confounding and frustrating because it may stand in sharp contrast to an adjudicator's requirements of linearity. Clients may feel pressure to fill in the memory gaps. They may also be receiving unsolicited advice from their community on "what to say," advice that may or may not be useful or accurate. Clients may also predetermine what pieces of their narrative are important and what pieces are not. Given that the client is unlikely to have legal experience, such judgment calls are not necessarily accurate. Clients may also withhold information because of a fear of judgment from their legal representative.

Finally, the testifying is likely to be terrifying to the client. Human beings are notoriously bad witnesses.[13] Under the best of circumstances, we do not necessarily remember events clearly or linearly. Having to do so under oath can fill us with anxiety. Indeed, I have seen professionals shaking at the thought of testifying at a deposition and subsequently fail miserably at giving linear, cohesive testimony – and this when the matter about which they are testifying is impersonal and the stakes are financial. In an asylum case, at stake is the life of the asylum seeker and perhaps that of her family as well. Moreover, disclosure taboos will be working overtime to silence a survivor testifying to a black-robed authority figure, subjected to cross-examination, all in a public forum.[14] Likewise, language issues can greatly impede testimony. The asylum seeker may not be able to communicate directly with the adjudicator, putting her at the mercy of an interpreter who she can only hope is accurate, understands the nuances of her history and does not have her own preconceived notions about the asylum seeker's history. In defensive asylum proceedings in the United States, it is the immigration court, and not the asylum seeker, that provides the interpreter. An asylum seeker will not know who that interpreter will be until she gets to court the day of her merits hearing. Consequently, in addition to being yet another stranger to whom the asylum seeker must recite her rape narrative, the interpreter might be of a different gender, increasing the shame and difficulty of the testimony.

Although all of these issues can be overwhelming to both the client and the lawyer, they can be tempered. At the very least, the lawyer can educate herself regarding the potentiality of these problems and insert into the process plenty

---

[13] As one expert in litigation psychology vividly framed the issue, the "average" witness may be "a dangerous grenade with the pin pulled out, ready to explode" (Singer 2012).

[14] Notwithstanding assurances of the confidentiality of asylum procedures, most survivors view a courtroom as a public forum.

of opportunities to dialogue with the client regarding the issues. The solution the dynamics necessitate, however, is an interdisciplinary legal team.

THE NECESSITY OF INTERDISCIPLINARY COLLABORATION

I was privileged to be a part of Isabelle's new legal team. Isabelle later told me that it was because of my approach that she could talk about the rape (Naomi 2012; interview by author). For example, I knew from my years as a social worker that interviewing success comes not solely from either hand-holding or confrontation. Regardless of how tragic a client's story, or regardless of how necessary a piece of information is to the legal case, an interviewer must know how to balance the two and have the skill to know when and how to use each technique and when and how to move from one response to the other. For example, I knew that the government attorney and the adjudicator in Isabelle's case would want to know why she did not come forward about the rape in Alex's asylum case.

The assumption underlying this question was that Isabelle simply fabricated the rape in order to get asylum for herself and her family. A rigid gendered legal framework cannot allow for the possibility that an asylum seeker cannot disclose sexual torture without certain safeties and trust established with her legal representatives who conduct the client interviews. Working within the current legal framework, then, necessitates exploring the disclosure taboos in order to explain the underlying mental health and cultural issues in a way that satisfies the adjudicator's fabrication concerns. Questioning the asylum seeker on her lack of disclosure, however, presents a risk that the question will lead the client to think that her legal representatives do not believe her.

Regardless of the sensitivity of the lawyer, it is almost inevitable that the client, while intellectually understanding why the lawyer is asking the question, may understandably have an emotional response to the questioning. The client may feel the lawyer is not really on her side, or that the interrogatory nature of the question makes it too difficult to continue the process. Lawyers may err on either a "Larry" approach, in which there is no thought to how the question can be asked in order to minimize its interrogatory nature; or the hypersensitivity issue discussed above in which the lawyer is hesitant to ask at all, which of course risks that the first time the question is asked is in the hearing with the adjudicator. Interdisciplinary training and continued work with mental health professionals can give the lawyer the skills in how, when and where to ask these difficult questions. Interdisciplinary training can encourage the lawyer to have a mental health professional available to the client to process a difficult interview. By enlisting a mental health professional as a continued source of support for the client, the client has someone on her team whose sole purpose is to offer support and develop coping mechanisms to get through the process itself, someone who does not need to ask the interrogatory questions.

Notably, however, my social work skills alone did not lead to the success of Isabelle's case. First and foremost, it was Isabelle's own persistence and courage. After Isabelle, it was the interdisciplinary approach with which my colleagues and I approached the case; in other words, it was the skill and knowledge of both professions in partnership with the client that created the space in which Isabelle could disclose her narrative and her story could subsequently be framed consistent with the requirements of the U.S. asylum law. This is not to say that the process was in any way easy on Isabelle. To the contrary, the legal system did what it always seems to do and revictimized Isabelle, Alex and their children by, first and foremost, forcing Isabelle to disclose a rape she had decided long ago never to disclose. Furthermore, Isabelle's narrative of that rape was subjected to microscopic examination and cross-examination. Present was that never-ending question always asked of rape survivors: did it really happen? Isabelle's case thus concretized for me that the only way through that system is via the creation of a new subsystem of interdisciplinary collaboration in which the asylum seeker's professionals are fluent in both the law and mental health.

It takes skill on the part of a lawyer and great strength on the part of a client to jointly navigate the disclosure taboos, the trauma, the shame and the lawyer's own preconceived notions about rape to frame the client's narrative in a way that is legally compelling and consistent with the system's requirements while simultaneously remaining willing to ask and answer those difficult questions, address the system's gendered framework and prepare for a proceeding that is likely to be more interrogative than investigative. The enormity of this task can be significantly eased with the use of an interdisciplinary approach. To gain an understanding of how to successfully work with a survivor, for example, the mental health professional and the lawyer together can begin to explore questions that seek to push the relationship beyond the gendered restrictions. These questions should become part of an attorney's regular practice and include such questions as:

How do I identify if my client is a rape survivor?

How do I establish trust or rapport with my client and overcome the consequences of trauma such that she will be able to tell me about the rape?

How do I explain the confusing law to my client?

How can I ensure that the interviews are accurately translated?

How can I best ensure that I understand the client's responses to disclosure and to the trauma of the legal process?

How do I genuinely respond to what I hear?

What response is sincere and respectful versus condescending or patronizing?

How much personal response is appropriate and how much will only serve to further embarrass or shame the client?

How do I overcome my own discomforts of hearing an account of rape?

Am I limited by my own cultural preconceptions about rape?

Am I limited by my own issues of outrage at my client's victimization and the likely impunity her persecutors enjoy?

In exploring these questions, the professionals can identify what limits the representation and can work together with the client so that she can feel as safe and supported as possible and so that the adjudicator sees an accurate and compelling account of persecution.

In Isabelle's case, for example, the system's definition of rationality called into question why she did not immediately flee her home country after the rape and why, at the very least, she did not come forward to make her own asylum claim once the family did escape. We anticipated that the immigration judge or the government attorney would ask about this as a credibility issue. We therefore spent many hours together ensuring not only that Isabelle was prepared to explain the issue but that we, as her lawyers, had sufficient expert testimony to present to the immigration judge that put the time lapses in context. Consequently, for example, we researched how the combination of a misogynistic culture with the disclosure taboos and the unsafe environment provided by Larry guaranteed that Isabelle could not have disclosed her rape during Alex's asylum case, and how the choice to leave was not Isabelle's to make but was left to Alex.

The mental health professional and the lawyer can also work together to minimize the harm of the legal environment. A lawyer cannot establish the kind of space in which a mental health professional works. Lawyers often meet with clients in conference rooms, for example, as opposed to an office of a mental health professional that is specifically designed to establish safety and comfort for the client. A mental health professional may also take some notes during a session with her client, but a lawyer cannot do her job without taking copious notes of what the client reports so that she can put the client's account of persecution into a persuasive and organized litigation package for the adjudicator. The mental health professional can, however, assist the lawyer in considering issues that can increase the client's sense of safety, alleviate stress and convey the importance of the client's well-being. Thus, the lawyer should consider logistics such as room size, where people sit, who is in the room, does the gender of who is present matter, what about meal times, travel times, interruptions, and distractions. How a lawyer addresses these considerations can become central to whether a client feels safe enough to disclose. These are questions that mental health professionals consider every day, making cross-professional work essential in asylum representations of rape survivors.

Likewise, the mental health professional can help the lawyer frame the interview questions to be productive, understand the responses and assess whether what appear to be holes or inconsistencies are simply manifestations of trauma. Similarly, the mental health professional can assist the lawyer in identifying signs of retraumatization, how much meaning and risk should be assigned to such symptoms and work with the client to formulate response options. Finally, the most difficult of interviews can take place in a mental health professional's office, where the client has access to both her professionals.

CONCLUSION

The past few years has seen an increase in an interest in interdisciplinary practice. There have been cross-discipline trainings across the country. Asylum clinics often have a mental health professional guest lecture on the topic of mental health issues in asylum claims. The lecture typically includes the expert testimony that a mental health professional can provide. By doing so, the lecture also introduces the students to the concept of the impact of trauma on memory and the particular methods of interviewing traumatized clients that may be successful in overcoming disclosure taboos and post-trauma symptoms and in establishing a safe environment in which the client can disclose the details of a trauma such as rape to the legal representatives. I have regularly done trainings for law students on the same topic. Lawyers are also conducting one-session trainings for mental health professionals to educate the professionals on asylum law and process in the United States.

Although these trainings are helpful, they are introductions. The feedback I regularly receive from participants is that one-session trainings are insufficient, and that even the consultations with an expert mental health witness regarding the testimony leaves the legal representatives in unfamiliar and often frightening territory. Law students regularly report that they are unsure how to respond to a client speaking, in particular, of brutal accounts of rape, or if and how to respond to indicators that the client is experiencing emotional trauma during the students' client interviews. Students have, for example, reported clients staring off into space or heavily grinding their teeth while speaking about history of atrocious sexual violence.

It seems to me that under these circumstances, the harsh asylum process can so easily go awry for either the client or the untrained lawyer or law student. When we are stuck and unsure of how to move the process forward, when the client seems so fragile it seems as if she could break with a breath, when the issues of disclosure taboos and self-edited narratives put the legal case at risk, or even when the brutality of what we are witness to is overwhelming, the natural solution is a partnership across professions. Such a partnership would include intense trainings and regularly scheduled and structured cross-disciplinary consultations that go beyond expert witnessing into the formation of interdisciplinary teams.

REFERENCES

Bryant, Susan J. and Jean Koh Peters. 2005. "Five Habits for Cross-Cultural Lawyering." In Kimberly Barrett and William George, eds., *Race, Culture, Psychology and Law*. Thousand Oaks, CA: Sage, 47–62.

Conroy, Melanie A. 2009. "Real Bias: How REAL ID's Credibility and Corroboration Requirements Impair Sexual Minority Asylum Applicants." *Berkeley Journal of Gender Law & Justice* 24: 1–47.

Courtois, Christine and Ford, Julian. 2013. *Treatment of Complex Trauma: A Sequence, Relationship-Based Approach*. New York: Guilford.

Freedman, Jane. 2007. *Gendering the International Asylum and Refugee Debate*. Basingstoke: Palgrave MacMillan.

Frydman, Lisa and Seelinger, Kim Thuy. 2008. "Kasinga's Protection Undermined? Recent Developments in Female Genital Cutting Jurisprudence." *Bender's Immigration Bulletin* 13: 1073–1105.

Halligan, Sarah L., Tanja Michael, David M. Clark, and Anke Ehlers. 2003. "Posttraumatic Stress Disorder Following Assault: The Role of Cognitive Processing, Trauma Memory, and Appraisals." *Journal of Consulting and Clinical Psychology* 71(3): 419–31.

Herlihy, Jane, Kate Gleeson, and Stuart Turner. 2010. "What Assumptions About Human Behaviour Underlie Asylum Judgments?" *International Journal of Refugee Law* 22(3): 351–66.

Hesford, Wendy. 2011. *Spectacular Rhetorics: Human Rights Visions, Recognitions, Feminisms*. Durham, NC: Duke University Press Books.

Immigration and Nationality Act. 1952. *US Code*. Section 101(a) (42).

Immigration and Nationality Act. 1952. *US Code*. Section 208(b)(1)(B)(iii).

Kelly, Nancy. 1993. "Gender-related Persecution: Assessing the Asylum Claims of Women." *Cornell International Law Journal* 26: 625–74.

Lopez-Galarza v. I.N.S. 1996. 99 F.3d 954, 959 (9th Cir.).

Matter *of D-V-*. 1993. 21 I&N Dec. 77, 79–80 (B.I.A.).

Meffert, Susan M., Karen Musalo, Dale E. McNiel, and Renée L. Binder. 2010. "The Role of Mental Health Professionals in Political Asylum Processing." *Journal of the American Academy of Psychiatry and the Law Online* 38(4): 479–89.

Mezey, Gill, and Ajoy Thachil. 2010. "Sexual Violence and Refugees." In Dinesh Bhugra, Tom Craig, and Kamaldeep Bhui, eds., *Mental Health of Refugees and Asylum Seekers*. Oxford: Oxford University Press, 243–61.

Musalo, Karen. 2002–03. "Revisiting Social Group and Nexus in Gender Asylum Claims: A Unifying Rationale for Evolving Jurisprudence." *DePaul Law Review* 52: 777–808.

Musalo, Karen. 2010. "A Short History of Gender Asylum in the United States: Resistance and Ambivalence May Very Slowly Be Inching Towards Recognition of Women's Claims," *Refugee Survey Quarterly* 29(2): 46–63.

Podkul, Jennifer. 2005. "Domestic Violence in the United States and Its Effect on US Asylum Law." *Human Rights Brief* 12: 16–46.

Singer, Amy. "Professionally Prepared for Witness Preparations?" *Trial.* http://www.trialconsultants.com/Library/ProfessionallyPreparedforWitnessPrep.html

United Nations. 1951. Convention Relating to the Status of Refugees, July 28. U.N.T.S. no.2545. *Treaty Series* 189: 137–221.

United Nations. 1967. Protocol Relating to the Status of Refugees, Jan. 31. U.N.T.S. no. 8791. *Treaty Series* 606: 267–92.

United Nations High Commissioner for Refugees. 2002. Guidelines on International Protection: Gender-Related Persecution within the Context of Article 1A(2) of the 1951 Convention and/or Its 1967 Protocol Relating to the Status of Refugees. http://www.unhcr.org/refworld/docid/3d36f1c64.html (Retrieved November 11, 2012).

Van der Kolk, Bessel A., and Rita Fisler. 1995. "Dissociation and the Fragmentary Nature of Traumatic Memories: Overview and Exploratory Study." *Journal of Traumatic Stress* 8(4): 505–25.

Wilson, John and Drozdek, Boris, eds. 2004. *Broken Spirits: The Treatment of Traumatized Asylum Seekers, Refugees, War and Torture Victims*. New York: Brunner-Routledge.

5

Anthropological Evidence and Country of Origin Information in British Asylum Courts[1]

Anthony Good

Decisions by governments and courts as to whether an asylum applicant has a "well-founded fear of being persecuted," as required by the 1951 Refugee Convention, usually depend to a significant extent on the analysis of what has come to be known as Country of Origin Information (or COI) about the prevailing situation in the applicant's home country. Does that information suggest that people like the applicant are at risk of persecution back home? For their part, faced with the difficult task of demonstrating that they themselves would be at risk *in future*, all that most asylum seekers can do is try to prove that they have suffered persecution in the past. The problem is that their personal narratives of suffering are often the only evidence they can produce on this. Decision makers (government officials or judges) must therefore decide whether their uncorroborated story is credible, both *internally*, without contradictions and confusions over dates and places; and *externally*, consistent with information about the situation in their home country (Weston 1998; UKBA no date, paragraph 4.3). This external aspect of credibility again requires that applicants' narratives be judged in relation to the available Country of Origin Information. COI therefore figures importantly in refugee status determination procedures generally, though there remain significant national differences in how it is produced and used (Gyulai 2011, p. 7).

The importance of such country information in asylum adjudication has always been recognized. Thus, the UNHCR *Handbook* (2011, p. 42) states that "A knowledge of conditions in the applicant's country of origin ... is an important element in assessing the applicant's credibility,"[2] while, more

[1] This research was supported by E.S.R.C. Research Grant no. R000223352, and AHRC Grant AH/E50874X/1, under its *Diasporas, Migration and Identities* Programme, the latter held jointly with Dr. Robert Gibb of Glasgow University.
[2] As another UNHCR publication, dealing directly with COI, puts it: "Decision-makers must assess an applicant's claim and his/her credibility and place his/her 'story' in its appropriate factual context, that is, the known situation in the country of origin" (UNHCR 2004, paragraph 9).

recently, the EuropeanUnion's *Qualification Directive* specified that asylum decisions must take into account "all relevant facts as they relate to the country of origin at the time of taking a decision on the application."[3] As UNHCR's Director of Protection recently put it, "it is clear that country of origin information ... is key to decision-making" (ACCORD 2013, p. 5), and the President of the British Asylum and Immigration Tribunal has stated that if an asylum judge "fails to relate an appellant's story to the background evidence on the appellant's country, he has necessarily applied the wrong approach" (*Visuvanathan Jeyakumar*). Even so, references to Country of Origin Information, employing capital letters and the acronym COI, only began to gain currency from around 2005 onwards, and despite the growing reification that the adoption of this terminology symbolizes, COI is still not very precisely specified. The European Country of Origin Information Network, for example, defines it merely as "information on conditions in countries of origin of asylum seekers."[4] The United Kingdom Border Agency (UKBA), while giving an equally broad definition, explains that its focus is on COI concerning "human rights issues and matters frequently raised in asylum and human rights claims."[5]

In this chapter, drawing on long-running field research in the courts (Good 2007) and the experience of acting since 1994 as a 'country expert' in over five hundred appeals involving Sri Lankan asylum applicants, I analyze the use of COI in asylum decision making by UKBA and the British asylum judiciary, and describe some of the problems that result from the divergent approaches to evidence adopted by social scientists and lawyers. The bulk of this COI concerns broad, generic issues, and is drawn from a variety of sources including news services, NGOs, government bodies, international agencies, and reports produced by experts. For example, as most Sri Lankan asylum applicants claim to have been tortured, virtually every case requires the decision maker to review and analyze the overwhelming body of information suggesting that ill treatment and torture are almost routine in Sri Lanka, even when a person is held in otherwise lawful detention. Applicants' lawyers are likely to present generic reports (such as UN Committee Against Torture 2011)

---

[3] *Directive 2011/95/EU of the European Parliament and of the Council of 13 December 2011 on standards for the qualification of third-country nationals or stateless persons as beneficiaries of international protection, for a uniform status for refugees or for persons eligible for subsidiary protection, and for the content of the protection granted*, Article 4(3)(a). http://eur-lex.europa.eu/LexUriServ/LexUriServ.do?uri=OJ:L:2011:337:0009:0026:EN:PDF [Retrieved November, 21 2013].

[4] http://www.ecoi.net/8.f-a-q.htm [Retrieved November 21, 2013].

[5] http://www.ukba.homeoffice.gov.uk/policyandlaw/guidance/coi/ [Retrieved November 21, 2013].

to the court, and in my own reports I add to this by linking this general material to the personal circumstances of the appellant and expressing my own opinions as to the plausibility of, for example, the torture methods described by applicants, or the means whereby they secured their release. In a few cases, moreover, there is country information pertaining directly to the applicant's personal circumstances, and this is potentially more telling than the analysis of generic issues, however expertly done.

In 2008, for example, I was asked for a report in connection with the appeal of a Tamil man from eastern Sri Lanka. Although never a member of the LTTE separatist group, he had been persuaded by friends to help LTTE cadres gain access to Fort Frederick in Trincomalee Harbor, where he worked as a civil servant. The UKBA caseworker seized upon this as wholly lacking in credibility, asserting that "there is no evidence to support your claim that your Department would be based in an army camp." On that basis his asylum claim was rejected. His solicitor asked if I knew the layout and operation of Fort Frederick, because this would "greatly help our client's claim." As it happened my wife and I had stayed at the rest-house in Fort Frederick on several occasions prior to the ethnic conflict. Far from being "an army camp" in the sense envisaged by the case worker, it was in fact a seventeenth-century Dutch fort, containing a few ancient cannon and herds of wild deer. My rebuttal of UKBA's assertion did not depend solely on this fortuitous personal experience however, because it took only a few minutes to locate a map of Trincomalee on UNHCR's *Refworld* database, clearly showing the government offices within the walls of the Fort.[6] On such apparently trivial details does the success or failure of an asylum claim depend.

THE REFUGEE STATUS DETERMINATION PROCESS
IN THE UNITED KINGDOM

UKBA administers asylum claims in the United Kingdom, on behalf of Home Office. Applicants undergo initial screening interviews to collect basic personal information, followed by far more detailed asylum interviews with Agency case owners, to establish the basic chronology of their story and test its internal credibility. If refugee status is then awarded no reasons are given, but most claims are refused and the case owner then writes a Reasons For Refusal Letter (RFRL) explaining and justifying that decision. Most Refusal Letters claim that the applicant's story lacks credibility, because of alleged internal or external inconsistencies in their account or because it conflicts with the available COI.

[6] www.unhcr.org/refworld/country,,,,LKA,,4918095a2,0.html [Retrieved November 22, 2013].

Such refusals generally entail rights of appeal before a First-Tier Immigration Judge from the Immigration and Asylum Chamber of the Tribunal Service. Most asylum applicants qualify for legal aid and so are legally represented. Their solicitor prepares the dossier of documents for the appeal, including their client's witness statement, but the advocate who actually argues the case in court is generally a barrister. UKBA is represented in court by a Home Office Presenting Officer (commonly referred to by practitioners as a 'Hoppo'), who is usually not a trained lawyer. Expert medical and country reports, if needed, are commissioned by the solicitor in the interval, which may last months or even years, between receipt of the Refusal Letter and the appeal hearing. This expenditure requires advance approval by the legal aid authorities, however.[7]

Hearings begin with a brief 'examination-in-chief,' in which the appellant confirms that their asylum interview transcript and witness statement are true and that they wish to submit them as evidence. The appellant is then cross-examined by the Hoppo, who asks very detailed questions in the hope of receiving replies that are, or seem, inconsistent with previous interviews and statements. These can then be used to cast doubt on the appellant's credibility. Very occasionally, other witnesses may then be called to give corroborative evidence. Experts normally give oral evidence only in legally important cases such as the Country Guideline hearings discussed later in this chapter. In their closing submissions, Hoppos generally attack the appellant's credibility, and invariably cite 'objective evidence' in the form of COI that is said to support UKBA's decision to refuse asylum. The appellant's barrister then tries to rebut the credibility points, and offers rival interpretations of the COI. The Immigration Judge later produces a written decision ('determination'), which should indicate, *inter alia*, how much weight was given to each major piece of country evidence.

A significant proportion of the decisions made by these First-Tier Tribunals are appealed, many of them successfully. The procedures for such second appeals have changed frequently over the years, but the forms taken by the hearings themselves have been rather more constant. In general, they involve a panel of two Senior Immigration Judges. No further evidence is taken from ordinary witnesses and no interpreters are provided: in most cases the appellant is not even present in court. Such appeals are ostensibly concerned

---

[7] In April 2013, the Ministry of Justice (2013) published a table of maximum hourly rates claimable through legal aid for expert witnesses of various kinds. However, none of the listed categories correspond to the 'country expert' role in asylum litigation, even though I had pointed out this lacuna in my capacity as a member of the Reference Group consulted during the drafting of the guidance. Moreover, all the hourly rates in the guidance, with the one exception of that for interpreters, are far greater than those typically claimed by country experts.

only with matters of law rather than fact, but in practice the boundary between the two is quite hazy; moreover, because asylum decisions must be made on the basis of the situation at the time of the hearing (*Ravichandran*), fresh COI is often submitted, including new or supplementary country expert reports.[8]

COI IN THE REFUGEE STATUS DETERMINATION PROCESS

Clearly, COI underlies both the credibility decisions made by UKBA and Immigration Judges, and their assessments of the risks involved in returning that person to their home country. The Home Office's Country of Origin Information Service (COIS) therefore produces reports, at roughly annual intervals, which summarize key country information for the twenty or so countries generating most asylum applications.[9] The *Country Reports* produced by COIS's predecessor, the Country Information and Policy Unit, had been repeatedly criticized for basic factual errors and highly questionable interpretations (Asylum Aid 1995, 1999; Immigration Advisory Service 2003, 2004). Partly to meet such criticisms, the Home Office set up in 2002 an independent Advisory Panel on Country Information to review these reports and recommend improvements designed to make them more accurate, balanced, and impartial.[10]

Largely in response to all this scrutiny, *Country Reports* now consist entirely of quotations from preexisting, mostly publicly available, electronic sources, as well as, more controversially, partially redacted information furnished by the British Embassy or High Commission in the country concerned, but with no comment or evaluation of the material by COIS staff themselves.[11] Although this represents

[8] Since June 2013, the determinations in such appeals, now heard by the Upper Tribunal Immigration and Asylum Chamber, have begun to be published on the Tribunal's website. Retrieved November 21, 2013 (https://tribunalsdecisions.service.gov.uk/utiac/decisions). By contrast, First-Tier Tribunal decisions are not readily available except to those directly involved.

[9] The latest *Country Reports*, together with ad hoc *Bulletins* on particular current issues, are routinely published on the UKBA website. Retrieved October 10, 2013 (http://www.ukba.home office.gov.uk/policyandlaw/guidance/coi/).

[10] For a retrospective analysis of APCI's work, see Immigration Advisory Service (2010a). The *UK Borders Act 2007* created an independent Inspectorate to monitor UKBA's effectiveness and efficiency, and in March 2009 APCI was replaced by an Independent Advisory Group on Country Information, reporting to the Independent Chief Inspector of the UKBA. It operates in a similar way to APCI, with some of the same personnel; see also the Independent Chief Inspector's report (2011) on the use of COI in UKBA decision making.

[11] In the case of Sri Lanka, these sources include the regular human rights assessments published by the U.K. Foreign and Commonwealth Office and the U.S. State Department; material from UNHCR, the UN Committee Against Torture, and other UN bodies; reports by bodies such as Amnesty International, Human Rights Watch and the International Crisis Group; and news reports from a wide range of local and international media (see UKBA 2012).

a clear improvement on the covert editorializing to which Asylum Aid and the Immigration Advisory Service (and, for that matter, the Advisory Panel; see Immigration Advisory Service 2010a, p. 84) had earlier drawn attention, there are of course still questions regarding the selection of sources and of passages to be quoted. Problems may also arise from the fact that the picture presented is not always coherent. The wider the range of sources quoted, the more likely it becomes that reports will contain opinions that are potentially or actually contradictory. Users of these *Reports*, be they judges, lawyers, Hoppos or UKBA case workers, may then find it difficult to reach balanced judgments on the relative plausibility of these different opinions, given that they themselves do not have detailed knowledge of the country in question.

At appeal hearings, Hoppos draw their country information almost entirely from these COIS *Country Reports*. Barristers generally cite them too, but usually submit additional documents such as generic reports by human rights bodies, medico-legal reports by doctors, or reports by 'country experts' such as anthropologists, political scientists, human geographers, and others with detailed knowledge about countries of origin.

Doctors who write medico-legal reports for asylum cases must demonstrate the appropriateness of their medical qualifications and specialized experience, as well as adhering to certain protocols, such as those governing post-traumatic stress diagnoses or the assessment of scarring.[12] Country experts in the United Kingdom, however, are almost entirely unregulated in terms of qualifications and training, and there are no protocols to be observed – only the very general rules over an expert's duties in civil litigation, as set out in section 35 of the *Civil Procedure Rules* (Ministry of Justice 2011a).[13] The practical application of these rules is explained in an associated *Practice Direction* (Ministry of Justice 2011b), the most crucial part of which is paragraph 1.3:

> An expert should assist the court by providing objective, unbiased opinion on matters within his expertise, and should not assume the role of an advocate.[14]

Experts are therefore left very much to their own devices when it comes to structuring their reports and even to deciding what may or may not properly be

---

[12] They must follow the DSM-IV protocol (American Psychiatric Association 2000) for PTSD diagnoses, and the Istanbul Protocol (UNHCR 2004) when assessing scarring. On the difficulties entailed by the latter requirement, see Kelly (2011, p. 85).

[13] Section 35.3 states: "(1) It is the duty of an expert to help the court on the matters within his expertise. (2) This duty overrides any obligation to the person from whom he has received instructions or by whom he is paid."

[14] The Tribunal has its own practice direction on expert evidence, much of which paraphrases the *Civil Procedure Rules* (Judiciary of England and Wales 2010, paragraph 10).

included in them. In general they get little or no advice from most instructing solicitors on such matters, even if they commit the cardinal sin of offering opinions on the appellant's credibility – a prime example of an issue that is the prerogative of the Immigration Judge. It is also a common complaint among country experts that they rarely receive copies of determinations for the cases on which they have written reports, even if they specifically request them from the solicitors in the hope of gaining helpful feedback on the utility and impact of their reports.[15] Like all other experts, I therefore had to develop my own strategies and structures, which evolved over the years as my understanding of the appeals process grew.

The general principles underlying the structure of expert reports, as I have now come to understand them, are set out in the *Best Practice Guide* recently produced with my Edinburgh colleague Tobias Kelly (Good and Kelly 2013).[16] Briefly, my reports, which are typically anything from forty to sixty pages long, now comprise numbered paragraphs.[17] They begin with a table of contents, listing the section headings and paragraph numbers within each section. An opening background section says when and by whom I was instructed and lists the documents shown to me. It then summarizes the appellant's narrative, and briefly considers whether this narrative is plausible and consistent with the background evidence. The bulk of the report then deals with my specific instructions, beginning each section by quoting verbatim from the instruction concerned. Reports contain significant amounts of generic material, because although it is of course important to tailor responses to their own unique situation, most asylum seekers are not high profile enough to figure in news reports or other documents that might corroborate their specific stories.[18] Moreover, the same issues tend to recur. Virtually every report has to discuss the prevalence of torture in the context of the Prevention of Terrorism Act and Emergency Regulations; the culture of impunity that this legislation helped

---

[15] Both deficiencies seem largely attributable to the heavy workloads and tight deadlines suffered by many immigration lawyers.

[16] This *Guide* appears to have been well received by lawyers, and there is a link to it on the web site of the *Directory of Experts on Countries of Origin* compiled by the Electronic Immigration Network and Immigration Law Practitioners' Association. Subscription only, http://www.ein. org.uk/experts/?q=experts [Retrieved November 21, 2013].

[17] The paragraph numbers are necessary because, in practice, the judge's attention will be drawn piecemeal to particular snippets of information in expert reports and other COI documents (see Good 2007, p. 212). Lawyers rarely ask judges to read whole sections or entire lines of reasoning. Indeed, it is common for lawyers to hand over marked-up copies of COI reports to the judge, in which the paragraphs they are asked to read have been highlighted with yellow marker pen.

[18] There are exceptions of course. For example, I have written reports on claims by two Members of Parliament and several reasonably well-known journalists.

create; the prevalence of sexual violence against male as well as female detainees; and the quality of official recordkeeping, which speaks to whether the Sri Lankan immigration authorities are likely to have on file any suspicions previously held against returning failed asylum seekers.[19] In such discussions, sources are obsessively cited and quoted to add weight to the analyses. Annexes to the report contain my *curriculum vitae*, and a declaration that I have observed the legal obligations of an expert – above all, this states my awareness that my overriding responsibility is to the court.

There is a tension built in to this system. Experts are required to adopt an objective attitude toward the evidence and their overriding duty is to help judges reach decisions. On the other hand, the legal process is adversarial and the lawyers representing asylum applicants always hire the experts; the Home Office almost never uses experts of its own.[20] This tension manifests itself in several ways. First, the divergent responsibilities described by Ardalan (this volume), when she contrasts the lawyers whose duty is to represent their clients, and the medical experts whose primary duty is to the tribunal, apply in much the same way to country experts.[21] Second, Hoppos see experts as hostile witnesses, and many judges, too, suspect experts of being 'hired guns' or even 'professional liars' (Heydon and Ockelton 1996, p. 384) aiming to provide evidence in favor of the claim, either because they are paid to do so or because of their political or humanitarian predispositions. In adversarial legal processes it seems inevitable that expert witnesses should face criticism from those who do not wish their opinions to influence the judge. If, as is usually the case, the expert is not actually present in court during the asylum appeal, the Hoppo will often attack both the report's contents and the expert's credentials. When experts *do* give oral evidence most Hoppos are ill equipped to sustain such critiques, but even so they will try to convince the judge that the expert's

[19] There is no space to discuss these substantive issues adequately here. However, as regards proving persecution based on sexual violence, the problems faced by applicants in the United Kingdom (Baillot, Cowan, and Munro 2009) resemble those explained by Marton (this volume), though the potential positive impact of expert evidence in underpinning such claims is arguably slightly greater in the United Kingdom than is described by Ruffer (this volume) for the United States.

[20] The Home Office does make extensive use of Language Analysis reports (Kam, this volume) but the Scottish Court of Session has ruled (MABN) that these do not meet the standards expected of expert evidence.

[21] The situations of country experts and medical experts are not identical, however, because the evidence involved is markedly different. Medical reports are almost always based on the expert's examination of, or interview with, the asylum applicant, but most country experts in the United Kingdom never meet the appellant (and would decline to do so if asked). In this way we do at least evade the charge routinely leveled by Hoppos at writers of medico-legal reports, that they have simply believed whatever the appellant told them (Henderson and Pickup 2012, paragraph 26.50).

opinion is biased or incomplete and should not be relied upon. As is often the case in legal argument, they may argue from entirely opposite premises on different occasions. This is purely a matter of pragmatism; the overriding aim is to win one's case, not to maintain logical coherence. For example, the Hoppo may seek to reduce the weight of the expert's opinion by arguing that it is out of date because the expert has not visited that country for some time; or, where this argument does not apply, may be little any recent evidence that the expert has personally uncovered as being purely anecdotal, and unsupported by documentary sources.

ETHNOGRAPHIC EVIDENCE IN THE COURTS

As the previous section made clear, most COI, even in expert reports, is obtained from public sources. However, I have also made three visits to Sri Lanka at my own expense with the specific intention of collecting information more directly, and this section illustrates the advantages and disadvantages of presenting such ethnographic information to the asylum courts. On each visit, I was accompanied by Tony Paterson, a British immigration solicitor specializing in asylum claims by Sri Lankan Tamils, who was also concerned to obtain witness statements from the relatives of some of his current clients. Ironically, I first met and interviewed him in 2001 during my initial research into uses of expert evidence in asylum appeals (Good 2007) precisely because, at that time, he was unique among immigration lawyers in *not* using country experts, but instead paying regular visits to Colombo to collect evidence for himself.

By way of brief background, the roots of Sri Lanka's long-running ethnic conflict lie partly in geography and demography. Tamils are concentrated in the north and east of the country while Sinhalese predominate in the Central Highlands and Southwest coastal strip. Sinhalese make up around 70 percent of the population, whereas only 20 percent are Tamils. The introduction of the universal electoral franchise thus meant that after independence the key to electoral success was to appeal in an increasingly chauvinistic way to the interests of the Sinhalese majority (Smith 1970; Brow 1996). In 1971, during my first period of residence there, Ceylon became the Republic of Sri Lanka under a Left Front government headed by Mrs. Bandaranaike's Sri Lanka Freedom Party. The new constitution abandoned earlier safeguards preventing ethnic discrimination; importantly, given the high priority Tamils give to education, quotas were introduced limiting their access to universities. The newly formed, separatist Tamil United Liberation Front (TULF) won several seats in the 1977 elections, but its relative powerlessness encouraged the appearance of militant 'Tamil Tiger' groups.

Tigers killed thirteen Sinhalese soldiers in Jaffna in 1983, sparking serious anti-Tamil riots in the south; the ethnic conflict is generally dated from this event (Wilson 1988; Spencer 1990). Violent Tamil resistance grew in scale, and in 1987 the Indian government (which had been covertly supporting some militant groups) attempted to mediate. An Indian peacekeeping force was sent to Sri Lanka but instead spent two years fighting the militants before withdrawing ignominiously. The extensive human rights violations for which it was responsible set a precedent for the behavior of both sides thereafter. The largest militant group, the Liberation Tigers of Tamil Eelam (LTTE), began assassinating constitutional politicians, as well as members of rival militant groups, whose survivors reformed as pro-government paramilitary groups like the Eelam People's Democratic Party. From 1990 onwards, the LTTE formed the *de facto* administration of the Jaffna peninsula and parts of the east coast. After more than a decade of military escalation, punctuated by brief ceasefires, a formal ceasefire agreement was signed by the government and LTTE in February 2002, but there was a gradual slide back into violence from 2005 onwards (Smith 2007). The government formally withdrew from the ceasefire in January 2008, precipitating the military conflict that ended in May 2009 with the complete military defeat of the LTTE, and the deaths of huge numbers of trapped Tamil civilians (Weiss 2011).

Our field visits took place at markedly different stages in this process. The first was in August 2003, when the ceasefire had been operating for a year and was still being largely observed. The land route linking the Jaffna peninsula and government-controlled areas in the south had been opened, and it was possible for us to travel through LTTE-controlled territory and, under TULF auspices, to visit the extensive High Security Zones in Jaffna, from which the entire civilian population had been forcibly evacuated. Because the situation was relatively relaxed at that time, none of our informants were at all concerned about remaining anonymous. Nonetheless, we ourselves were under surveillance: Colombo police even phoned a Tamil lawyer in London to ask questions about us. We therefore had to bear in mind the potential risk we posed to our informants. This was particularly relevant for my solicitor companion because, in seeking information that he could submit directly as evidence to British courts, he could not merely interview people and make his own notes, as I did, but had to produce signed witness statements. Many of these contained allegations of human rights violations by the army or police. Such statements were sometimes immediately faxed back to London, and the paper copies were then handed over so the statement-givers could personally destroy them.

Our February 2006 visit also took place while the ceasefire was officially still in effect, but being far less rigorously observed. I travelled with my wife to the east coast city of Batticaloa, not only to find out more about the human rights situation in the east, but also because I had a doctoral student working there. In Batticaloa I was also able to see the effects of the tsunami just over a year earlier, and to witness the astonishing density of the military presence on Eastern highways. On this visit, people in Colombo were still willing to speak freely and allow use of their names. In Batticaloa, by contrast, where a factional split in the LTTE had occurred a few months earlier, leading to widespread killings, disappearances and abductions, people were extremely cautious about revealing information and anxious that their names should not be used. On our third visit in February 2010, however, although the conflict was by then over, almost no one from the NGO sector, even in Colombo, was willing to be quoted by name because of the levels of threat and harassment against news reporters or NGO activists working on human rights violations. For this reason too, our visit was confined to Colombo and it did not seem appropriate to produce a public-domain report.

Many different issues arose during these three visits that had a bearing on the evidence in my subsequent expert reports. I shall mention just one of these, from the 2003 visit. The Sri Lankan government had created a national Human Rights Commission (HRC) in 1996, and UKBA's Reasons for Refusal Letters regularly cited the creation of the HRC as evidence of improvement in the human rights situation. A typical paragraph read:

> A National Human Rights Commission was established in 1996, tasked with monitoring government human rights practices, ensuring compliance with constitutional fundamental rights provisions and investigating complaints of human rights violations. Although the Commission has been criticised for failing to pursue aggressively its broad mandate, it has undertaken numerous visits to places of detention.

Undoubtedly this was indeed a positive step, though the legislation establishing the HRC did not comply fully with international humanitarian law, and there were problems over implementing its provisions. For example, although HRC staff could visit authorized detention centers, some prisoners were held in unauthorized places. Most crucially, HRC's mandate did not cover pro-government militias, which work in tandem with the security forces and do much of their dirty work as regards abductions and disappearances.

It was clearly important, therefore, to assess at first hand the conditions under which HRC was operating, and during our 2003 visit to Jaffna I spent a day in the local HRC office. A UN human rights trainer, assigned to this office, told me that there were problems over the narrow operational definition of torture used by HRC, which was limited to physical ill treatment. Staff complained that too much time was wasted on complaints concerning familiar South Asian grievances like salary arrears, promotions, transfers, and appointment procedures. I was shown HRC's log books in which complaints were recorded and actions taken were noted. When a complaint of torture was received, HRC's response was to undertake mediation rather than seeking to impose sanctions; the two parties were brought together and the officer was asked to admit the truth of the allegation and pay small amounts of compensation. The advantage for the soldier concerned was that the matter went no further; they faced no disciplinary proceedings.

HRC's Regional Coordinator Mr. Chandrasekara, who was by common consent one of its most committed and effective officials, was subject to army harassment. He was often stopped at military checkpoints while travelling on official business, and had made formal complaints. I was shown a letter from the Jaffna Military Commander, referring to an incident when Mr. Chandrasekara had refused to allow an armed soldier to travel in his vehicle during a visit to a High Security Zone, on the grounds that HRC had to maintain visible independence and neutrality. Mr. Chandrasekara maintained that he was entitled to move around unescorted, but the letter asserted in strong language that were he to make similar demands in future, soldiers had been ordered to refuse him entry to the Zone without needing to refer the matter to senior officers. Attempts by the security forces to restrict the movements of HRC staff, and potentially compromise their neutrality, escalated after my visit. In September 2004, Mr. Chandrasekara was assaulted by a police officer in Jaffna police station while investigating a complaint. The case against the policeman was never heard because Mr. Chandrasekara relocated to Canada (U.S. State Department 2005). Nor was he the first HRC official forced to flee the country under threat. The director of its Vavuniya office had left the country in 1999 after receiving death threats (U.S. State Department 2002).

This kind of information is of great importance in assessing HRC's capacity to oversee the kinds of improvements in human rights observance constantly referred to in Refusal Letters. It is also precisely the kind of information, concerning daily practice rather than paper regulations, that an anthropologist is especially qualified to provide. One day observing the workings of an office scarcely qualifies as fieldwork. Even so, it provided me with insights that have been helpful in assessing numerous asylum cases ever since. In particular, it has allowed me to illustrate to judges the practical difficulties involved in monitoring human rights observance on the ground.

As regards the weight attached by the court to the evidence in such fieldwork-based reports, however, there is often a curious reversal from the situation in academia. When anthropologists present seminar papers to their peers, the element most immune from criticism is their own ethnography; as James Clifford pointed out, "I was there" is a clinching argument unless you are willing to question the researcher's competence or honesty (Clifford 1988, p. 25; Good 2006a, p. 101). In legal contexts, however, ethnographic observations are liable to be dismissed as 'anecdotal,' and prime authority tends to be accorded to documentary evidence. For example, the first two field visits just described led to generic, public domain reports for general use in connection with Sri Lankan asylum claims. In those reports, I explicitly disavowed any claims to completeness and explicitly avoided drawing conclusions of my own. I also made clear that I was simply reporting what was said or shown to me by particular, named informants.[22] My 2006 *Visit Report* (Good 2006b) therefore consisted almost entirely of paragraphs like the following, in which my informants' names were included in parentheses:

> With this context in mind, interviewees were asked about the significance of scarring, and about police body searches of persons detained or otherwise under suspicion. The police manual requires them to remove the belts, neckties and shoes of detainees, so they have opportunities to see parts of the body not normally visible (Chandralal, Xavier). Police also examine the chests, elbows, and knees of detainees looking for rough skin possibly indicative of paramilitary training. They routinely carry out body searches (using female officers in the case of female suspects), although strip searching, which was formerly quite common, has been rare recently (Xavier, Ganeshalingam, Chandralal, Nandarajan).

Even so, one panel of judges, faced with this *Visit Report* in a case (*Santhirakumar Subramaniam*) where I had not been asked for a specific report on the claimant, responded as follows:

> Turning now to the expert evidence adduced on the appellant's behalf, we are bound to say, with respect to Professor Good, that we are not impressed with his report. Although Professor Good is plainly qualified by his experience and background ... to give expert evidence on the matters covered by it, *he has fallen into the trap of expressing his views freely but failing to identify his sources, except in the most general terms* (italics added). In that regard, it is not sufficient for an expert merely to make *ex cathedra* pronouncements on the various issues placed before him. If his views are to be given any significant weight, he must also state with sufficient clarity *how* he knows these opinions to be true. Failure to do so is bound to devalue the evidential weight of his opinion.

[22] Thus, my 2006 *Visit Report* (Good 2006b) stated on its title page: "In this report, I distinguish clearly between what I observed for myself and what I was told by others. Where assessments are those of particular persons, this is indicated where possible."

I can only interpret this response, which at first seemed bewildering, as a kind of genre mistake; a complete failure to recognize the nature and status of the material and its sources, who were of course people rather than documents.

JUDICIAL EVALUATION OF COI

Virtually all asylum appeal determinations make references to COI, though sometimes these may only be very brief, leaving it unclear precisely what COI was before the Tribunal and how this has been analyzed and assessed.[23] In their determinations, Immigration Judges use COI for a variety of purposes, such as corroborating information about specific places and individuals; evaluating the weight of expert reports; assessing general credibility; and estimating future risk (Townhead, in Immigration Advisory Service 2009, p. 36). However, as noted earlier, the more comprehensive the COI in terms of the range of sources covered, the more likely it is to contain assessments and opinions that are potentially or actually contradictory. Partly for this reason, a checklist of criteria for evaluating country information was developed by the International Association of Refugee Law Judges (2009, pp. 150–1), under the general headings of the relevance and adequacy of the COI; its sources; its nature and type (which rather oddly turned out to refer mainly to impartiality and balance); and whether it had received prior judicial scrutiny.

A checklist in an academic article does not have the force of law, of course, even when the authors are judges, but the topic was also authoritatively considered by the European Court of Human Rights in paragraph 120 of, appropriately enough, a Sri Lankan case, NA *v. United Kingdom*:

> In assessing such material, consideration must be given to its source, in particular its independence, reliability and objectivity. In respect of reports, the authority and reputation of the author, the seriousness of the investigations by means of which they were compiled, the consistency of their conclusions and their corroboration by other sources are all relevant considerations.

These criteria have now been adopted in the United Kingdom. The determination in the important 2009 case *TK* states, at paragraph 5, that "at least within the context of Article 3 jurisprudence, judges should now be assessing COI by the standards set out by the Court [in] NA," which it summarizes as "accuracy, independence, reliability, objectivity, reputation, adequacy of methodology, consistency and corroboration."

---

[23] This does not apply to recent Country Guideline cases (see later in this chapter), whose *raison d'être* is the analysis of COI and that have adopted the practice of appending full bibliographies.

Certain COI issues constantly recur in asylum appeals by claimants of particular nationalities. It is clearly inimical to justice if that information is assessed differently in different appeals (Thomas 2008, 2011), so from 2000 onward the Tribunal began designating certain appeals as Country Guideline cases, with a view to assessing the COI on commonly arising issues.[24] As paragraph 12.2 of the Tribunal's *Practice Directions* explains, such cases are to be treated as authoritative in other, subsequent appeals relating to the same issue and depending upon the same or similar evidence (Judiciary of England and Wales 2010, paragraph 12.2).

A Country Guideline determination thus provides a kind of 'factual precedent'[25] for judges hearing similar cases. In the Court of Appeal, Lord Justice Laws accepted that this was an 'exotic' notion in English law, but nonetheless thought it to be potentially 'benign and practical,' subject to certain safeguards:

> A principal safeguard will lie in the application of the duty to give reasons with particular rigour. [O]pinion evidence will often or usually be very important, since assessment of the risk of persecutory treatment in the milieu of a perhaps unstable political situation may be a complex and difficult task in which the fact-finding tribunal is bound to place heavy reliance on the views of experts ... (*S & Others*)

Many early Country Guideline cases utterly failed to live up to such standards. Some cited only one source, the COIS *Country Report* (*MG*, for example; Immigration Advisory Service 2004, p. 47).

The same cannot be said now – *TK*, for instance, cites 450 sources – but it is still possible to query the comprehensiveness and balance of the sources used, for which, of course, the lawyers are at least as responsible as the Tribunal. In *FS*, for example, a Country Guideline case on apostasy in Iran, the Tribunal considered a large body of COI in a seemingly fair and balanced fashion. Yet the religious material before it came entirely from Christian sources; not a single source represented the views of Muslim scholars. As a result, the tribunal's analysis was unavoidably riddled with orientalist presumptions such as the conflation of *Iranian* law and *Islamic* law (Good 2009, pp. 42–3).

The ultimate question in asylum appeals is whether the asylum applicant would face a 'real risk' of persecution if returned home. Such risk assessments

---

[24] Current Country Guideline determinations appear on the Tribunal website http://www.judiciary.gov.uk/Resources/JCO/Documents/cg-list-last-updated-240713.pdf [Retrieved November 21, 2013].

[25] The Tribunal (*NM & Others*) is unhappy with this term on the grounds that, unlike true precedents, findings in Country Guideline cases are always at the mercy of fresh evidence or changed situations.

must be based on the country situation on the date of the hearing (*Ravichandran*); consequently, Country Guideline cases risk being "out of date on the day they are promulgated" (Yeo, in Immigration Advisory Service 2005, p. 16). In my view, such cases arguably have a place for issues where changes are unlikely in the short or medium term (cultural attitudes toward divorce or rape, for example), but seem inappropriate for matters where the situation might change at any moment, such as the level of risk faced by Tamils if returned to Colombo, which was a principal issue in the last four Country Guideline cases dealing with Sri Lanka.

Whatever its merits in promoting consistent decision making, the Country Guideline system poses problems for 'country experts,' as I have already experienced on two occasions:

> the Appellant's representatives ought to have ensured that Dr. Good's report addressed . . . the Practice Directions (*JDJ*).
> Leaving aside our disappointment that both [experts] (especially Professor Good) should have seen fit to go over old ground (*TK*).

The problem here is that while lawyers may be required to treat such 'factual precedents' as authoritative, experts clearly cannot do so because, with the greatest of respect, the opinion of a British judge as to the prevailing situation in a given country or region carries no weight at all, *as evidence*, for a country expert. In forming and justifying their opinions on the issues, it is impossible for experts to ignore material simply because it was considered and pronounced upon in an earlier Country Guideline determination. If Immigration Judges wish to reserve to themselves the right to decide what COI is relevant to an expert's opinion, there seems little point in commissioning expert reports at all.

ON THE 'OBJECTIVITY' OF COI

That final point applies all the more strongly because the skills involved in analyzing material such as COI are notably underdeveloped among legal professionals. William Twining points out that techniques for assessing factual evidence receive little emphasis in legal training, and that "an imbalance exists between the amount of attention devoted to disputed questions of law . . . and the amount devoted to disputed questions of fact . . . in legal processes generally" (2006, p. 15). Moreover, the cases within which legal fact-finding takes place "are artificially constructed units extracted from more complex and diffuse contexts" (Twining 2006, p. 447). As Conley and O'Barr note (1990, pp. 9, 11), this abridged raw material is then "treated as transparent, transformed into a window through which the law views the set of constructed meanings it calls 'facts'." Moreover, this process generally ignores litigants' own discourses in favor of legal terminology. The assessment of factual evidence by judges thus tends to reflect "a tradition of relatively complacent commonsense empiricism" that devotes relatively little attention to the problems and issues involved in the collection, processing, presentation, and weighing of factual information (Twining 2006, p. 28).

Social scientists are often likely to find themselves at odds with such 'commonsense,' undertheorized legal approaches to factual evidence, which seem likely to be especially problematic in asylum adjudications because of the centrality of the asylum seeker's narrative. For example, the standard practice in British asylum courts, of referring to COI as 'objective evidence,' causes disquiet among expert witnesses because it appears to take no account of the processes of contextualization, interpretation, even construction, to which such knowledge is subject (Good 2007, pp. 223–4).[26] However, although it is disconcerting to hear one's analyses being characterized by lawyers and judges in this way, it is important to recognize that lawyers use a notion of objectivity quite different from that of philosophers and social scientists. For lawyers 'objectivity' seems to be a pragmatic, not a metaphysical concept. Rather than implying something external to the observer, and therefore capable of independent verification, it has similar status to the notion of 'the Reasonable Man' for Barotse judges (Gluckman 1955). For lawyers, in effect, objectivity is the subjectivity of the Reasonable Man. In claiming objectivity for one's expert reports, one would therefore merely be stating that no reasonable expert on Sri Lanka would be likely to reach different conclusions.

Home Office reasoning often displays particularly naive forms of 'common-sense empiricism,' as illustrated in the 2006 Country Guideline case *LP*, in which I gave written and oral evidence. Its lawyers were seeking to minimize the weight of expert evidence by Dr. Chris Smith, a British security specialist with excellent contacts among Sri Lankan police and military, whose report drew directly on interviews he had conducted with key officials like the Inspector General of Police. In its written submissions, the Home Office argued that the role of 'country experts' in asylum cases differed from that of experts in other civil litigation. Normally, it argued, experts use their specialist knowledge to interpret, for example, medical diagnostic findings. It went on:

---

[26] The Tribunal (*TK*, paragraph 7) questioned this terminology for a different reason, that "to refer to such evidence as 'objective' obscures the need for the decision-maker to subject such evidence to scrutiny to see if it conforms to the COI standards just noted" (a reference to *NA*, discussed earlier). This still appears to assume that objectivity is attainable when certain criteria are met.

The role of a 'country expert' in an [asylum appeal] is rather different. Here, the issue relates to conditions in a specified country or region. It is unlikely that any specialist knowledge is required in order to *interpret* the information. Rather the role of a 'country expert' is to assist with the provision of the 'raw data,' in terms of providing comprehensive and balanced factual information. ... Whilst the [tribunal] may be assisted by the opinion of a 'country expert,' it is important that the tribunal is provided with the factual material upon which that opinion is based, in order to conduct its own assessment of the conclusions to be drawn from it. (italics in original)

This was clearly an attempt to limit country experts to mere gatherers of factual information for judges to interpret. Moreover, the reference to 'raw data' laid the ground for an argument advanced in court, that Dr. Smith's evidence should not be accepted unless he also provided his interview notes made at the time. This argument was no doubt largely tactical, but the very fact that it was deemed worth advancing presupposed the positivistic assumption that these notes would be freer from bias and, by extension, that COI might exist as a form of 'raw data' 'out there' in the world. Interestingly, though, COIS itself does not always do this. Although its stated methodology is to include interview transcripts as addenda in its own country visit reports (Swift 2008), the most recent COIS/Foreign and Commonwealth Office report on Sri Lanka (Home Office 2009) includes only paraphrases of interviewees' replies (Good and Gibb 2013).

LP's barrister resisted this demand, saying that, "a filtering process needs to be applied to the evidence and that is why an expert is needed," but even this does not seem to go far enough. The process is not simply one of purifying a 'truth' that has become contaminated by selectivity or bias; the fact is that the provision, as well as the assessment, of COI are both, fundamentally and inevitably, interpretive processes. Similarly, Redmayne (2001, pp. 14–16) points out that not all biases are 'motivational' (where expert witnesses might be biased because they want one side to win); there are also, inevitably, 'cognitive' biases whereby the very perception of the evidence is affected by the scientific and professional paradigms within which the expert was trained or acculturated (Polanyi 1958; Kuhn 1962; Bloor 1976). Of these two forms of bias, judges focus only on the first. For example, some Immigration Judges were already questioning the objectivity of COI even before the comments in *TK* cited earlier, and for 'two main reasons: political agendas and selective information' (Immigration Advisory Service 2010b, p. 56). This was true at least as far back as the 2001 determination by Mr. Justice Collins, then President of the Tribunal, who stated, in *Slimani*, that experts "all suffer from the difficulty that very rarely are they entirely objective in their approach. ... Many have fixed opinions about the regime in a particular country." In short, judges consistently see experts as biased in a purely motivational sense, a failing from which they seem to regard themselves as mercifully free. They seem wholly unaware of the possibility of cognitive bias, which of course applies to them equally.

Happily, the judges in *LP* concluded that "in this jurisdiction experts are not merely the providers of raw data but they can be the interpreters of it as well." Although the Home Office argument was mainly aimed at Dr. Smith, it would have raised problems for me too if the judges had accepted it. There is no decision in English law as to whether anthropologists' field notes are privileged documents, and if the court had demanded access to my notes I would have been forced to test the water by refusing on grounds of professional ethics. Just to add an extra frisson, I had realized while listening to these arguments in court that the notebook in which I was transcribing proceedings was the very one used on my 2006 visit to Sri Lanka, so I actually had with me the evidence that the Home Office was unsuccessfully trying to elicit!

This incident brings into sharp focus some of the problems discussed in this chapter, arising from the key role played by COI in asylum decision-making, and the reification that this involves. Administrative and judicial decision makers are predisposed, through their training and because of the binary decision making in which they are engaged, toward a form of 'commonsense' or 'naive' empiricism. Their approach to country information risks losing sight of the fact that, even though it is usually presented to them in seemingly 'objective' and generalized documentary form, most such information derives ultimately from specific, localized events, as directly observed by media reporters, human rights activists, locally based diplomats, or country experts, who have then interpreted these observations within socially constructed frameworks of meaning, imbued with their own moral, professional, motivational and cognitive biases.

Cases[27]

> FS and others (Iran, Christian Converts) Iran CG [2004] UKIAT 00303.
> JDJ v. Secretary of State for the Home Department (SSHD) HX/32391/2002 & HX/60178/2003 (unreported: June 12, 2008).
> LP (LTTE area, Tamils, Colombo, risk?) Sri Lanka CG [2007] UKAIT 00076.
> MABN & Anor v. The Advocate General for Scotland Representing SSHD & Anor [2013] ScotCS CSIH 68 (July 12, 2013)

---

[27] Where no internet citations are given, the full texts of reported decisions listed here may be found on the British and Irish Information Institute database. http://www.bailii.org/. See also footnote 24 regarding Country Guideline cases [Retrieved November 22, 2013].

MG (Desertion, Punishment) Angola CG [2002] UKIAT 07360.

NA v. United Kingdom – 25904/07 [2008] ECHR 616.

NM and Others (Lone women, Ashraf) Somalia CG [2005] UKIAT 00076.

'Ravichandran': *R. v. The Immigration Appeal Tribunal & Anor ex p. Rajendrakumar* [1996] Imm A.R. 97 [1995] EWCA Civ. 16.

S. and Others v. SSHD [2002] EWCA Civ. 539 [2002] INLR 416.

Santhirakumar Subramaniam v. SSHD, AA/04813/2006 (unreported: August 17, 2006)

Slimani v. SSHD 01/TH/00092. (http://www.unhcr.org/refworld/docid/404f15034.html) [Retrieved March 23, 2011].

TK (Tamils, LP updated) Sri Lanka (Rev. 1) CG [2009] UKAIT 00049.

Visuvanathan Jeyakumar v. SSHD, 18779 (unreported: May 20, 1999).

REFERENCES

ACCORD. 2013. *Researching Country of Origin Information: Training Manual, 2013 Edition*. http://www.coi-training.net/handbook/Researching-Country-of-Origin-Information-2013-edition-ACCORD-COI-Training-manual.pdf [Retrieved November 21, 2013].

American Psychiatric Association. 2000. *Diagnostic and Statistical Manual of Mental Disorders*. 4th edn. Washington, DC: American Psychiatric Association.

Asylum Aid. 1995. *No Reason at All: Home Office Decisions on Asylum Claims*. London: Asylum Aid.

Asylum Aid. 1999. *Still No Reason at All: Home Office Decisions on Asylum Claims*. http://www.asylumaid.org.uk/wp-content/uploads/2013/02/Still_No_Reason_At_All.pdf [Retrieved November 24, 2013].

Baillot, Helen, Sharon Cowan and Vanessa E. Munro. 2009. "Seen but Not Heard? Parallels and Dissonances in the Treatment of Rape Narratives Across the Asylum and Criminal Justice Contexts." *Journal of Law and Society* 36(2): 195–219.

Bloor, David. 1976. *Knowledge and Social Imagery*. London: Routledge and Kegan Paul

Brow, James. 1996. *Demons and Development: The Struggle for Community in a Sri Lankan Village*. Tucson: University of Arizona Press.

Clifford, James. 1988. *The Predicament of Culture*. Cambridge, MA: Harvard University Press.

Conley, John M. and William M. O'Barr. 1990. *Rules Versus Relationships: The Ethnography of Legal Discourse*. Chicago: Chicago University Press.

Gluckman, Max. 1955. *The Judicial Process Among the Barotse of Northern Rhodesia*. Manchester, UK: Manchester University Press.

Good, Anthony. 2006a. "Writing as a Kind of Anthropology: Alternative Professional Genres." In G. De Neve and M. Unnithan, eds., *Critical Journeys: The Making of Anthropologists*. Aldershot, UK: Ashgate, pp. 91–115.

Good, Anthony. 2006b. *Report on Fact-Finding Visit to Sri Lanka: 10th–20th February 2006*. http://www.ein.org.uk/members/country-report/report-fact-finding-visit-sri-lanka-10th-20th-february-2006; subscription only [Retrieved November 24, 2013].

Good, Anthony. 2007. *Anthropology and Expertise in the Asylum Courts*. London and New York: Routledge-Cavendish.

Good, Anthony. 2009. "Persecution for Reasons of Religion under the 1951 Refugee Convention." In Kirsch, Thomas G. and Bertram Turner, eds., *Permutations of Order: Religion and Law as Contested Sovereignties*. Farnham: Ashgate, pp. 27–48.

Good, Anthony and Tobias Kelly. 2013. *Expert Country Evidence in Asylum and Immigration Cases in the United Kingdom: Best Practice Guide.* University of Edinburgh. http://www.san.ed.ac.uk/__data/assets/pdf_file/0003/124698/BPG_type set_3.pdf [Retrieved November 21, 2013].

Good, Anthony and Robert Gibb. 2013. "Do the Facts Speak for Themselves? Country of Origin Information in French and British Refugee Status Determination Procedures." *International Journal of Refugee Law* 25(2): 291–322.

Gyulai, Gabor. 2011. *Country Information in Asylum Procedures: Quality as a Legal Requirement in the EU*. 2nd edn. Budapest: Hungarian Helsinki Committee.

Henderson, Mark and Alison Pickup. 2012. *Best Practice Guide to Asylum and Human Rights Appeals*. http://www.ein.org.uk/bpg/contents; subscription only [Retrieved November 24, 2013].

Heydon, J. D. and Mark Ockelton. 1996. *Evidence: Cases and Materials*. 4th edn. London: Butterworths.

Immigration Advisory Service. 2003. *Home Office Country Assessments: An Analysis*. London: Immigration Advisory Service.

Immigration Advisory Service. 2004. *Home Office Country Reports: An Analysis*. (http://www.ilpa.org.uk/resources2.php?action=search&advanced=&&page=620; subscription only) [Retrieved November 25, 2013].

Immigration Advisory Service. 2005. In Yeo, Colin, ed., *Country Guideline Cases: Benign and Practical?* http://www.freemovement.org.uk/wp-content/uploads/2012/01/Country-Guideline-cases-benign-and-practical.pdf [Retrieved November 24, 2013].

Immigration Advisory Service. 2009. In Williams, Elizabeth, Jo Pettitt, Laurel Townhead and Stephanie Huber (eds.), *The Use of Country of Origin Information in Refugee Status Determination: Critical Perspectives*. http://www.refworld.org/pdfid/4a3f2ac32.pdf [Retrieved November 24, 2013].

Immigration Advisory Service. 2010a. *The APCI Legacy: A Critical Assessment*. http://www.refworld.org/docid/4b90d9a12.html [Retrieved November 21, 2013].

Immigration Advisory Service. 2010b. In Tsangarides, Natasha, ed., *The Refugee Roulette: the Role of Country Information in Refugee Status Determination*. http://www.refworld.org/docid/4b62a6182.html [Retrieved November 24, 2013].

Independent Chief Inspector of the UK Border Agency. 2011. *The Use of Country of Origin Information in Deciding Asylum Applications: A Thematic Inspection*. http://icinspector.independent.gov.uk/wp-content/uploads/2011/02/Use-of-country-of-origin-information-in-deciding-asylum-applications.pdf [Retrieved October 10, 2012].

International Association of Refugee Law Judges. 2009. "Judicial Criteria for Assessing Country of Origin Information (COI): A Checklist." *International Journal of Refugee Law* 21(1): 149–68.

Judiciary of England and Wales. 2010. *Practice Directions: Immigration and Asylum Chambers of the First-Tier Tribunal and the Upper Tribunal*. http://www.judiciary.gov.uk/Resources/JCO/Documents/Practice%20Directions/Tribunals/IAC_UT_FtT_PracticeDirection.pdf [Retrieved 10 October 2012].

Kelly, Tobias. 2011. *This Side of Silence: Human Rights, Torture, and the Recognition of Cruelty*. Philadelphia: University of Pennsylvania Press.

Kuhn, Thomas S. 1962. *The Structure of Scientific Revolutions*. 2nd edn. Chicago: Chicago University Press.

Ministry of Justice. 2011a. *Civil Procedure Rules, Part 35: Experts and Assessors*. http://www.justice.gov.uk/guidance/courts-and-tribunals/courts/procedure-rules/civil/contents/parts/part35.htm#IDAHO0HC [Retrieved November 21, 2012].

Ministry of Justice. 2011b. *Civil Procedure Rules, Practice Direction 35: Experts and Assessors*. http://www.justice.gov.uk/guidance/courts-and-tribunals/courts/procedure-rules/civil/contents/practice_directions/pd_part35.htm [Retrieved November 21, 2012].

Ministry of Justice. 2013. *Guidance on the Remuneration of Expert Witnesses*. http://www.justice.gov.uk/downloads/legal-aid/funding-code/guidance-on-remuneration-of-expert-witnesses_-April-2013.pdf [Retrieved November 21, 2012].

Polanyi, Michael. 1958. *Personal Knowledge*. Chicago: Chicago University Press.

Redmayne, Mike. 2001. *Expert Evidence and Criminal Justice*. Oxford: Oxford University Press.

Smith, Chris. 2007. "The Eelam Endgame?" *International Affairs* 83: 69–86.

Smith, Donald E. 1970. *Religion and Political Development: An Analytic Study*. Boston: Little, Brown and Company.

Spencer, Jonathan. 1990. *Sri Lanka: History and the Roots of Conflict*. London and New York: Routledge.

Swift, Nick. 2008. "Fact Finding Missions – Methodology and Guidance." *11th Meeting of the Advisory Panel on Country Information, 2008*. http://apci.homeoffice.gov.uk/PDF/eleventh_meeting/APCI.11.6%20%20FFMs%20(methodology%20&%20guidance).pdf [Retrieved January 14, 2012].

Thomas, Robert. 2008. "Consistency in Asylum Adjudication: Country Guidance and the Asylum Process in the United Kingdom." *International Journal of Refugee Law* 20: 489–532.

Thomas, Robert. 2011. *Administrative Justice and Asylum Appeals: A Study of Tribunal Adjudication*. Portland, OR: Hart Publishing.

Twining, William. 2006. *Rethinking Evidence: Exploratory Essays*. (2nd edn.) Cambridge: Cambridge University Press.

UKBA. 2009. *Report of Information Gathering Visit to Colombo, Sri Lanka 23–29 August 2009*. http://www.unhcr.org/refworld/docid/4aeo66de2.html [Retrieved January 12 2012].

UKBA. 2012. *Sri Lanka Country of Origin Information (COI) Report*. http://www.ukba.homeoffice.gov.uk/sitecontent/documents/policyandlaw/coi/srilanka12/ [Retrieved November 21, 2013].

UKBA. No date. *Considering Asylum Claims and Assessing Credibility*. http://www.ukba.homeoffice.gov.uk/sitecontent/documents/policyandlaw/asylumprocessguidance/consideringanddecidingtheclaim/guidance/considering-protection-.pdf?view=Binary [Retrieved November 21, 2013].

UN Committee Against Torture. 2011. *Consideration of Reports Submitted by States Parties under Article 19 of the Convention – Sri Lanka*. http://www.refworld.org/docid/4efo88252.html [Retrieved November 21, 2013].

UNHCR. 1997. *UNHCR Note on the Principle of Non-refoulement*. http://www.refworld.org/docid/438c6d972.html [Retrieved November 21, 2013].

UNHCR. 2004. *Country of Origin Information: Towards Enhanced International Cooperation.* http://www.unhcr.org/refworld/docid/403b2522a.html [Retrieved November 21, 2013].

UNHCR. 2011. *Handbook and Guidelines on Procedures and Criteria for Determining Refugee Status.* http://www.unhcr.org/refworld/docid/4f33c8d92.html [Retrieved November 21, 2013].

UNHCR. 2004. *Istanbul Protocol: Manual on the Effective Investigation and Documentation of Torture and Other Cruel, Inhuman or Degrading Treatment or Punishment.* (http://www.ohchr.org/Documents/Publications/training8Rev1en.pdf) [Retrieved August 26, 2014].

U.S. State Department. 2002. *2001 Country Reports on Human Rights Practices: Sri Lanka.* http://www.state.gov/j/drl/rls/hrrpt/2001/sa/8241.htm [Retrieved October 13, 2012].

U.S. State Department. 2005. *2004 County* [sic] *Reports on Human Rights Practices: Sri Lanka.* http://www.state.gov/j/drl/rls/hrrpt/2004/41744.htm [Retrieved October 13, 2012].

Weiss, Gordon. 2011. *The Cage: The Fight for Sri Lanka and the Last Days of the Tamil Tigers.* London: The Bodley Head.

Weston, Amanda. 1998. "'A Witness of Truth': Credibility Findings in Asylum Appeals." *Immigration and Nationality Law and Practice* 12(3): 87–89.

Wilson, A. Jeyaratnam. 1988. *The Break-Up of Sri Lanka.* Honolulu: University of Hawaii Press.

PART II

PRACTICES AND TECHNOLOGIES FOR MEDICO-PSYCHO EXPERTISE

6

Expert as Aid and Impediment: Navigating Barriers to Effective Asylum Representation

Sabrineh Ardalan

As soon as Muhammed, a young man from Cameroon, hit puberty, he realized that he was attracted to other men.[1] He knew he had to hide these feelings or he would be ostracized, attacked, or even killed if his family learned that he was gay. At first he tried to date girls to stop the kids in his class from insulting him for being feminine. But he did not have feelings for girls and could not force himself to stay in relationships with them. When he was in university, Muhammed started secretly dating his classmate Christopher. Although Muhammed was scared of being discovered with Christopher, spending time with him was the only thing that made Muhammed happy, and he took the risk.

When a friend stumbled on the boys kissing one day, Muhammed pleaded with that friend not to tell anyone, but the friend refused. He dragged Muhammed to his parents' house and told Muhammed's father what he had seen. From the rumors he had heard in the community, Muhammed's father had suspected that his son was gay. He started yelling homophobic slurs at Muhammed and punching and kicking him. When Muhammed's father left the house to consult with his tribal and religious chiefs about what punishment to impose, Muhammed escaped his house. Soon thereafter, Muhammed fled to the United States.

I met Muhammed at the Harvard Immigration and Refugee Clinical Program (HIRC), where I supervise law students and represent clients in their applications for asylum and other forms of humanitarian relief. A team

---

[1] Throughout this chapter, the names of asylum applicants, along with any identifying and home country information, have been changed to protect confidentiality. The case examples discussed in this chapter draw on my experiences at the Harvard Immigration and Refugee Clinical Program (HIRC). HIRC has engaged in direct representation of asylum-seekers, as well as appellate litigation and policy advocacy, for thirty years. For a description of HIRC, see http://www.harvardimmigrationclinic.org.

of law students and I worked closely with Muhammed, meeting for several hours each week over the course a year to elicit his story and prepare his case for adjudication. In addition to drafting Muhammed's affidavit, the students also conducted extensive research on conditions for LGBT individuals in Cameroon and began looking for evidence to corroborate his testimony.

Under the Refugee Convention, Muhammed's credible and persuasive testimony alone should have been sufficient to establish eligibility for asylum. But, as the editors' introduction to this volume makes clear, adjudicators increasingly expect corroboration of an applicant's story from outside sources, leaving lawyers to seek outside experts and other evidence to bolster their clients' claims and credibility. Given the distorted evidentiary requirements in asylum cases, including adjudicators' demands for extensive corroboration, it is critical that our interactions with other experts are effective – our clients' lives often depend on it. Yet, there is a natural tension between lawyers, whose role is to advocate zealously for clients, and other experts who may see their roles in the asylum process differently. It is inevitable that we sometimes disagree.

In Muhammed's case, our legal team identified a need for three types of outside experts: a country expert to document both the pervasive violence against LGBT individuals in Cameroon and the failure of the state to protect those individuals; a medical expert to document the scars Muhammed sustained from his father's beatings; and a psychological expert to connect Muhammed's nightmares, headaches, and isolation in the United States to the trauma he suffered in Cameroon.[2]

Our communications with the country expert and medical evaluator were productive, and they drafted affidavits that effectively supported Muhammed's asylum case. But our collaboration with a forensic psychological evaluator proved more complicated. The psychologist, who met with Muhammed and drafted a forensic evaluation, described him in terms that, in many respects,

---

[2]   It is important to note that asylum applicants who have access both to lawyers and to other experts are a rarity – not the rule. Advocates and adjudicators alike must consider the potential impact on unrepresented asylum applicants of the increased demands for corroboration, including expert evidence. The regular submission of expert testimony and evaluations in immigration proceedings may unfairly raise the bar for the majority of asylum applicants who are unrepresented or underrepresented and do not have the resources to submit expert evidence. As a result, asylum advocates must think creatively about how to expand representation and how to improve the asylum adjudication process. A recent New York immigration court study presents a model for holistic representation that includes funding for both legal and nonlegal services, such as expert testimony and mental health services (NYIRS 2012).

contradicted our experiences with Muhammed over many months. He described Muhammed as an upbeat, forthcoming, and optimistic man who told a clear and consistent story about the past harm he had suffered. The psychologist stated that Muhammed had largely recovered from the Post-Traumatic Stress Disorder (PTSD) and depression he suffered upon his arrival in the United States.

Yet, in dozens of meetings at HIRC, Muhammed was reticent, reserved, and withdrawn. He would often cry when discussing his isolation here in the United States, his separation from his long-time boyfriend, and his fears of being forced to return to his home country. It was hard for him to remember dates and sequences of the attacks he suffered, and he would completely shut down when he started to recall the threats and beatings from his father. While at times he was hopeful about his future, the meetings with HIRC often left him despondent, with terrible headaches and nausea; he tried to block them out of his mind after he left the office each week.

From my perspective as Muhmmed's attorney, these divergent accounts had the potential to undermine Muhammed's asylum case. If Muhammed was able to recover from the trauma so quickly, an adjudicator might question the severity of the harm suffered. The evaluation's description of Muhammed as "forthcoming" and "consistent" in his narrative could also be problematic; what if Muhammed shut down emotionally or had difficulty remembering dates and sequences of events in court, as he had at HIRC meetings and as often occurs? Although the psychologist understood my concerns, he was taken aback at having to reconsider the way he had framed his evaluation. He had not wanted to victimize Muhammed and had tried to depict him as the strong, resilient survivor that, in many ways, he was.

When I asked Muhammed about his meetings with the psychologist and about the optimism the psychologist described, Muhammed explained that he had felt very comfortable talking to the psychologist. He noted that it was unusual for him to connect with someone so quickly, but the psychologist made him feel very safe and protected. Muhammed felt supported and understood. While it was reassuring for me that the psychologist believed Muhammed was doing well in terms of recovering from his PTSD and depression, the evaluation's emphasis on hope, happiness, and optimism was incongruous with the portrait Muhammed presented at HIRC meetings – and possibly damaging to his case.

We asked the expert to meet with Muhammed again, but he refused. He told us that he thought we would coach Muhammed in how to answer his questions, thereby undermining Muhammed's sincerity and the expert's objectivity. In the end, the expert did agree to correct factual errors in his account of Muhammed's experiences in Cameroon; he also included an explanation of the connection between Muhammed's ongoing PTSD symptoms and his continued isolation here in the United States. However, the expert refused to revise his original conclusions. Because the psychologist had based those conclusions on his medical expertise, he did not believe it appropriate to revisit them in response to concerns raised by Muhammed's attorneys.

Interactions between attorneys and experts in asylum cases are often fruitful, but Muhammed's case highlights an important reality: lawyers and other experts see their work and view "evidence" through different optics. In some cases, experts see themselves as partners in the asylum process, working toward a common goal of helping an applicant obtain asylum. In other cases, experts are sympathetic to clients, but see their role primarily as "truth tellers," providing an objective perspective on the conditions in a given country, or the effects of PTSD on an applicant. In those instances, experts' sense of integrity may be violated when lawyers ask for revisions to their reports to reflect differing perspectives.

In this chapter, I argue that attorneys and experts should work together throughout the asylum process to understand each other's respective roles and to ensure, whenever possible, that their goals are aligned. Expert testimony can be critical to the success of an applicant's claim, but prepared without close collaboration with attorneys, such testimony has the potential to undermine an asylum seeker's case. In some instances, where differences of opinion cannot be reconciled, the attorney-expert relationship may not be salvageable.

I open this chapter by explaining the importance of expert testimony in recent years given adjudicators' increasing demands for corroboration of asylum claims. I then describe specific examples from HIRC's direct client representation that highlight the ways in which close collaboration between lawyers and other experts can help asylum applicants in presenting their claims. Next, I address the sometimes-conflicting perspectives of experts and attorneys in HIRC cases, and the need for increased transparency and communication among experts and lawyers about their roles and responsibilities in asylum representation. I conclude by arguing that explicit protocols need to be adopted in order to improve collaboration between experts and attorneys in the asylum process and to mediate the divide between objectivity and advocacy that is often at issue in these cases.

THE PARADIGM SHIFT TO AN EXPERT REQUIREMENT

Over the past fifteen years, adjudicators have increasingly demanded extensive corroboration of an asylum applicant's claim.[3] In many jurisdictions, the submission of extensive evidence, and in particular of psychological, medical, and country condition expert testimony, has become a functional requirement for a successful asylum application. As discussed further below, such expert evidence serves three key purposes in asylum adjudication.

First, courts often rely on expert testimony to overturn decisions by adjudicators who improperly denied applicants' asylum claims in the first instance. In *Mukamusoni v. Ashcroft*, for example, the court of appeals cited the testimony of a psychological expert in finding that the asylum applicant, a Rwandan woman who was repeatedly detained, interrogated, and beaten by soldiers, had provided sufficient corroboration to establish eligibility for asylum. The court vacated the original decision and ordered the adjudicator to reconsider the applicant's claim in light of the forensic psychological evaluation, which was "literally replete with information which supports the substance of Mukamusoni's testimony," including evidence of "ulcers developed in prison, her independently sought HIV testing in light of her fear of having contracted AIDS from her rapes, [and] trauma-induced PTSD symptoms such as nightmares, hopelessness, sleeplessness, distrust of others, etc."[4] In other similar cases, appellate courts have ordered adjudicators to revisit denials of asylum protection where adjudicators have failed to admit expert evidence or refused to give it adequate weight in making asylum determinations.[5]

Second, adjudicators may turn to expert testimony to allay their concerns about applicants' credibility, particularly following widely publicized stories

---

[3] The Board of Immigration Appeals, the administrative appeal body for immigration cases in the United States, first set forth the parameters for reasonable corroboration in its 1997 decision in *Matter of S-M-J-*, 21 I&N Dec. 722 (BIA 1997): 725–6. Congress codified *Matter of S-M-J-* and reiterated these requirements with the REAL ID Act of 2005.

[4] *Mukamusoni v. Ashcroft*, 390 F.3d 110 (2004): 122. Similarly, in *Cece v. Holder*, a different court of appeals relied on the testimony of a country expert, a professor in Balkan history, to overturn the initial adjudicator's denial of asylum, finding that a young, single Albanian woman targeted by members of a criminal gang would not be able safely relocate within Albania if forced to return. The expert, a professor in Balkan history, "described a very serious problem of human trafficking for prostitution in Albania in which gangs, often with the protection, and at times the participation of the police, kidnap women ..." *Cece v. Holder*, 733 F.3d 662 (2013): 667.

[5] *Tun v. Gonzales*, 485 F.3d 1014 (2007): 1028–29; *Niam v. Ashcroft*, 354 F.3d 652 (2004): 660. In *Tadesse v. Gonzales*, for example, the Seventh Circuit returned the asylum case to the original immigration judge to allow the torture counselor who had evaluated the applicant and identified the applicant's symptoms as "characteristic of survivors of rape and torture" an opportunity to testify *Tadesse v. Gonzales*, 492 F.3d 905 (2007): 911.

about some instances of fraud in asylum cases.[6] Because an applicant's testimony is often the central – if not the only – source of evidence in asylum cases, adjudicators often focus on inconsistencies in an applicant's story in order to determine whether the applicant's claim is genuine or fraudulent.[7] Legislation and case law require that such inconsistencies be viewed holistically – in light of the "totality of the circumstances," and considering "all relevant factors."[8] Adjudicators, however, often fail to follow these strictures, improperly finding that any inconsistency – even if tangential to the claim or immaterial – undermines an applicant's credibility (Anker 2013, p. 183; Einhorn and Berthold, this volume).[9]

As Hawthorne Smith, Stuart Lustig, and David Gangsei explain in their chapter in this volume, experts may provide critical context for those inconsistencies. A psychological expert, for example, can play an important role in explaining why an applicant's trauma history – not a lack of credibility – resulted in testimonial inconsistencies. The more distressing an event, the more likely an asylum seeker is to remember "central details . . . at the expense of peripheral details" (Herlihy and Turner 2009, p. 178–79). Inconsistencies frequently arise when people describe traumatic events, particularly when a significant period of time elapses between each re-telling (Jacobs and Lustig 2010; Herlihy, Scragg, and Turner 2002, p. 326). Due to the enormity of the backlog in the U.S. immigration system, asylum seekers are often forced to wait years for their cases to be heard, thereby increasing the likelihood of gaps

---

[6] In July 2011, the *New York Times* ran a front-page article describing the "shadowy industry dedicated to asylum fraud" that "thrives in New York" (Dolnick 2011). The next month, the *New Yorker* profiled Caroline, a young African woman, who successfully applied for asylum in the United States based on a story she had invented. Although Caroline likely had a valid asylum claim based on the attacks her family suffered due to their support for a prominent opposition leader, she embellished those facts and claimed to be a rape survivor in order to improve her chances of being granted asylum (Mehta 2011).

[7] Under the REAL ID Act of 2005, adjudicators can consider any inconsistency in making an adverse credibility determination. REAL ID Act of 2005, Public Law 109–113, 119 U.S. Statutes at Large 231 (2005). The Act states that, "considering the totality of the circumstances, and all relevant factors, a trier of fact may base a credibility determination on the . . . consistency between the applicant's or witness's written and oral statements . . ., the internal consistency of each such statement, the consistency of such statements with other evidence of record . . ., and any inaccuracies or falsehoods in such statements, without regard to whether an inconsistency, inaccuracy, or falsehood goes to the heart of the applicant's claim, or any other relevant factor."

[8] REAL ID Act § 101(a)(3)(B)(ii); 8 U.S.C. § 1158(b)(1)(B)(ii).

[9] HIRC recently took on the case of a Burundian woman who was denied asylum in the first instance due to an apparent inconsistency between her testimony that her sisters were killed in the genocide and her testimony that a sister had accompanied her to her visa interview. For the Burundian woman, the female cousin who accompanied her to the visa interview was, in fact, her sister, although biologically she was not. The inconsistency was significant enough from the adjudicator's perspective to undermine the Burundian applicant's credibility and her claim.

in memories. Expert testimony is thus often essential to proving that, despite these gaps and inconsistencies, an applicant is not malingering.

Country experts can also help adjudicators understand inconsistencies in applicants' testimony. When an applicant is unfamiliar with Western notions of time, a country expert can provide an adjudicator with the cultural context necessary to explain why an applicant may experience difficulties recounting events in a linear manner (Kalin 1986, p. 236). As Anthony Good notes in his chapter in this volume, a country expert can attest to whether an applicant's narrative is consistent with the expert's information about conditions in the applicant's country of origin. In addition, a country expert's specialized knowledge is often invaluable to filling in gaps in human rights reports and explaining why changes to laws often cited in reports have not yet improved conditions on the ground.

Third, expert testimony is particularly useful in establishing why an applicant was unable to file for asylum within his or her first year in the United States, as required under U.S. law. An adjudicator may excuse an applicant's failure to file for asylum within his or her first year in the United States, if the applicant can demonstrate, inter alia, that he or she suffered a "serious illness or mental or physical disability, including any effects of persecution or violent harm suffered in the past, during the [one]-year period after arrival," that prevented the applicant from timely filing for asylum.[10] A mental health expert can document "the presence of psychiatric disorders or symptoms related to trauma exposure" and demonstrate how those conditions "may adversely impact an asylum seeker's capacity to file an application and to cogently present [his or her] story" (Piwowarczyk 2001, p. 156–7).

THE NEED FOR COLLABORATION

Throughout this volume, doctors, psychologists, country experts, adjudicators, and immigration practitioners alike have heralded the importance of expert evidence in establishing asylum eligibility (Chelidze et al. 2014: Ch. 7, infra, Smith et al. 2014: Ch. 8, infra, Good 2014: Ch. 5, supra, Einhorn and Berthold 2014: Ch. 1, supra). Drawn from experiences at HIRC, the three case examples described below highlight the ways in which HIRC attorneys have successfully worked with medical, psychological, and country experts to document physical and mental scars; explain inconsistencies and gaps in memory; prove exceptions to the one-year filing deadline; and assess the dangers an applicant would face if forced to return home.

---

[10] INA § 208(a)(2)(D); 8 C.F.R. § 208.4(a).

In the case of a young man from Uganda named Robert, medical and psychological evaluations were indispensable to documenting the physical and psychological effects of the human rights violations he had suffered. Robert fled to the United States after being repeatedly abducted, detained, and tortured by Ugandan government security forces. Robert had extensive scars from his time in detention, but the details he provided about his abduction and torture varied significantly with each retelling. When he came to HIRC, he had no evidence to document his claim – he had nothing other than his passport and a college transcript. Given the lack of other corroboration, along with Robert's difficulties recounting his experiences, I knew expert testimony would be particularly critical to proving that Robert had suffered past persecution and had a well-founded fear of future persecution.[11]

The medical expert who examined Robert found a scar on the back of Robert's head, consistent with a blow that Robert had described from the butt of a gun. The doctor also identified scars on Robert's knees, calves, lower back, and hip area, consistent with the whippings and electric shocks Robert suffered while in detention. These findings by the doctor helped demonstrate to the adjudicator that Robert had suffered severe physical harm rising to the level of persecution. The doctor's forensic physical evaluation and photographs he took of the scars were the only non testimonial evidence of the past physical harm inflicted on Robert.[12]

The psychologist who evaluated Robert wrote an affidavit documenting his trauma history and explaining the reasons why Robert was unable to recount his past experiences in a coherent, linear manner. In her expert report, the psychologist emphasized the significant effects of trauma on Robert's memory. She noted that Robert became very emotional when describing his past, and his memories often flooded together. She observed that while Robert's fragmented memories might appear as confusion or even dissembling about specific events, his difficulties with recall were, in actuality, a symptom of severe PTSD.

The psychologist recommended that we ask the adjudicator for a continuance to postpone Robert's testimony to a later date so that Robert could see a

---

[11] Under U.S. asylum law, a finding of past persecution gives rise to a presumption of future persecution, which the government can rebut by showing either that country conditions have changed or that the applicant could relocate safely within the country. 8 U.S.C. § 1101(a)(42); 8 C.F.R. § 208.13(b)(1)(i)(A); 8 C.F.R. § 1208.13(b)(1)(i)(A).

[12] Fears of applicants lying and concerns about bias in witnesses may lead immigration judges to privilege "objective" documentary evidence of harm suffered or feared, including, for example, authenticable photos and police reports, over testimonial evidence of experts or other witnesses (see Smith et al., this volume). As such, adjudicators may give greater weight to forensic medical evaluations, which document actual physical scars, than to psychological evaluations, which are based on the most critical, and at the same time potentially most difficult evidence to assess – the testimony of the applicant.

psychologist and start therapy to ensure that he did not break down completely while preparing to testify. As Miriam Marton explains in her chapter in this volume, such interdisciplinary collaboration is often essential in asylum cases to help clients disclose painful memories in a safe setting. The psychologist in Robert's case worked closely, with me and the student team, to sensitively elicit the details of his past torture, without re-traumatizing him.

As Robert's case underscores, a psychological expert can help explain to attorneys and adjudicators alike the effects of trauma on an asylum seeker's memory and demeanor and the reasons why an applicant's testimony may be inconsistent or incoherent (see the chapters by Chelidze et al., and Smith et al., in this volume; also, Gangsei and Deutsch 2007, p. 81). Such experts are particularly important in asylum cases since adjudicators may consider applicants' demeanor and any inconsistencies in written or oral testimony in determining whether applicants are credible.

A forensic psychologist can also, as noted, explain the relationship between the effects of the trauma suffered or feared and an applicant's inability to come forward and timely apply for asylum. Mary, for example, a domestic violence survivor from Kenya, was eight years past her one-year filing deadline, when she came to HIRC. She had only opened up about the violent beatings and rapes her husband had inflicted after reconnecting with a childhood friend, a social worker who could tell that Mary was suffering. The friend did not want to pry, but over time, she managed to convince Mary to talk to her about some of her past experiences and her fears of return to Kenya.

When HIRC students and I began meeting with Mary, we realized we would need a psychological evaluation to explain why Mary was unable to apply for asylum during her first year in the United States. In meeting with Mary, we quickly observed how painful it was for her to recount what had happened and referred her to a psychologist for counseling and a forensic evaluation. The psychologist provided HIRC with an evaluation that documented Mary's severe PTSD and ongoing avoidance of the painful memories of her past. The evaluation explicitly connected the horrific abuse Mary had suffered in Kenya to her tremendous fear of speaking of the past, even here in the United States. The evaluation underscored that given Mary's severe trauma, she could not have come forward and applied for asylum earlier. The adjudicator relied on this psychological evaluation in finding that Mary qualified for an exception to the one-year filing deadline. The psychological expert was thus critical to Mary's ability to proceed with her asylum claim.[13]

---

[13] If an asylum applicant fails to meet an exception to the one-year filing deadline, he or she cannot proceed with an asylum claim. Rather, the applicant is limited to applying for

In Mary's case, we also had to find a country expert to explain why the
Kenyan authorities would not and could not protect Mary if she were forced to
return. While Kenya had passed national laws against domestic violence, we
knew from our conversations with Mary and country condition evidence, that
in practice, the laws were not consistently enforced at the local level. HIRC
students contacted a political science professor whose research focused on
gender violence in Kenya, and he agreed to testify in Mary's case. He
explained to the adjudicator why, based on his knowledge of Kenya, Mary's
fear of being subjected to further violence or even death in Kenya was well
founded. The country expert was able to corroborate Mary's account of
Kenyan authorities' unwillingness to intervene in situations involving domestic violence. Mary's husband had ties to the police, and the country expert was
able to attest to the increased danger she would face if she contacted the
authorities.[14]

As Good notes in his chapter, country expert reports are often critical to
clarifying or rebutting information presented in country condition reports – in
particular, information in country reports prepared by government officials,
which may be biased or incomplete. For example, in a HIRC case involving a
gay man from central Africa, there was a dearth of information on violence
against LGBT individuals. The 2009 U.S. State Department reports on
human rights practices noted that "there were no reports" of violence or
discrimination against LGBT individuals in the applicant's home country,
and the government attorney used this statement to argue that violence was not
occurring. The country expert HIRC asked to testify was, however, able to
explain the actual meaning of this statement.

She noted that LGBT individuals in the applicant's home country were too
scared to come forward and report the attacks they suffered. She explained that
human rights groups were not investigating and documenting such abuses,
given competing priorities regarding human rights violations and homopho-
bia within the local human rights community.[15] The adjudicator found
that the applicant's fears of harm if forced to return to his home country

---

withholding of removal and protection under the Convention Against Torture, neither of
which provides for family reunification or a pathway to citizenship (Anker 2013, pp. 8–9).

[14] There is no requirement that an applicant seek state protection if it would be futile to do so or if
reporting to the authorities would cause further harm. Asylum Officer Basic Training Course,
2009, "Female Asylum Applicants and Gender-Based Claims" 24–25, retrieved June 30,
2014 from http://www.uscis.gov/sites/default/files/USCIS/Humanitarian/Refugees%20%26%
20Asylum/Asylum/AOBTC%20Lesson%20Plans/Female-Asylum-Applicants-Gender-Related
-Claims-31aug10.pdf.
[15] Galya Ruffer's description of her field research on rape and sexual violence in the Democratic
Republic of Congo similarly underscores the differences between official narratives of human
rights abuses in a particular country and actual conditions on the ground (Ruffer, this volume).

were well-founded and pointed to the expert's testimony that a dearth of information in official reports "does not mean that such acts do not occur since there are no avenues through which a person could report" an attack (Ardalan 2013, p. 10).

TRUTH-TELLING VERSUS ADVOCACY

As attorneys, we request affidavits from country experts, doctors, and psychologists with one goal in mind: to help our clients win asylum. In pursuing this goal, we often assume that other experts are on our "team."[16] Although that is sometimes the case, some experts may have different assumptions about their roles. Doctors and psychologists, for example, are trained to objectively describe injuries and to explain what might have caused them.[17] For country experts, preserving their impartiality before the tribunal may be a central concern.[18] Attorneys may view clients through different lenses than other experts and may suggest changes to expert affidavits to ensure consistency between an expert's affidavit and the applicant's case. Experts may, however, balk at taking direction from members of another profession, even with the best of intentions. The four cases described herein draw from the experiences of HIRC attorneys and highlight these challenges in cross-disciplinary representation.

As was the case with Muhammed, conflicts may arise between lawyers and experts regarding how to present and describe an applicant's history, demeanor, trauma, and testimony. At her initial meeting with attorneys at HIRC, Maryum, a Pakistani client, described ongoing loss of appetite, sleeplessness, and recurring nightmares from the time she started receiving threatening calls and messages in Pakistan to the present. Clinic attorneys requested a forensic psychological evaluation to assess whether these symptoms were related to the threats that Maryum had suffered as a result of

---

[16] In some other fields, such as in cases involving the Social Security Administration, which employs its own set of internal experts, the division between advocacy and objective evaluation may be more clearly delineated (Hubley 2008, p. 368). In contrast, in the immigration context, lawyers commission expert affidavits and therefore often assume the affidavits will align with the legal objectives and framing of the case.

[17] As the American College of Physicians has observed, "the expertise, the objectivity, and the credibility of the medical profession are essential to persons who seek political refuge. ... Physicians' testimony will be assessed by the immigration judge using criteria such as the qualifications of the physician ... and the relevance and the reliability of the evidence brought forth in the testimony" (American College of Physicians 1995, p. 609).

[18] Some government attorneys may challenge experts as "hired guns" whose opinions support an applicant's claim because they receive payment or because their mission and objectives align with the applicant's.

her activism and to the harms she feared if forced to return to Pakistan. The psychologist had one interview with Maryum and drafted a lengthy affidavit, diagnosing Maryum with PTSD and emphasizing the deleterious effects that returning to Pakistan would have on Maryum's mental health.

Although the evaluation was very helpful in terms of offering a diagnosis for Maryum's symptoms, the evaluation was, in critical respects, inconsistent with the facts presented by Maryum and with the legal theory of her case. The psychologist focused extensively on the childhood abuse that Maryum had suffered, portraying her as a submissive victim. This description was, however, at odds with Maryum's outspokenness and her strength as a female activist, upon which the legal theory of her case was built.

From a young age, Maryum had rebelled against her conservative father. Maryum's mother stood up for her and encouraged her to pursue a British education. Because of this, Maryum's mother came under attack from her husband. As the eldest child, Maryum tried to protect her mother, which further angered her father; and Maryum was also subjected to insults and beatings. The psychologist who evaluated Maryum specialized in childhood abuse. As a result, the psychological evaluation focused heavily on the beatings that Maryum suffered at the hands of her father. In contrast, Maryum's asylum claim was based primarily on the threats she received after she studied in the United Kingdom and returned to Pakistan to work with an international organization to promote women's rights.

I contacted the psychologist and noted that some of the facts and events described in the evaluation were inconsistent with the information students and I had elicited from Maryum in dozens of client meetings. The psychologist quoted Maryum as saying she "accepted" the violence within her family, because she could not stop it. But when I reviewed the evaluation with her, Maryum vehemently denied accepting the violence, and in fact, said that she had spent her life standing up for herself, her mother, and other Pakistani women. The evaluation also stated that Maryum had received seven to ten threatening phone calls and texts, but Maryum did not remember how many she had received. In speaking with the psychologist, I suggested taking out the quote and some details, including the number of threats, since they did not comport with Maryum's recollection.

The psychologist was taken aback at my comments and requests for deletions and clarifications. As the chapters in this volume by Chelidze et al., and by Smith et al. describe at greater length, forensic medical and psychological evaluations typically include a detailed section that sets forth the applicant's entire life story.[19] Mental health experts and forensic doctors are instructed that history taking and relaying should be rigorous and extensive (Jacobs and Lustig 2010; Jones and Smith 2004, p. 385). The quotes the psychologist had attributed to Maryum were based on her transcription of Maryum's words at the time of the evaluation. She believed that she had accurately captured what Maryum had told her, and she was not inclined to revisit her description. She felt that I had usurped her role as the expert. She had volunteered to conduct the psychological evaluation pro bono and had already spent more time than she had anticipated on the case. The psychologist had expected I would review her affidavit and submit it as she had written it with only minor revisions.

In speaking with the psychologist, I explained that, as it currently stood, I would not be able to submit her evaluation. I noted that, unfortunately, under U.S. law, any inconsistency between the evaluation and Maryum's affidavit, including the divergent descriptions of Maryum's reactions and the minor factual differences regarding the number of threats, could be used by an adjudicator as a basis for making an adverse credibility determination and denying Maryum's asylum claim.[20] Eventually the psychologist reluctantly agreed to cut the parts of her evaluation that were inconsistent with Maryum's recollection, but she was not pleased with this outcome. In agreeing to do a psychological evaluation for Maryum's asylum case, she had seen her role as

---

[19] HIRC attorneys often request that evaluators keep the personal history section of their affidavits brief in order to minimize the potential for inconsistencies with the lengthy affidavit HIRC lawyers and students prepare. An analogous, lengthy description in an evaluation may therefore be unnecessary and potentially problematic. Where an applicant is unrepresented and/or where the attorney does not take the time to interview the client extensively or prepare a lengthy affidavit for the applicant, a detailed description of the facts by the psychological or physical evaluator may in fact help the applicant. As Smith et al. describe in their chapter in this volume, history-taking by forensic evaluators may elicit previously undisclosed information directly related to the applicant's claim. Yet, regardless of length, it is critical that evaluators and attorneys work together to ensure that there are no factual inconsistencies between the oral and written testimony submitted in support of the applicant's case.

[20] It is important to note that the term "consistent" may have different meanings for doctors, psychologists, and attorneys. A psychologist or medical doctor may consider an asylum applicant's testimony to be consistent when the applicant's account is internally consistent and is consistent in terms of the major events described. Doctors and psychologists often expect omissions and variations in minor details, particularly in applicants suffering from PTSD, and consider such variations to be a natural and expected part of an applicant's narrative. Yet, as De Jesús-Rentas, Boehnlein, and Sparr explain, "discrepancies in history are often used as a key reason for rejecting asylum claims. ... An unintentional minor inconsistency between the facts in the forensic report and the applicant's petition may cloud the judge's perception of the applicant's credibility" (2010, p. 494–6).

that of an independent, objective expert whose evaluation would complement the legal case; she had not anticipated being asked to revisit her evaluation to address legal concerns that were outside of her purview.

At HIRC, we spend hundreds of hours with clients and observe in depth how they tell and retell stories and how recounting past experiences and fears affects them physically and psychologically.[21] Our observations sometimes conflict, however, with those of the forensic evaluators who may only meet with a client once or a handful of times.

In another case, HIRC attorneys represented an extraordinarily strong and resilient Guatemalan woman activist who often presented as if she was unaffected by the threats she received prior to fleeing her country. When describing the events of the past, she rarely broke down into tears except when discussing her fears for her family. She developed strong coping mechanisms, including regularly jogging and leading church groups, which helped her manage her fears. But for years, living in the United States, did not disclose to anyone, not even to her own family, the complete picture of why they could not return to Guatemala.

The forensic psychological evaluation HIRC initially obtained described why the client was forced to leave Guatemala, including the past threats she received, but stated that she was asymptomatic and did not exhibit any signs of PTSD. This description was, however, at odds with what HIRC attorneys had learned in extensive meetings with the client about her nightmares and intrusive memories, as well as avoidance tactics that she employed in her daily life. The evaluation's failure to identify and describe any effects of trauma on the applicant presented a significant obstacle to proving that she met an exception to the one-year filing deadline. It was only after extensive conversations with the forensic psychologist explaining what we had observed and knew about her and her symptoms that the psychologist agreed to interview her again to better understand how the trauma she had suffered prevented her from coming forward to apply for asylum earlier.

Close collaboration and mutual respect between lawyers and experts is particularly vital in the context of the one-year filing deadline. In order to find that an applicant meets an exception to the one-year filing deadline, adjudicators often expect experts to include a clear statement linking applicants' PTSD to their inability to come forward and apply for asylum within their first year in the United States. Yet, this type of conclusion may be difficult for mental health professionals to attest to, regardless of their training

---

[21] Eliciting client testimony is a work in progress until the hearing date; essential details and memories often come back to clients as the date of the hearing approaches and as clients prepare to testify.

and expertise. In asking experts to assess whether an applicant's mental or physical disability prevented the applicant from filing an asylum application within his or her first year here, mental health professionals have to draw what is essentially a legal conclusion. Although psychologists are experts on the symptoms manifested and the impairments suffered, they may not understand the type of assessment an adjudicator is looking for. Lawyers may have a better understanding of the information an adjudicator needs to reach a decision regarding whether an applicant meets an exception to the one-year deadline.

As a result, attorneys may be placed in the difficult position of having to explain adjudicators' demands for additional corroboration to experts who may not fully understand the legal basis for the demand. In one instance, for example, an adjudicator requested a supplemental affidavit from a forensic psychologist to address in greater depth the one-year filing deadline issue. The asylum case involved a gay man who had suppressed his past history of persecution for many years until he was detained by immigration following a traffic stop. The psychologist did not understand the reason for the adjudicator's request and insisted that his initial affidavit was clear enough for the adjudicator to understand why the applicant had been unable to apply for asylum earlier. The psychologist had described at length the applicant's severe PTSD symptoms and isolation in his initial evaluation and believed that this description should have sufficed to show that the applicant met the criteria for an exception to the one-year deadline. He had presented his diagnosis and did not know what else he could add. Through discussions with HIRC attorneys, the psychologist eventually understood that the adjudicator needed an additional statement explicitly linking the applicant's PTSD to his inability to come forward earlier in order to grant the applicant asylum.

Ideological differences may also arise in working with country experts with divergent perspectives on human rights conditions in applicants' home countries. A country expert who has, for example, been involved in efforts to reform state institutions may be reluctant to criticize those institutions for failing to protect individuals from persecution. In a case involving a woman who fled to the United States to escape her abusive husband, HIRC consulted with a human rights advocate about whether she might be able to provide an expert affidavit. The human rights advocate declined to provide an affidavit because she had worked with government officials to establish protections for women against domestic violence, including shelters for women who fled abuse. Her optimism about the safeguards for women in the applicant's home country stood in stark contrast, however, to the experiences of the HIRC client. The HIRC client had sought protection from the authorities, but they had refused to intervene. As a result, HIRC students sought out another expert who had studied violence against women in the region, and she was able to confirm that the client's experiences were consistent with her understanding of the lack of political will to enforce protections for women. She corroborated the client's account that authorities view domestic violence as a private family affair, not to be intervened in by the state.

PROTOCOLS FOR COLLABORATION BETWEEN LAWYERS AND EXPERTS

Given the importance of expert testimony in today's asylum process and the potential for misunderstanding between lawyers and other experts, guidelines need to be developed to mitigate tensions and improve collaboration in asylum cases. Experts and lawyers must respect each other's respective professional roles and boundaries and work closely together, whenever possible. Without explicit protocols, however, such collaboration between attorneys and other experts can be fraught with tension. As the case examples given in this chapter illustrate, clear and extensive information sharing is necessary to ensure that attorneys and other experts alike understand each other's respective ethical and professional obligations.

As legal experts, it is our responsibility to effectively communicate to other experts our expectations for their testimony in immigration proceedings, as well as potential challenges to their expertise and conclusions that the adjudicator and government attorney may raise. Attorneys need to set forth at the outset their main objectives for the expert testimony, including the specific questions they hope to have answered, so that experts can try to address them. Similarly, doctors, psychologists, and country experts need to make clear what they perceive their role to be, what their objectives are in providing expert testimony, what they plan to address in their testimony, and how they would like to communicate with and receive feedback from attorneys. Ideally, these conversations between lawyers and other experts should occur prior to the drafting of an expert affidavit or forensic evaluation, so that all parties can better understand the perspectives each professional brings to the process.

Extensive communication between experts and attorneys is often necessary from the time a lawyer first contacts an expert through finalization of the affidavit for filing and testimony in court.[22] Unfortunately, such communication

---

[22] Chelidze et al. suggest in their chapter that once a medical affidavit is drafted, it can be submitted to the court. Yet from my perspective as an attorney, the process from the drafting of the affidavit to its filing in court can be complicated and at times, contentious, and often requires extensive communication between experts and attorneys.

generally occurs in an ad hoc manner. For example, our experience working with the Maryum's psychological evaluator would have benefited from a lengthier discussion at the outset with the expert regarding the focus of her legal claim. In Muhammed's case and in the case of the Guatemalan woman activist, the process might also have been smoother if we had shared our observations of the clients' demeanor and history with the mental health experts prior to the evaluation process.

In communicating with other experts, attorneys need to respect experts' objectivity and opinions and avoid suggestions or changes that impinge on experts' impartiality. In order to ensure consistency with the other factual descriptions presented in a client's asylum application, including the applicant's own personal statement, attorneys may need to closely review the client history presented in an expert affidavit and make suggestions to eliminate any inconsistencies. Experts may, however, balk at the methods attorneys use, that is, track changes and comments, to give feedback. As a result, attorneys should determine from the beginning what type of feedback other experts will be open to and the best way to provide it.

Attorneys and experts each speak the language of their own trade, and, in some instances, mediators may be necessary to navigate the divide. Staff at nonprofits, including HealthRight International, Survivors International, and Physicians for Human Rights, which train medical doctors and mental health clinicians to perform forensic evaluations, can facilitate communication among lawyers, doctors, and psychologists in the asylum process. Attorneys may also benefit from training on the process of preparing medical and psychological evaluations so that we are better equipped to interact with doctors and mental health professionals. Specific parameters should be established so that, on the one hand, attorneys understand the bounds within which they may make suggestions and ask for revisions and, on the other hand, experts understand the reasons for attorneys' requests, including the flawed credibility and corroboration requirements of the asylum system. Clear communication and close collaboration is essential to ensure that experts and attorneys work together effectively.

REFERENCES

American College of Physicians. 1995. "The Role of the Physician and the Medical Profession in the Prevention of International Torture in the Treatment of Its Survivors." *Annals of Internal Medicine*, 122(8): 607–13.

Anker, Deborah, ed. 2013. *Law of Asylum in the United States*. Eagan, MN: Thomson Reuters.

Anker, Deborah E. 2002. "Refugee Law, Gender and the Human Rights Paradigm." *Harvard Human Rights Journal*, 15: 133–54.

Ardalan, Sabrineh. 2013. "Country Condition Evidence, Human Rights Experts, and Asylum-Seekers: Educating U.S. Adjudicators on Country Conditions in Asylum Cases." 13–09 *Immigration Briefings* 1.

De Jesús-Rentas, Gilberto, James Boehnlein and Landy Sparr. 2010. "Central American Victims of Gang Violence as Asylum Seekers: The Role of the Forensic Expert." *Journal of the American Academy of Psychiatry and the Law*, 38: 490–498.

Dolnick, Sam. 2011. "Immigrants May Be Fed False Stories to Bolster Asylum Pleas." *The New York Times*, June 11, 2011.

Einhorn, Bruce. 2010. "The Gift of Understanding." *Albany Government Law Review* 3: 149–168.

Gangsei, David and Ana C. Deutsch. 2007. "Psychological Evaluation of Asylum Seekers as a Therapeutic Process." *Torture* 17: 79–87.

Good, Anthony. 2004. "'Undoubtedly an Expert'? Anthropologists in British Asylum Courts." *Journal of the Royal Anthropological Institute* 10: 113–33.

Herlihy, Jane, Peter Scragg, and Stuart Turner. 2002. "Discrepancies in Autobiographical Memories – Implications for the Assessment of Asylum Seekers: Repeated Interview Study." *British Medical Journal* 324: 324–27.

Herlihy, Jane and Stuart W. Turner. 2009. "The Psychology of Seeking Protection." *International Journal of Refugee Law* 21: 171–92.

Hubley, Nathaniel O. 2008. "The Untouchables: Why A Vocational Expert's Testimony in Social Security Disability Hearings Cannot Be Touched." *Valparaiso University Law Review* 43: 353–405.

Jacobs, Uwe and Stuart Lustig. 2010. "Psychological and Psychiatric Opinions in Asylum Applications: Ten Frequently Asked Questions by Fact Finders." 15–15 *Bender's Immigration Bulletin* 2.

Jones, David Rhys and Sally Verity Smith. 2004. "Medical Evidence in Asylum and Human Rights Appeals." *International Journal of Refugee Law* 16: 381–410.

Kalin, Walter. 1986. "Troubled Communication: Cross-Cultural Misunderstandings in the Asylum-Hearing." *International Migration Review* 20: 230–241.

Meffert, Susan M., et al. 2010. "The Role of Mental Health Professionals in Political Asylum Processing." *Journal of the American Academy of Psychiatry and the Law* 38: 479–489.

Mehta, Suketu. 2011. "The Asylum Seeker." *The New Yorker*. August 1, 2011.

New York Immigrant Representation Study (NYIRS) Steering Committee. December 2012. "A Model for Providing Counsel to New York Immigrants in Removal Proceedings." *Cardozo Law Review*. http://www.cardozolawreview.com/content/denovo/NYIRS_ReportII.pdf [Retrieved December 6, 2013].

Paletta, Damian. 2011. "Doctor Revolt Shakes Disability Program." *The Wall Street Journal*, November 21, 2011.

Physicians for Human Rights. 2001. "Examining Asylum Seekers: A Health Professional's Guide to Medical and Psychological Evaluations of Torture." [Retrieved November 19, 2013].

Piwowarczyk, Linda. 2001. "Seeking Asylum: A Mental Health Perspective." *Georgetown Immigration Law Journal*, 16: 155–71.

Ramji-Nogales Jaya, Andrew I. Schoenholtz and Philip G. Schrag. 2009. *Refugee Roulette: Disparities in Asylum Adjudication and Proposals for Reform*. New York, NY: New York University Press.

U.N. Convention relating to the Status of Refugees, opened for signature July 28, 1951, 19 U.S.T. 6259, 189 U.N.T.S. 137.

U.N. High Commissioner for Refugees. 1992. "Handbook on Procedures and Criteria for Determining Refugee Status." http://www.unhcr.org/3d58e13b4.html [Retrieved November 19, 2013].

U.N. Protocol relating to the Status of Refugees, opened for signature Jan. 31, 1967, 19 U.S.T. 6223, 606 U.N.T.S. 267.

Wiebe, Virgil and Sarah S. Brenes. 2011. "Mental Health Professionals and Affirmative Applications for Immigration Benefits: A Critical Review of Administrative Appeals Office Cases Involving Extreme Hardship and Mental Harm." 11–04 *Immigration Briefings* 1; 11–27 U of St. Thomas Legal Studies Research Paper 1.

7

Documenting Torture *Sequelae*: The Weill Cornell Model for Forensic Evaluation, Capacity Building, and Medical Education

Khatiya Chelidze, Nicole Sirotin, Margaret Fabiszak, Terri Gallen Edersheim, Taryn Clark, Luis Villegas, Patriss Wais Moradi, and Joanne Ahola[1]

Mr. C. was referred to the Weill Cornell Center for Human Rights (WCCHR) by Physicians for Human Rights (PHR) for a psychiatric evaluation as part of his application for asylum. He was evaluated by a psychiatrist, who also served as a medical director of WCCHR, and one medical student participant-observer. Mr. C was referred to PHR by his attorney and to the attorney by Human Rights First, an independent human rights organization.

Mr. C. is a forty-one-year-old man with a four-year history of anxiety, disturbed sleep, difficulty with memory and concentration, as well as persistent pain in his lower back, knees, and shin. Mr. C. fled the People's Republic of China approximately four years earlier to seek asylum in the United States after being tortured for his political beliefs. Mr. C. became involved in politics as a college student and was interested in the teachings and career of a noted political activist who was later arrested and censured by the Chinese government.

After Mr. C. distributed information and news about this activist among his friends via email, plainclothes officers arrested Mr. C. at his home. Mr. C. was taken to a windowless room where the officers questioned him about his political activities for what seemed like hours. The police officers thumb-cuffed him and lifted his hands over his head. The posture reminded Mr. C. of a person being hanged. The officers beat him with a rubber baton on his legs, abdomen, and back. They kicked his legs with their leather shoes, and his shin began to bleed. They then bashed his head against a wall, and at some point, Mr. C. fell unconscious. He was released later that night, and his wife took him to the hospital. At the hospital, Mr. C. recalls having an X-ray

[1] **ACKNOWLEDGMENTS:** The authors express thanks to Prof. Dan Smulian, Dr. Oliver Fein, Dr. Yoon Kang, Dr. Shelli Farhadian, Dr. Ellie Emery, Dr. Alexandra Tatom, Dr. Carol Storey-Johnson Alejandro Lopez, Carmen Stellar, Jiyeong Jeong, and WCCHR.

performed on his leg and getting stitches on the back of his head. Two days later, he was discharged from the hospital, and he and his family escaped to the United States shortly thereafter.

WCCHR's evaluation of Mr. C. was performed in accordance with the standards set forth in the United Nations document known as the Istanbul Protocol, formally titled the *Manual on the Effective Investigation and Documentation of Torture and Other Cruel, Inhuman or Degrading Treatment or Punishment*. Mr. C. was found to suffer from two psychiatric disorders, post-traumatic stress disorder (PTSD) and major depression, both felt to be consequences of the torture he reported. A medico-legal affidavit was drafted by the medical student and revised by the examining psychiatrist. Some months later, Mr. C. had a hearing in immigration court. The psychiatrist attended the hearing as an expert witness in case oral testimony was needed. The participating medical student and one other student board member of WCCHR observed the hearing.

Mr. C. was granted asylum.

INTRODUCTION

Worldwide, there may be between ten million and one hundred million torture survivors. Many torture survivors flee their country of origin and seek asylum. The United States accounts for approximately 15 percent of all asylum-seeker acceptances in the OECD in recent years (OECD 2013, p. 340). Asylum seekers in the United States constitute a diverse demographic group, ranging from children to adults and hailing from all continents. Because no statistics are officially recorded, an unknown number of asylum seekers in the United States are also torture survivors (Eder 2004, p. 281). These men, women, and children now carry the psychiatric and/or physical consequences (*sequelae*) of their abuse. However, only a small percentage of U.S.-residing torture survivors are evaluated by a health care professional for their specific torture *sequelae*.

Over four hundred thousand foreign-born survivors of torture from 112 countries (Eisenman 2012) reside in the United States. In 1996–1997, the U.S. Congress passed the first Torture Victims Relief Act (TVRA) with strong bipartisan support. The TVRA, signed into law in 1998, authorized funding to support both domestic and overseas programs that engage projects or activities specifically designed to treat victims for the physical and psychological effects of torture. In 1998, Congress also passed the Foreign Affairs Reform and Restructuring Act (FARRA), implementing Article Three of the Convention Against Torture (CAT) in immigration and extradition contexts in the U.S. Since the passage of the TVRA and the FARRA, domestic efforts to provide support to victims of torture residing in the United States have proliferated. The National Consortium of Torture Treatment Programs lists over thirty organizations in sixteen states that work to advance the knowledge, technical capacities, and resources devoted to the care of torture survivors.

The unmet need for specialized clinical and psychiatric evaluation of torture survivors is particularly apparent in urban areas (Hexom et al. 2012). Previous studies have found that between 10 and 15 percent of foreign-born patients who present to urban primary care centers and emergency departments are survivors of torture, yet few are recognized as such by healthcare professionals (Crosby et al. 2006). Many such individuals reside in the New York metropolitan area (Metalios 2008). New clinics and modalities of care are emerging throughout the United States and beyond to help improve the representation of asylum seekers who are also torture survivors. WCCHR is one new modality for providing forensic evaluations for this population..

Torture survivor clinics provide tailored care to torture survivors (Lustig et al. 2007). Asylum seekers present all too frequently with mental illness, as the chapter by Hawthorne Smith, Stuart Lustig, and David Gangsei in this volume demonstrates. Estimates of mental illness among asylum seekers suggest a high burden of disease; approximately 30 percent suffer from PTSD, and 70 percent suffer from anxiety or major depressive disorders (Eder 2004). Evidence from other countries suggests that those with less social support after the initial asylum claim is filed report the highest rates of mental illness (Gerritson et al. 2006). The WCCHR is a medical student-run human rights clinic dedicated to providing forensic evaluations to survivors of persecution seeking asylum in the United States. The clinic is a program of Weill Cornell Medical College (WCMC) in New York City.

Clinics that formally collaborate with agencies providing legal representation to asylum seekers are in high demand (Stadtmauer et al. 2010). The employment of forensic medical evidence in asylum adjudication is transforming refugee status determination globally (Wallace and Wylie 2014). As the demands of asylum adjudication in the United States become increasingly specific and empirical, greater numbers of torture survivors need professional documentation of their conditions to substantiate their claims. The WCCHR was founded to fulfill the specific requirements of torture survivors seeking asylum as requested by their legal counsel. Run by medical students while supervised by faculty, the WCCHR was designed to increase the capacity of medically-trained personnel to meet the urgent needs of torture survivors. Torture survivors in New York City constitute a highly vulnerable population that needs the support and recognition of the medical community. Education, language, and often the very effects of torture can prevent asylum seekers from providing sufficient testimony (Eder 2004). Medical affidavits, which are legal documents used to record both physical and psychological evidence of torture, have emerged as a fundamental component of torture survivors' narratives in asylum claims.

This chapter provides an overview of the organization and practices of the WCCHR. We first provide a brief history of the establishment and formation of the center. We then outline the "clinical model" in place and the process of forensic evaluation in a student-run clinical setting. We address some of the challenges encountered during the first several years of operation. We look to the future and anticipate how the WCCHR model may be strengthened, expanded, or implemented elsewhere. The WCCHR model highlights the relationship between health and human rights and promotes the inclusion of human rights education into the medical school curriculum. Students graduate with a knowledge of the basic tenets of human rights and an appreciation for the inseparable connection between the right to safety and freedom from persecution and the right to health. The WCCHR graduate becomes part of a workforce of medical professionals with a core commitment to health and human rights.

THE FOUNDATION OF THE WEILL CORNELL CENTER FOR HUMAN RIGHTS

WCCHR was founded in 2010 when four medical students from WCMC proposed the creation of a clinic to learn about human rights and the needs of asylum seekers and to provide much-needed assistance to this underserved population. The students sought out PHR, a U.S.-based international human rights organization with more than twenty years of experience working with asylum seekers through their volunteer Asylum Network, to partner with them in this endeavor. The students then obtained the support of the Dean of Affiliations at WCMC, recruited several experienced asylum clinicians through PHR to serve as medical directors, and asked select faculty to join a small advisory board. WCCHR began evaluating asylum seekers during its first month of existence. Created as a student club, WCCHR ran on an annual budget of approximately $400 for its first several years, using borrowed space for evaluations and meetings. Over the ensuing four years, the student board grew from four students to twenty-four, and the number of faculty evaluators grew from two to twenty-three. Close to 150 evaluations have been conducted to date. WCCHR is the first student-run asylum clinic at a U.S.

medical school and has been heralded as a model for future asylum evaluation programs.

The WCCHR model has a similar structure to many academic law school clinics in that it serves the public interest and involves a mentored partnership between faculty and students. For example, the Safe Harbor clinic at the Brooklyn Law School, a frequent collaborator of WCCHR, is a clinic where students work in teams, supervised by faculty members, to represent clients in cases affecting their legal status in the United States. Many of these cases involve applications for asylum. Law students are involved with conducting research on the political and historical backgrounds of the countries of origins of their clients, conducting interviews and helping to prepare applications for asylum and presenting claims before an asylum officer or immigration judge. When a team determines that a client may benefit from a medical or psychological evaluation, the Safe Harbor Clinic will often partner with PHR to have WCCHR conduct these evaluations. This represents a unique partnership between medical students and law students operating in service learning activities overseen by faculty advisors. In addition, this has prompted a collaborative teaching model. The Safe Harbor Clinic faculty director has been involved in training WCCHR students on asylum law, and WCCHR faculty and student board members have led classes on the role of forensic medical evaluations in asylum cases for Safe Harbor students.

The work of WCCHR revolves around the forensic evaluation. The purpose of a forensic evaluation is delineated in the Istanbul Protocol. This document describes the responsibility of the evaluator to perform the following: delineate the nature of the persecution as described by the applicant; describe the symptoms experienced following the trauma; document clinical signs of torture observed during the evaluation; provide an explanation of the findings in the context of the applicant's history; ensure that the applicant's story is consistent with the symptoms reported; explain problems with testimony that may have resulted from trauma; provide written and oral testimony; and educate the judiciary on the medical consequences, or *sequelae*, of torture. It is crucial to note that this is not a doctor-patient relationship. The purpose of the evaluation is *not* to provide medical, gynecological, or psychiatric services; rather, the goal is to determine whether trauma experienced by the applicant in the past is consistent with current clinical findings. Typically, physicians specializing in internal medicine, family medicine or gynecology conduct medical and gynecological evaluations, although physicians and surgeons of any specialty may conduct evaluations. Psychiatrists or other qualified mental health professionals, such as psychologists and licensed clinical social workers, typically conduct psychiatric evaluations.

There are as many forms of persecution practiced as there are individuals experiencing persecution. Thus, applicants present with diverse signs of trauma, both visible and invisible. A medical evaluator may examine an applicant's body for common signs of torture: burn marks, lacerations, bullet wounds, crush injuries, signs of beatings, stress positions, suspension, or electrocution. A gynecological or medical evaluator can determine whether the applicant has experienced female genital cutting and can look for signs of anal or vaginal rape (Arnold 2009). However, practitioners of torture are increasingly sophisticated in their methods and are careful not to leave any physical marks (Warfa 2011). Hence, trauma may manifest only in an applicant's mental state. In such cases, psychiatric evaluations are crucial in assessing the effects of trauma on an applicant's mental health and determining whether an applicant's presentation is consistent with his or her story. Psychiatric evaluators may find and describe signs of post-traumatic stress disorder, major depression, panic disorders, anxiety disorders, and substance abuse disorders.

WCCHR is unique in that it functions not only to provide forensic evaluations but also to teach students as a part of their medical education. Forensic evaluations conducted by WCCHR involve a client, an evaluator, at least one student participant-observer and a professional interpreter, if necessary. The medical students observe and take notes while the clinician conducts the evaluation. After the clinical interviews, the students draft the medico-legal affidavit. The evaluator edits, signs, and submits the affidavit, which becomes part of the client's application for asylum. The type of evaluation (medical, gynecological, or psychiatric) provided varies according to the client's needs, and a client may have more than one type of evaluation in support of his or her case. In addition to submitting a written affidavit, evaluators may be called upon to give oral testimony by telephone or in court, which students are also encouraged to observe.

Forensic evaluations are respected evidence in a court of law; they assist judges in assessing the credibility of the applicant. Without a forensic evaluation or an attorney to support an asylum seeker's case, the probability of that case being accepted averages approximately 24 percent, depending on the court circuit and other factors. A forensic evaluation supporting a case raises the case's chance for acceptance to 90 percent, making the work of providing medical, gynecological, or psychiatric evaluations invaluable to survivors of torture seeking asylum (Physicians for Human Rights 2012).

As of June 2014, WCCHR has conducted more than 150 evaluations for more than 130 clients from 39 countries. Of these clients, 35 have been granted asylum or another form of legal protection, and the remaining clients are awaiting a decision or have not yet had an asylum interview or court hearing. One hundred percent of WCCHR's clients who have been to interviews or court hearings have been granted asylum or another form of humanitarian relief. WCCHR has also begun a continuing care program, which helps clients find resources for both clinical care and other necessities. Aside from its contribution to the asylum applicants, the direct beneficiaries of the work conducted by WCCHR, this model has multiple benefits for the students and faculty and helps train health professionals to work in this important field.

THE CLINIC MODEL

Foremost, the WCCHR model increases the workforce of professionals knowledgeable and passionate about working with asylum seekers and survivors of torture. Since its inception, WCCHR has trained 262 students from Weill Cornell Medical College and other medical schools such as the College of Physicians and Surgeons at Columbia University, the Perelman School of Medicine at the University of Pennsylvania, the Alpert Medical School at Brown University, and the School of Medicine at New York University at biannual training events. Additionally, other medical schools, such as the University of Michigan Medical School, the Perelman School of Medicine at the university of pennsylvania, the College of Physicians and Surgeons at Columbia University, and the Alpert Medical School at Brown University, have invited WCCHR faculty in conjunction with PHR to hold trainings at their institutions. Many other professionals in allied fields have been trained, including psychologists, social workers, law professors, and nurse practitioners. WCCHR currently has twenty-three active evaluators and has trained a total of forty-three psychiatric, medical, and gynecological evaluators at WCMC faculty trainings in addition to the faculty trained at other medical schools by WCCHR and PHR. Trainings provide information on basic asylum law, how to conduct forensic evaluations, affidavit writing and, for the medical students, ways to start similar clinics at their schools. WCCHR also provides advanced trainings and seminars on asylum law, how to testify in court as an expert witness, and other relevant topics. The trainings aim to expand the workforce of students and faculty doing this work and have already led to the founding of sister clinics at medical schools such as the University of Pennsylvania, University of Michigan, Columbia University and Brown University. Students involved with WCCHR graduate with an understanding of how to recognize physical and psychological signs of torture and the legal issues that asylum seekers and survivors of torture may face.

One of the greatest strengths of the WCCHR model, and the aspect that most contributes to the clinic's sustainability, is its reliance on volunteer work. All members of WCCHR are involved on a volunteer basis, resulting in a clinic that needs few financial resources to operate. This also results in the virtually unlimited capacity to extend membership to all interested students, leading to an increasing cohort of participants that is replenished yearly with an incoming class. A number of volunteers are organized into a dedicated board comprised of members with clearly delegated tasks. The board is responsible for coordinating case scheduling and follow-up, faculty recruitment and training, research projects, fundraising, public relations and other clinical and organizational operations. A panel of volunteer faculty advisors supports the student board. Three medical directors act to perform evaluations, train new evaluators and advise the board when necessary, leading to a collaborative team of students and faculty.

WCCHR provides a powerful teaching tool that has created opportunities for students and rewards for faculty. The model introduces medical students to advanced clinical concepts early in training, emphasizing the psychosocial aspects of patient care. Most students involved in WCCHR begin working with the organization in the first month of medical school; the first asylum evaluation they participate in is almost always both their first clinical encounter and first psychiatric encounter. They observe experienced faculty using their most expert and flexibly employed interviewing and examination skills while creating a trusting alliance with an asylum applicant who may be psychologically fragile and from a culture different from that of the evaluator. Students participate in a pro bono endeavor, again paralleling the law school social justice clinics. They learn to write medico-legal affidavits and are able to appreciate the role of the health professional as an expert witness. They take on as much leadership responsibility in this student-run organization as they wish. They hone their skills in writing, teaching, mentoring, researching, presenting findings at professional conferences and designing programs.

Faculty members find that they get to know their students well, through both the close clinical collaboration in the asylum evaluation and in running and developing the human rights center. Clinicians have the opportunity to do pro bono work in human rights and to work with extremely vulnerable individuals. They are also able to hone their writing, forensic and leadership skills. Students and faculty are enriched by collaborative work for a cause to which they can contribute with passion and commitment.

Finally, beyond participating in the trainings and evaluations, students are encouraged to deepen their knowledge of the asylum field by completing research projects and literature reviews. These projects are conceived by matching student interests with the expertise of the medical directors or leaders in the asylum community. One example of this work is a novel examination of the impact that laws, such as the one-year bar in the asylum process, have upon different groups of asylum seekers. The one-year bar is a legal measure stating that asylum seekers must apply for asylum within one year of arriving in the United States. Although there are two exceptions allowed within this legal structure, since its initiation in 1996, it has long been contested that this law places an unnecessary and discriminatory barrier to seeking asylum for those who need it most. In order to more carefully analyze these claims, two WCCHR students worked with one medical director and partnered with HealthRight International, a global health and human rights organization. HealthRight provides services to those seeking asylum through their Human Rights Clinic. By partnering with HealthRight, WCCHR students were able to work in concert with asylum experts and benefit from HealthRight's long history in the asylum field. Through this work, the students discovered that asylum seekers who had been subjected to gender-based violence were more likely to miss the deadline set by the one-year bar compared to those seeking asylum based on other forms of persecution. They presented these findings at the 2013 Conable Conference and are in the process of drafting a manuscript for publication.

These opportunities to delve deeper into the asylum field provide an invaluable context to the work that is being done at WCCHR. Achieving a better understanding of asylum enables WCCHR to better meet the needs of the constantly evolving asylum community. WCCHR is working with the administration of WCMC to expand its ability to meet these needs in several ways.

First, a research database of all the asylum cases WCCHR has worked on is in development. When finished, this database will provide a rich opportunity to perform quantitative research in this field. Its users will be able to trace trends in cases and case outcomes, leading to a better understanding of the asylum field.

Research projects and literature reviews can be carried out at any point throughout the medical school curriculum. However, WCCHR also offers an elective during the final year of medical school to provide protected research time in which students are able to dedicate themselves fully to a project. WCCHR has worked with faculty of the medical school to integrate forensic evaluations into the official curriculum as an option for an area of study for students. The long-term goals of integrating asylum work into the curriculum include ensuring not only that WCCHR benefits from greater student involvement but also that students begin to contribute to the field of asylum as a whole. Involving medical students in this process early in their equation helps ensure that these future physicians will integrate forensic evaluations into their profession in a way that will benefit the vulnerable population of asylum seekers.

CHALLENGES OF THE CLINIC MODEL

WCCHR is a young organization; many aspects of its operations have changed since its inception and will continue to evolve as it grows and strives for improvement. Creating an organization such as WCCHR involves inherent difficulties in logistics, funding and staffing. In light of these issues, the model has several potential drawbacks. First, any volunteer-based organization is susceptible to experiencing problems with turnover and staff retention. Of note, WCCHR requires substantial time of its physician faculty advisors and medical directors, who counsel the board and perform evaluations on a volunteer basis. Logistical issues – finding clinical space, obtaining methods for secure file storage, finding meeting space – can be difficult to address and require a high degree of motivation to overcome. Additionally, funding sources can be limited due to the nature of the organization as a medical school program receiving money from the student government, grants and donations. Each of these issues will be addressed in turn.

WCCHR's volunteers are the backbone of its operation. The organization is highly dependent on their presence and dedication. As a student organization, this model contends with the constant turnover that comes from board members graduating, leaving the board to pursue other projects, or requiring more time to dedicate to academics. These transitions are inevitable, and the model has implemented methods of dealing with staffing issues. First, interviews are held with every student applying for a board position. These serve to assess experience and commitment level. On the other end, transitions between incoming and outgoing board members are staggered. For example, the outgoing executive director will train the incoming director for the first half of the academic year, then will officially hand over the title of executive director while still being available for advisement during the second half of the year. Taking these steps to ensure smooth incoming and outgoing transitions has worked well for the model, and the organization continues to grow and expand the size of its board.

As is common in academic medical schools, faculty time is usually compensated through clinical revenue or research funding, with some exceptions for teaching. Thus far, WCCHR has relied on faculty to donate their time for participation in all aspects of the clinic: conducting evaluations, conducting training sessions, participating in WCCHR networking events and assisting in other organizational operations. This model has limitations, as it is dependent on individual faculty members' decisions on how much time they allot to these important activities. Other incentives that could work include a small degree of funding provided by the medical college to faculty members to free them from clinical duties to participate. Alternatively, external funding could be sought, either through research grants or foundation dollars that could be used to support faculty time.

Institutions that pursue this model may find logistics – finding space, scheduling, coordinating – to be an additional challenge. These are challenges that are best overcome with a structured, organized board of dedicated members and tenacious collaboration with the administration of the institution. WCCHR borrows its clinical space from the Margaret and Ian Smith Clinical Skills Center of Weill Cornell Medical College, a state-of-the-art patient simulator suite and standardized patient center. This space is used to help students of the medical college build clinical skills and contains exam rooms where evaluators and students associated with WCCHR can conduct forensic evaluations. Meeting spaces are found in classrooms around the medical college, and lecture halls are used for trainings. Logistical issues are unique to the institutions and organizations that experience them and should be dealt with on a case-by-case basis.

Finally, without any way to generate clinical revenue, the organization is constantly looking for funding. The volunteer staff and borrowed space do not require payment, but the organization uses revenue to subsidize materials and food for trainings, to host networking events for professionals working with asylum applicants and for future plans to provide more services to the asylum applicants themselves.

STRATEGIES FOR FUTURE SUCCESS

Many factors have come together to make WCCHR a successful organization. WCCHR could not have come into existence without a partnership with PHR. PHR has many years of experience to share with a fledgling human rights clinic and contributes to many aspects of the clinic's operations, including lending the expertise necessary for WCCHR to train clinicians to conduct evaluations. Additionally, PHR screens potential cases presented by legal representatives and is the referral source for many of the asylum applicants WCCHR evaluates. The relationship between WCCHR and PHR is a groundbreaking and powerful one, as it represents the joining of an academic institution and a nonprofit human rights organization to advance human rights.

Crucial to the proper functioning of this model is a well-organized and carefully chosen group of students to serve as the board and dedicated faculty to serve as advisors. The board of WCCHR coordinates every aspect of the organization and is divided into two branches: clinical operations, which manages case scheduling, continuing care, faculty recruitment and student and faculty training, and organizational operations, which manages research, fundraising, public relations, and monitoring and evaluation.

Most communication between board members takes place through email, but regular meetings are crucial to the productive exchange of ideas. The members of clinical and organizational operations meet once a month in small groups. The board as a whole meets once a month to inform members of large-scale changes and upcoming events and opportunities. These meetings also give board members a chance to update the board on their activities and facilitate communication among members. Every member of the board has clearly delegated responsibilities and a supervisor who oversees tasks. This model of organization has been invaluable to the success of WCCHR and continues to act as the fundamental support for its operation on a day-to-day as well as a long-term basis.

CONCLUSION

WCCHR is innovative in several ways. As the first medical-student run asylum clinic, it provides a much needed model for how an academic medical institution and a nongovernmental organization can partner to assess and understand the health needs of an underserved population and to assist in addressing their medical and legal needs. This model serves to expand the number of clinicians who understand how to identify signs and symptoms of trauma and who understand the forensic and clinical needs of this population. WCCHR has trained over 250 medical students, and this number will only rise as other medical schools adopt the WCCHR model. These students will create a critical mass of health professionals who are experienced and knowledgeable in the health needs of victims of torture and other forms of persecution.

The WCCHR model highlights the relationship between health and human rights and promotes its inclusion into the medical school curriculum. Medical students are learning the basic tenets of human rights and the connections between one's right to safety and freedom from persecution and the right to health. WCCHR is training a workforce of medical professionals who have a strong background in health and human rights. Students involved in WCCHR possess the concrete skills needed to identify signs and symptoms of trauma and have learned to work collaboratively in an interdisciplinary way with other health professionals, nonprofit organizations and those in the field of law to effect positive change for an underserved population.

Mr. C.'s history of persecution detailed at the beginning of this chapter is not a unique story. With thousands of individuals seeking asylum in the United States every year, it is critical to establish a structure that provides an unbiased evaluation of the asylum application. Expert evaluations have the capacity to provide evidence and contribute clarity to what is often a complex asylum process. WCCHR provides one example of a way in which health care professionals can not only contribute to an individual asylum seeker's application but also create the opportunity to train medicals students throughout the process. This education forms the foundation for students' continued participation in the asylum process. The granting of asylum for Mr. C. becomes an example of what can be accomplished at the intersection of legal services, medical services, and a group such as WCCHR. With steady progress and expansion, it is possible for Mr. C.'s example to become the standard of care.

REFERENCES

Arnold, Frank. 2009. "Treatment and Management of Wounds and Scars of Torture." *Wounds* 5.4: 60–71.
Campbell, Thomas A. 2007. "Psychological Assessment, Diagnosis, and Treatment of Torture Survivors: A Review." *Clinical Psychology Review*, (June); 27(5): 628–41.
Crosby, Sondra S., Norredam, Marie, Paasche-Orlow, Michael K., Piwowarczyk, Linda, Heeren, Tim, and Grodin, Michael A. 2006. "Prevalence of Torture Survivors Among Foreign-Born Patients Presenting to an Urban Ambulatory Care Practice." *Journal of General Internal Medicine.* (July); 21(7): 764–8.
de C. Williams, Amanda C., Amris, K., and Van der Merwe, J. 2003. "Pain in Survivors of Torture and Organized Violence." *Progress in Pain Research and Management* 24 (2003): 791–802.
Eder, Katherine J. 2003. "The Importance of Medical Testimony in Removal Hearings for Torture Victims." *DePaul Journal of Health Care Law*, 7(2): 281–314.
Eisenman, D. P., Keller, A. S., and Kim, G. 2000. "Survivors of torture in a general medical setting: how often have patients been tortured, and how often is it missed?" *The Western Journal of Medicine*, 172(5): 301–4.
Gerritsen, Annette A. M., Bramsen, Inge, Deville, Walter, Van Willigen, Loes, H. M., Hovens, Johannes E., and Van der Ploeg, Henk, M. 2006. "Physical and Mental Health of Afghan, Iranian and Somali Asylum Seekers and Refugees Living in the Netherlands." *Social Psychiatry and Psychiatric Epidemiology.* (September); 41(1),18–26.
Hexom, Braden, Fernando, Dinali, Manini, Alex F., and Beattie, Lars K. 2012. "Survivors of Torture: Prevalence in an Urban Emergency Department." *Academic Emergency Medicine* (September); 19: 1158–65.

Lustig, Stuart L., Kureshi, Sarah, Deluchi, Kevin L., Iacopino, Vincent., Morse, and Samantha C. 2007. "Asylum Grant Rates Following Medical Evaluations of Maltreatment Among Political Asylum Applicants in the United States." *Journal of Immigrant Minority Health* (February) 10: 7–15.

Metalios, E. E., Asgary, R. G., Cooperman, N., Smith, C. L., Du, E., Modali, L., and Sacajiu, G. 2008. "Teaching Residents to Work with Torture Survivors: Experiences from the Bronx Human Rights Clinic." Journal of General Internal Medicine, 23(7): 1038–42.

OECD 2013. *International Migration Outlook 2013.*

Physicians for Human Rights. 2012. *Examining Asylum Seekers.* Cambridge, MA.

Stadtmauer, Gary J., Singer, Elizabeth, and Metalios, Eva. 2010. "An Analytical Approach to Clinical Forensic Evaluations of Asylum Seekers: The Healthright International Human Rights Clinic." *Journal of Forensic and Legal Medicine.* (January); 17(1): 41–5.

UNHCR. 2001. *Istanbul Protocol: Manual on the Effective Investigation and Documentation of Torture and Other Cruel, Inhuman or Degrading Treatment or Punishment.* New York, United Nations: Office of the High Commissioner for Human Rights.

UNHCR. 2013. *U.N.H.C.R. Asylum Trends 2012.* http://www.unhcr.org/5149b81e9 .html.

Wallace, Rebecca M. M., and Karen Wylie. 2014. "The Reception of Expert Medical Evidence in Refugee Status Determination," *International Journal of Refugee Law* 25: 749–67.

Warfa, Nasir, et al. 2011. "Contemporary Methods of Torture and Sexual Violence Medical Record Analysis." *World Cultural Psychiatry Research Review*: 112–18.

8

Incredible Until Proven Credible: Mental Health Expert Testimony and the Systemic and Cultural Challenges Facing Asylum Applicants

Hawthorne Emery Smith, Stuart Lorin Lustig, and David Gangsei

New York City police officers were hunting for a rapist who was terrorizing women in the South Bronx. Late one evening they viewed a man entering an apartment building in the neighborhood in question. Officers yelled out to the man and asked him to identify himself. The young black man was frightened and reached into his back pocket to pull out his identification. As the man pulled out his wallet, officers feared that he was pulling out a gun. Police officers fired 41 rounds, and struck the man with nineteen of them. The man, a young African immigrant named Amadou Diallo, fell dead. There was great upheaval and protest within the local community, especially among communities of color, protesting racial profiling and police tactics.

Lost in the social turmoil was the fact that Mr. Diallo was living legally in the United States as an asylee. He had won his asylum case claiming to be Mauritanian. During his testimony, he had described seeing his parents murdered and his family forcibly uprooted and sent across the border to Senegal. However, when Mr. Diallo was killed, his parents arrived to mourn him and were frequently seen in the local media, hailed as models of dignity and compassion.

But the fact that his parents were still living, and that they were from Guinea (as was Mr. Diallo), raised questions among asylum adjudicators about the veracity of asylum claims put forth by Africans in general, and particularly those claiming to come from Mauritania. Credibility was called into question, and this remains an important area where the dialectical relationship between expert evaluators and adjudicators can play a valuable role in clarifying issues of consistency, psychological functioning, and the probability of the veracity of an applicant's claim.

The authors of this chapter, who work with a substantial number of African asylum seekers within their clinical populations, try to bridge the potential disconnect between their clients' trauma narratives, which are frequently viewed as internally consistent and plausible by the mental health clinicians who have been participating in the documentation process, and the realistic concerns of adjudicators regarding exaggeration and fraud as perpetrated by some asylum applicants (Jacobs, Evans, and Patsalides 2001a). The authors discuss concerns raised by adjudicators, as well as the clinical perspectives that seek to shed light on these questions and allay some of the suspicions maintained about the applicants and their supporting documentation.

Mental health expert reports are relied upon globally by lawyers who represent asylum applicants, as well as by asylum officers and immigration judges, who assess the credibility of reported histories of torture, gender-based persecution and other forms of trauma. Expert opinions regarding the presence of profound challenges to an applicant's emotional and behavioral functioning, reflected in the presence of Post-Traumatic Stress Disorder (PTSD), Major Depressive Disorder, or other stress related syndromes, are also commonly considered as factors relevant to providing relief for applicants who have missed the one-year filing deadline or whose cases are complicated in other ways. Concerns exist, however, about how to treat the observations and insights from mental health experts and how to weigh these clinical data in relation to the overall body of evidence in the case. This is particularly salient in regard to asylum seekers from African countries, as some widely reported cases of fraud or malingering have been associated with cases from this region and have fostered what some may call a "culture of disbelief" within the asylum process (Dolnick 2011; Mehta 2011; Souter 2011).

As scholars and practitioners, we are cognizant of the fact that standards and practices in carrying out psychological evaluations of asylum seekers vary considerably among clinicians in their role as experts in immigration proceedings. This chapter endeavors to expand the discourse so that more experts and adjudicators are speaking the same language and working from the proverbial "same page" when considering these complex cases. The authors will attempt to respond to common issues and concerns they have encountered in the two decades they have been engaged in this work. The chapter is organized around common questions or themes that arise when engaging in this challenging work.

There will be process-oriented themes such as: operating within one's bounds of competence; maintaining the role of expert rather than advocate; effectively communicating one's written and/or verbal findings; and striking a balance between the historical narrative and the psychological findings in an expert report.

The authors also explore cultural and intrapsychic issues, such as: explaining potential inconsistencies in a survivor's trauma narrative; the effects of cultural

and emotional marginalization on African asylum applicants; and helping a
client to find his or her voice in an intimidating situation.

This chapter emphasizes that high quality evaluations can be prepared both
by mental health clinicians who provide ongoing treatment and by clinicians
conducting evaluations independent of a treatment relationship. In both
cases, these evaluations are valuable additions to the asylum adjudication
process and merit considerable influence when done ethically, competently
and within the bounds of the clinician's professional expertise.

To this end, there are limits to what a clinician can say with certainty.
Evaluators cannot conclusively rule out the possibility of fraud and deception,
but can shed a great deal of light on the probability of such occurrences based
on sound clinical observation and judgment. Clinicians cannot definitively
identify the cause of an applicant's psychological distress, but can speak to the
consistency of an applicant's psychological presentation with what would be
expected from someone who has undergone the sort of traumatic events that
he or she reports.

These nuanced distinctions are central to the ongoing dialectical relationship between the clinician expert witness and the asylum adjudicators. This is
especially pertinent in the case of many African asylum applicants, where
detailed corroborating documentation may not be as readily available, and
adjudicators may be less familiar with the intricacies of current events and
social stressors facing the applicants. In such circumstances, more weight may
be placed on the expert testimony as a "make or break" threshold for the
assessment of an applicant's credibility. As clinicians struggle to stay within the
bounds of their competence, adjudicators must also strike a delicate balance
and be careful to not be swayed by their own assumptions or preconceptions,
or rely too heavily on clinical conclusions that have their own inherent
structural and logistical limitations.

LOGISTIC AND SYSTEMIC ISSUES IN PROVIDING PSYCHOLOGICAL TESTIMONY

Despite external pressures, clinicians who participate as expert witnesses or
evaluators in asylum cases need to recognize that their job is not to "win the
case." Even when evaluators are sought by potential clients or immigration
lawyers who are seeking "one of those PTSD letters," or because of the
"success rate" of a particular clinician or program, clinicians must remain
faithful to the true intent of their evaluations (Lustig et al. 2008). The clinician's job is to provide the most detailed, accurate, and insightful report and
testimony possible in order to support adjudicators to make the most

informed, nuanced, and appropriate decision based on the evidence at hand. No more, no less. Clinicians lose much of the influence that they possess as experts when they appear to be an advocate rather than an objective evaluator of psychological processes.

As such, clinicians must acknowledge that as they are not witnesses to the reported traumatic events in the client's home country, they can only speak of reported facts, not past events. The clinician generally has no premorbid contact with the applicant, so no comparisons can be made between an applicant's current psychological functioning and how they may have comported themselves before the reported traumatic events. Therefore, clinicians cannot assert causation but must focus on the consistency of reported history, observed behavior, clinical engagement, and psychological symptoms (Smith 2007).

Recognizing the difference between being an expert and an advocate can be a crucial part of the dialectical communication between clinician and adjudicator in the asylum process. Respecting and being cognizant of the limits of what an expert can attest to may allow all parties to engage in the process from a positive perspective where the focus is on the evidence that is presented, as opposed to the definitive conclusions that cannot be provided.

In this regard, asylum adjudicators may express concern that all mental health evaluations presented to them appear favorable to the asylum applicant. Does this mean that the evaluators are advocates intent on convincing the adjudicators to grant their clients asylum? The overarching answer to this question is "no." The positive skew on the evaluators' reports is largely because mental health clinicians decline to provide an opinion in cases where psychological evidence in support of an asylum claim appears to not be credible or does not hold together clinically. For example, many evaluations are conducted by staff of organizations whose primary responsibility is treatment, not forensic evaluations. For such programs, only clients who have engaged in ongoing treatment in a sincere and committed manner, and where the clinician's observations can shed light on the forensic processes, will receive an affidavit or expert testimony from the clinician (Smith 2007). In cases in which clinicians are conducting evaluations apart from a treatment relationship, it is clear that referring attorneys for applicants do not request written reports in cases in which the clinician does not find credible and documentable evidence of injury consistent with torture. Thus, among evaluations submitted to adjudicators, the overall weighting toward evaluations supporting applicants' claims does not imply an advocacy bias on the part of the evaluators. It is certainly not true, as is sometimes alleged, that all evaluators will make a positive report regardless of the nature and facts of the case.

Adjudicators may also question whether clinicians who choose to evaluate asylum seekers, whether as volunteers, independent contractors, or as staff members of torture treatment organizations, begin with a bias in favor of the applicant. Here, it should be emphasized that all mental health professionals are subject to the codified training and ethical standards of their respective professions. Ethical standards and training require that clinicians record accurately what they are told and what they observe and that they interpret these findings according to commonly accepted scientific principles as they manifest in each individual case. Regardless of how well "vetted" a case may appear to be by a referring human rights organization or attorney, clinicians never assume a specific clinical outcome in advance of the assessment. Clinicians come to their clinical conclusions independent of the referring agent or agency, and regardless of whether the evaluation is provided on a pro bono or a fee for service basis. Indeed, professionals typically view their credibility as professionals to be just as important as the credibility of the asylum seekers.

Human rights organizations (e.g., charities or nonprofit agencies, such as Survivors International, Physicians for Human Rights, and HealthRight International) which manage volunteer networks of clinicians willing to provide evaluations emphasize the importance of the evaluator adhering to ethical principles by remaining impartial, as is appropriate in a forensic setting (HealthRight International 2011; Physicians for Human Rights 2012). Professionals in this field also know that a clinician who attempts to help one client by misrepresenting or exaggerating findings not only damages his or her own credibility but also hurts other survivors whose legitimate cases may now be viewed with skepticism or disbelief by adjudicators.

Immigration judges and asylum officers who have read numerous mental health evaluations of applicants may wonder, given the variation in human experience, why psychological reports often contain such similar conclusions. Despite differences in report format and style and the variations evaluators identify among both historical facts and individuals' experience of them, mental health professionals often write about the same clinical conditions in similar ways. Because they are assessing specifically for the presence or absence of signs and symptoms of trauma that would corroborate a prior history of victimization and that are consistent with the scientifically accepted criteria for diagnosis, their reports repeatedly and necessarily describe those symptoms as they are identified in each individual case. An analogy would be a group of physicians writing about patients with high blood pressure; the elevated measurements would be similarly repetitive. Those readings are simply the manifestation of the clinical condition (Jacobs and Lustig 2010).

Adjudicators who have been presented with mental health evaluations that differ substantially in style and format may wonder whether standard methods exist for these clinical examinations and reports. Guidelines have been published for health professionals on how to properly examine asylum seekers in particular and trauma survivors in general. One example is the Istanbul Protocol, a guide to medical and psychological investigation and documentation of torture and its effects, which was developed for the United Nations Office of the High Commissioner for Human Rights by an international team of experts and is widely recognized as a standard for the field (Iacopino et al. 1999). Other examples include the Physicians for Human Rights 2001 "Examining Asylum Seekers," a manual focused specifically on evaluation of asylum seekers in the United States, as well as other professional literature (e.g. Jacobs, Evans. and Patsalides 2001). It is preferable that health professionals are familiar with and utilize these guidelines.

Having said this, it is important to assert that reports that do not fulfill all the strictest standards cited here should not be considered invalid. Many health practitioners who are not familiar with all the complexities of medico-legal or psycho-legal work nevertheless do a thorough job of examining an asylum applicant and have both clinical experience and specialty knowledge regarding torture, trauma, and their effects. It is understood that adjudicators consider expert mental health opinions as one part of the body of evidence to consider in deciding the ultimate issues at hand. The opinions expressed by expert clinical evaluators should be assigned the weight they are due in the legal process.

Variations in evaluations also reflect the reality that mental health examiners come from different professions and have diverse training and professional habits, and that the issues requiring evaluation may be as varied as the applicants themselves. For example, it is very different to evaluate the consequences of a head injury sustained from a beating during torture compared to the emotional consequences of years of incarceration in abusive conditions. An examiner who might be the right expert for one case may not be right for a different one.

As such, a good standard to keep in mind is that the clinical conclusions should follow from the data in the report and clearly explain the basis for the opinion expressed. Evaluations ideally address the consistency between allegations and findings. In other words, an examiner who concludes that an asylum seeker suffers from PTSD should clearly present the data for that conclusion, such as instances of the various reported symptoms and accompanying behavioral observations and the consistency of these with what could be expected from the alleged torture or abuse. The conditions of the evaluation should be clearly stated, including the number and length of interviews conducted, whether interpreters were used, what sources of information were consulted and what records were reviewed; in other words, all of the elements one can expect from a document submitted for legal purposes. Furthermore, evaluations should be written in language that is clear and understandable by nonclinicians, as opposed to jargon decipherable only by other health professionals.

Another area for consideration with implications for credibility is the use of psychological tests and assessment measures with asylum seekers. Understandably, adjudicators sometimes look for such objective documentation. However, there are significant challenges associated with using such tests on an African immigrant population. Examiners must contend with considerable linguistic, cultural, socioeconomic, and educational diversity in these endeavors. Consequently, many standard assessment methods might not be appropriate for use, or would have to be modified according to the specific demands of such cases. Many asylum seekers come from cultures that are very different from those in which such tests were developed, and often have limited formal education. Therefore, they differ substantially from what researchers and test developers call the "normative sample," which is the group of people on whom the test norms are based. In such situations, test results that might look scientific and objective may not actually be valid. The process is often further complicated by the need to use interpreters, or to translate written tests into languages in which their psychometric properties have not been measured.

Professional standards of ethics and practice require clinicians to utilize methods that have sufficient validity. Furthermore, as health practitioners, clinicians have a duty to protect examinees from unnecessary stress. Many asylum seekers are in such emotional distress that the verbal exploration of their history and experience and their described and demonstrated symptoms produce more than sufficient evidence for a valid assessment. Even where tests or assessment measures are appropriate, their use, in the judgment of many clinical evaluators, would be an undue burden, leading clinicians to abstain from the use of procedures they might have planned to use in advance. For all these reasons, internationally recognized standards for evaluating survivors of torture, such as the Istanbul Protocol, establish the clinical interview as the standard for assessment methodology. Within that framework, some evaluators use tests or symptom assessment measures as supplements to the clinical interview, while not relying on them for conclusive diagnoses.

To emphasize, credibility is an essential component to the success of an asylum application. It cuts across historical, personal, psychological, and institutional domains. Expert psychological evaluators focus primarily on the applicant's reported and observed symptoms, as well as their emotional reactions and comportment as they relate to their trauma narrative, their behavior, and their ability to testify appropriately in the asylum process. In addition, evaluators often have access to the applicant's reported trauma history through declarations prepared with referring attorneys or other official documents.

Opinions differ among professional expert evaluators about how much of the historical narrative should be included in the written psychological evaluation. Some experts provide a detailed account of trauma history. In such cases, it is essential that information documented come directly from the evaluator's interview rather than being copied from other sources. Other experts provide a summary of the most significant elements of the trauma narrative to contextualize the symptoms and clinical observations, aware that a detailed account is provided elsewhere. In such cases it is essential that the evaluator explore the complete trauma history verbally even if he or she does not fully recount it in the written report. Where the evaluator is also providing ongoing treatment, this information will likely have emerged organically in the treatment process. In those cases the trauma history might be presented in a brief summation of reported events while the crux of the report will focus on the applicant's course in psychological treatment. In fact, an attorney may ask that an evaluator's recitation of the reported traumatic events be brief, so as to avoid the inadvertent inconsistencies between documents that may arise in the normal process of repeated narration of traumatic memories in the high-stress and often prolonged asylum process. Either approach – the detailed account or the summary – is valid. The decision develops as part of the dialectical relationship between evaluators, attorneys and adjudicators in relation to their specific preferences for documenting, presenting and receiving evidence. In either approach, the clinical impressions form the basis of the psychological evaluation and the subsequent findings.

Sometimes an adjudicator may question why a clinician provides a complete account of the survivor's trauma history, suggesting that this is redundant and uncorroborated by other evidence. They may observe that history shared in this format will be "reported history" and not verifiable statements of fact. Furthermore, the applicant's narrative is usually covered within their legal documents, and review by adjudicators of what may be perceived as a duplicate narrative may place a greater time burden on an already overburdened system.

Notwithstanding these observations and independent of what is included in written form, it is always critical for the clinician to explore the personal and trauma history directly with the asylum seeker, whether or not the applicant has come to the evaluation with a written copy of their narrative that was taken in another context (perhaps by their legal team or another clinician). This exploration provides an essential means of observing and assessing the applicant's cognitive and emotional process, as well as shedding further light on the question of consistency.

Concerning the review of applicant's declarations and other documents that narrate relevant events, some evaluators review such documents before conducting an evaluation interview, whereas others prefer to wait until after their initial interview. Either approach is valid and ethical. If the applicant's verbally presented narrative is significantly inconsistent with previously written accounts, or if there are significant gaps, the evaluator must assess why this is the case, possibly in terms of an applicant's current deficits in psychological functioning, or possibly in terms of malingering or exaggeration. This discussion will return to the latter topic further on.

In addition to delving into the content of the narrative, clinicians must also mine the wealth of observational data available in the process of how the narrative is related, inconsistencies and all. Simply stated, clinicians need to observe the process of how a story is related, as well as the content of what is related. Just as a physician who evaluates physical injuries sustained during torture has to know the precise details of what reportedly happened in order to evaluate the degree of consistency between the physical evidence of the injury and how the injury was inflicted, a mental health examiner also needs to carefully observe the way a person behaves as he or she tells their story, and consider how that person may have changed as a result of traumatic events. This includes how a survivor relates to the examiner or therapist within the room, how they may have related to their family and others while events were unfolding, as well as other pertinent aspects of their stories. In many cases, by virtue of having more time than adjudicators to interview the applicant as well as having specialized interviewing skills, the history taken by mental health clinicians uncovers relevant facts that were not included in previously prepared written documents and that help to explain the psychological symptoms included in their reports.

Several examples from clinical practice shed light on this dimension. There have been cases where history-taking by a mental health evaluator uncovered previously unreported information that was painful to reveal but was directly related to the asylum claim. For example, an African asylum seeker had an extreme psychological reaction subsequent to being sexually molested by police officers due to his sexual orientation. The intensity of his emotional reaction to this abuse rendered this applicant unable to share his trauma history or testify in his asylum proceedings. It was through the careful and gradual uncovering by the treating clinician of other incidents of trauma in the survivor's life (including being raped while he was a child), that the clinician was able to provide testimony allowing adjudicators to understand the extreme nature of the applicant's retraumatization; they were then able to see his apparently suspicious and uncooperative demeanor in the asylum process in a different light.

In another example, a survivor of chattel-based slavery in a North African country could not even recall all seven of his children's names when he first came to the treatment program for an intake interview. The clinician observed that the survivor's memory improved and his thinking became more linear and detailed only as he became more comfortable and progressed in treatment. Despite this improvement, when the applicant was placed in the high-stress environment of the asylum hearing, he became emotionally overwhelmed and regressed to the point where he was a "terrible witness," barely able to communicate let alone remember important details. His inability to coherently tell his story cast doubt upon his credibility. The treating psychologist was called in to talk about how this decompensation was actually consistent with the applicant's presentation in treatment and during anxiety-provoking situations and as such supported rather than undermined his reported trauma history.

In this same case, one of the prime examples of perceived discrepancy in the applicant's narrative, and a major sticking point in the proceedings, was when the applicant had spoken in a therapy session about the death of his elder brother when the "master" refused to provide medical care after a poisonous snakebite. This had happened many years before the events that were outlined in the survivor's asylum application took place, and was not mentioned in his legal submission for asylum. When the government attorney labeled this omission as an unreported discrepancy that undermined the applicant's credibility, the psychologist testifying as an expert witness was able to put the event in the context of a life filled with multiple traumas, and placed the omission in the context of the extreme difficulty this client had manifested in revealing his traumatic experiences. The clinician pointed to consistency in the client's clinical presentation, including the tentative and gradual nature of how the applicant was able to eventually share his narrative in the course of therapy. When the government attorney asked the applicant why he had only shared this story with his clinician, and not shared these background details during cross-examination; the applicant simply responded, "Because my doctor took the time to ask me."

These examples illustrate that the purpose of a clinical evaluator taking a complete history is to verify, clarify, and shed light, and to study from a psychological perspective the asylum seeker's emotional comportment, thought processes, and incidental memories, all of which can be extremely helpful in understanding his or her testimony. As previously stated, the balance in how much of the historical narrative is shared within the written psychological evaluation depends on the context of the report, the focus of the findings and the ongoing dialectical process between evaluators and adjudicators.

CULTURAL AND INTRAPSYCHIC ISSUES FOR ASYLUM APPLICANTS

The question of credibility and inconsistency looms large for asylum seekers. There are a great number of potential questions in an asylum case, but many of these can be boiled down to three main questions. If asylum applicants are able to respond to these questions adequately, in terms of being consistent and verifiable, it can go a long way toward satisfying their burden of proof in their case. The three questions are: "Are you the person you claim to be? Do you come from the country from which you claim to have come? Have you undergone the experiences you claim to have survived?" (Smith, Kuck, and Beck 2011).

When there are inconsistencies in an asylum case regarding factual details or dates, if there are inconsistencies between verbal and written testimony, or if there are inconsistencies between different written documents, it can cast doubt on the whether the applicant can actually answer these three important questions truthfully and satisfactorily. And if doubt is cast on one aspect of a person's story, it might stand to reason that the other aspects are called into doubt as well, even where answers there may have been seen as consistent. Given these factors, adjudicators may reasonably wonder why mental health clinicians frequently submit opinions in support of claims containing such inconsistencies. This is an issue of major importance since asylum law allows adjudicators to find lack of credibility for even minor inconsistencies, even where these are not material to the facts of the case. The authors have seen cases where denial of asylum has been based on such inconsistencies.

Research findings indicate that people are commonly quite inconsistent over time in the narration of the same event, even when narrating stories they believe to be true, especially with respect to dates, times, sequence of events, and other details. Research also shows that this is even more true for traumatic as opposed to nontraumatic narratives, even when there is no political or financial benefit, and that the length of time between renditions is associated with more discrepancies in trauma narratives (Herlihy, Scragg, and Turner 2002).

In addition, some applicants suffer from considerable cognitive impairment, which may predate their traumatic experiences, or be exacerbated by the trauma they have experienced. Such impairment can affect memory and testimony (Jacobs and Iacopino 2001). From the medical/psychological perspective, experienced evaluators also know that some trauma survivors are reluctant to divulge the very details that clarify and strengthen their case. The reasons for this may include feelings of shame, which may be culturally determined, or traumatic avoidance and fear (Smith and Keller 2007). These reactions may be compounded by the circumstance of being inter- viewed by persons of authority, such as immigration officers or judges (Lustig 2008). Many asylum seekers are afraid to divulge their full story upon arrival in this country (e.g., during an interview at the border or airport) because their history of persecution or torture renders them afraid of officials, or because they fear information they provide will be transmitted to their home country, endangering family members and associates (Ardalan and Clark 2014; Smith and Keller 2007). In one instance, a clinician received a referral of an asylum seeker who had not divulged two violent sexual assaults, as well as the murder and disappearance of two other family members (that the survivor witnessed directly), for over thirty years.

Another disturbing dynamic impinges on some asylum seekers. Some of the most severe cases of persecution that evaluators may see are nevertheless cases in which a frightened torture survivor, who has a very strong and legitimate claim to asylum from the outset, is misled by an unscrupulous advocate into believing that, if he or she does not embellish the facts, he or she will be denied asylum and be deported back to where the torture took place. In a related scenario, there have been a significant number of cases in which the applicant was barely mentally competent, and for whom many "facts" had been supplied by supposedly well-meaning third parties who understood only part of the story. This "assistance" generally leads to more doubt being cast on the applicant's credibility, and is harmful to the process.

These complicated and multidirectional interactions are particularly salient for African asylum applicants. African torture survivors often speak with trepidation of "*les conseils de la rue*," which is French for "street advice." This means that the rumors, urban legends, and myths that are trafficked in the hair salons and taxi stands of the expatriate African community can be harmful to those seeking recourse through the asylum process. Many African immigrants with whom the authors have worked clinically share the notion that "the only thing worse than a lack of information is misinformation."

Many African survivors are told to avoid applying for asylum, or are given false information by other expatriates. This can have major impact on one's

ability or willingness to apply for asylum before the twelve month filing
deadline. Some African immigrants have even described a scenario in which
Africans who have been in the country for a significant amount of time "want
to see others suffer like they did," and may withhold or falsify important
information.

Acting on misguided advice or misinformation has ruined many an African
asylum applicant's chances at being seen as credible by adjudicators. When
these dynamics are involved, psychological evaluations, particularly those
provided by clinicians who are engaged in ongoing treatment, may be the
best opportunity to explore the multiple contexts (intrapsychic, educational,
and communal) that can shed light on apparent contradictions and inconsistencies in an applicant's narrative.

Careful exploration by clinicians often reveals that certain discrepancies
have very understandable and psychologically plausible explanations. Some
asylum applicants have received limited or substandard education and fail
to comprehend the intended meaning of particular questions. A significant
portion of African asylum seekers presenting for treatment or evaluation have
had limited literacy skills. There may also be differences in the importance
placed on exact dates in particular cultures. For example, many clients from
Guinea over the age of forty have the documented birth date of January 1, as
exact dates of birth were not frequently noted in official birth records.

Other applicants have had their stories poorly translated initially or at some
point in the process. The resulting inaccuracies may be related to elements of
the applicant's narrative or even to specific demographic information. Cases
have been denied or delayed because the interpreter confused the words "since"
and "until." In one case, a judge denied asylum because of discrepancies
regarding the dates of birth of an applicant's children. These discrepancies
were caused because the dates of birth were transcribed in the "month-day-
year" format used in the United States, as opposed to the "day-month-year"
format used uniformly elsewhere. Over time, evaluators and adjudicators
become very familiar with these kinds of issues.

Many torture survivors who have entered the United States and who may
already be suffering from avoidance and withdrawal symptoms associated
with PTSD, or a lack of proactive initiative associated with depression, may
also fail to apply for asylum within the mandatory one-year filing period. Some are
so distrustful of other Africans (especially those from their home country) that they
may not seek out the immigration-related information that exists within their
community. If they do reach out, survivors may be guided toward "*notarios*" or
"volume lawyers" or others who may provide substandard service to already
marginalized communities, resulting in the presentation of poorly prepared and

inaccurate applications (Dolnick 2011). All these hazards can threaten legitimate asylum claims.

In such cases, clinicians may spend many hours with applicants. When seeming discrepancies resolve with clarifications, or can be well explained on the basis of clinical findings, a clinical evaluation and report and/or expert witness testimony that help to contextualize these discrepancies will be provided. When discrepancies seem to get worse over time, or cannot be well explained on the basis of clinical findings, clinicians will typically express their concerns to the applicant's attorney. Clinicians may decline to prepare a report, or the attorneys may choose to not submit the report that is provided, as it would not be viewed as beneficial to their client's case. Again, the clinician's responsibility is to provide the most accurate and insightful evaluation possible, based on his or her clinical observations and knowledge; not to become an advocate, who argues for asylum regardless of the merits of the case.

This notion of credibility cuts to the heart of the asylum adjudication process. It is particularly salient for African survivors, for whom the assumption of credibility is not a given. There are complex factors at play here. Because of the widespread poverty throughout continental Africa, there are those who believe that Africans would "say anything" to get to a country where they would have better economic opportunities. Citing high profile New York cases like the aforementioned Amadou Diallo case in the Bronx and the 2011 episode involving Dominique Strauss-Kahn in Manhattan, both of which cast doubt on the veracity of African asylum applicants, some feel as though there is a "guilty until proven innocent" or at least an "incredible until proven credible" burden that African applicants carry (Eligon 2011; Mehta 2011; Souter 2011). Their powerlessness is compounded when their realities – even in the macro-political sense – are ignored or overlooked. This is especially pertinent for African applicants, as the plight of their countries may be less familiar to Western based evaluators and adjudicators.

Examples from asylum applicants from Côte d'Ivoire and Guinea illustrate how there may be a disconnect between what is published in Western media outlets, or what is generally reported or understood to be transpiring in a particular country, versus the reality being lived by the affected populations. Both of those countries had presidential elections around 2010 that were associated with widespread violence and societal schisms, but that were deemed as "free and fair enough" for the international community.

As such, it became more difficult for asylum applicants from these countries to win their cases, or even to retain adequate legal representation, because it was assumed that circumstances were greatly improved. This was belied by the almost daily incidents of continued ethnic tension, sectarian violence, and score settling in both countries. Despite these ongoing difficulties and violent realities, it became increasingly difficult for these clients even to find legal representation from pro-bono legal representatives in the aftermath of the elections. Some legal practitioners felt that those cases will be "hard to win," and therefore could affect their firm's success rate, or perhaps be discouraging to the young lawyers assigned to these pro-bono cases. These factors can add to the frustration and potential retraumatization of applicants who feel that they are stuck and invisible. Similarly, many applicants from Guinea who had experienced extensive trauma at home due to their political activities or ethnic affiliation complained that they were assumed to be economic refugees rather than truly fleeing persecution, and therefore not considered legitimate applicants for asylum.

Another example of the special challenges facing African asylum applicants was touched upon at a recent gathering in Dar es Salaam, Tanzania, where mental health professionals operating in conflict-affected areas in East Africa, spoke about the "believability" aspect of the African experience. Participants noted that it is relatively easy for the outside world to believe the mass trauma it hears about from Africa, as there are frequent images in the media of widespread deprivation, mass migrations, refugee camps, and other scenes of hardship and tragedy. This does not necessarily translate, however, into emotional understanding or believing the narrative of a particular individual who has lived through these same harrowing experiences. It is as if the personal nature of the trauma narrative makes it too close, as it brings the horror of man's inhumanity toward others to a very intimate level that is uncomfortable for the listener. This dynamic can affect evaluators, adjudicators, and the general public.

At the same time, it is precisely the individual nature of a narrative that allows an applicant to stand out from the masses as someone with a credible personal story. For example, among asylum seekers from Somalia there is often a broad general pattern of persecution – rape, murder, robbery, torture, confiscation of property, and death threats perpetrated by majority clan militias against defenseless minority clan individuals and families. Adjudicators hearing many such cases may come to see them as too repetitive and even generic to substantiate any individual claim. The mental health clinician's effort in documenting individual differences in trauma and the specific and individual psychological reactions to those events supports each applicant to be perceived in his or her own right.

Credibility may also hinge on issues of cross-cultural definitions. In the case of African asylum applicants, perhaps one of the more complex issues concerning credibility and plausibility concerns the invocation of family and familial relationships. A number of factors that may increase people's suspicions about African asylum applicants concern differences in cultural and legal constructs, and family and kinship paradigms regularly assessed and documented in clinical evaluation. Because of cultural differences, the learning curve in this area is often steep for evaluators and adjudicators alike. As an example, in refugee resettlement programs working with survivors from the Horn of Africa, there have been high levels of perceived "fraud" where family ties reported in applications are not supported by DNA testing.

This information invites deeper cross-cultural investigation, for example, into the question of what constitutes a family. Patterns of adoption and affiliation differ among African societies, and can be held in stark contrast with Western definitions (e.g., Guyer 1981; Vaughan 1983). In many African societies, if an adult dies, his children are automatically adopted by his sibling. The deceased's children become the children of his sibling. There is no formal adoption process with papers, signatures, or an official governmental stamp. This may lead to discrepancies between the numbers of "officially recognized" children in an asylum application, and the total number of children that the applicant considers to be part of his or her immediate family. When educated about such issues, adjudicators and evaluators may help to explain and bridge the gaps between conceptualizations of family, so that these discrepancies will be seen in the context of cross-cultural adaptation as opposed to a falsification of familial documentation.

In the example described earlier regarding the former enslaved individual from North Africa, part of the government attorney's complaint concerned the definition of the "brother" who had died from snakebite. The applicant had already listed his siblings in his asylum application forms, but included only his living siblings who were from the same mother and father. The "brother" who had died was of mixed parentage. The client had explained during his treatment that in his country, slave women were often "given" to visitors to the master's household regardless of whether the woman was already a mother, married, or betrothed. As such, there were many "outside" babies from these "visits." The deceased "brother" and the applicant had the same mother, but different fathers. The applicant did not initially list his brother as a sibling because he was fearful that the immigration officials would not consider them to be "true" brothers due to the difference in parentage and because the brother had died so long ago. Without the input of the treating clinician, who was able to get at this detailed information during months of treatment, the client may have been viewed as inconsistent (at least) or a perjurer (at worst).

Recognizing the central importance of credibility in assessing asylum claims, and given that adjudicators have understandable concerns about fraud, it is not surprising that they may wonder whether applicants are lying to their clinical evaluators, whose reports may simply propagate these falsehoods. This raises the issues of malingering and deception.

Malingering is the clinical term that describes the false production or exaggeration of symptoms, whereas deception is a more general term (Resnick 2008). Malingering has been defined by the American Psychiatric Association (2000, p. 739) as "intentional production of false or grossly exaggerated physical or psychological symptoms, motivated by external incentives, such as avoiding military duty, avoiding work, obtaining financial compensation, evading criminal prosecution, or obtaining drugs."

To malinger convincingly is actually not so easy, provided that the examiner has some experience and training. It may seem that it would be easy to learn what the symptoms of a certain disorder are, such as PTSD, and to simply recite them, but that is a superficial understanding. There is a nuanced and subtle balance between what an interviewee self-reports and what a clinician observes that helps to defend against being fooled by exaggerated claims.

Along with expert opinion on the topic, clinical experience demonstrates that, faced with a careful and detailed inquiry, the person who is not actually suffering from the condition is under tremendous pressure to improvise and very likely becomes evasive, flustered or irritated in the process, whereas the person who genuinely has the condition feels increasingly understood and supplies more and more material (Sussan 2006). Clinicians consider the "internal consistency" of reported symptoms, which means that some symptoms typically do or do not occur together, a distinction that is difficult for laypeople to know. In addition to symptoms clinicians are also interested in "signs," which are objective markers of clinical conditions that can be observed directly, not just reported. For example, low energy is a reported symptom, while psychomotor retardation (being visibly slowed down by depression) is a sign. The possibility of malingering might be suggested by an unusual degree of familiarity with all the symptoms of a disorder while being unwilling to acknowledge the absence of any symptoms and by failing to exhibit any signs that should accompany the reported symptoms (Knoll and Resnick 2006).

Theorists and seasoned evaluators caution clinicians to be vigilant toward some of the classic behaviors of malingerers. Resnick et al. (2008, p. 116) stated, "malingerers may overact their parts by giving excessively dramatic reports of their symptoms." Malingerers may manifest dramatic voice changes to convey their feelings. They may consistently emphasize reported suicidal ideation and intent. They may focus on the more dramatic aspects of PTSD, such as nightmares and flashbacks and overlook equally common but less well-known symptoms such as avoidance and withdrawal (Resnick 2003). Behaviorally, clinical observers also explain that malingerers tend to be defensive and uncooperative with evaluators, as though the interview is an adversarial relationship or a high-stakes game of wits.

Clinicians routinely consider the possibility of malingering when conducting evaluations and utilize observation and interview methods that specifically probe for this possibility. Since much of the literature on malingering focuses on exaggerated reporting of symptoms, it is notable that many African asylum applicants are reticent to discuss their trauma histories, have trouble articulating them, or may even downplay the severity of their symptoms, as opposed to eagerly presenting a rehearsed list of symptoms. These observations can be very useful to highlight within the context of an asylum process, to show that the applicant does not seem to be "faking bad" to garner a specific secondary gain.

Programs that provide ongoing treatment to torture survivors have an entire course of treatment through which to gather information and observation that bolster their assessment of applicants' truthfulness and consistency. Factors clinicians may observe include, for example, do the applicants engage in treatment consistently and sincerely? Do they attend sessions frequently? Are they compliant with their medications, if medications have been prescribed? Is there some reduction in symptoms (both observed and reported) as they progress in treatment, or are they "always in crisis"? Clinicians who see clients who engage sincerely, and who observe variations in functioning based on the course in treatment and verifiable ongoing external stressors can make a stronger argument against the suggestion of malingering.

Deception is a bit trickier, and the dialectical relationship between evaluators and adjudicators is well served when both parties recognize the inherent limitations in totally eradicating doubt about the possibility of deception. The poet William H. Smith once said, "If you want to find the fool in the room, find the person who feels that he or she cannot be fooled." Clinicians must keep this sense of humility in mind when conducting evaluations, and adjudicators must understand that there is no "magic bullet," questionnaire, or tell-tale sign that will eradicate all ambiguity or doubt about an applicant's reported experiences.

As stated at the beginning of this chapter, clinicians do not have premorbid (prior to the reported trauma) contact with the applicants. Clinicians were not present to witness the reported traumatic experiences. Clinicians cannot assert causation but must limit themselves to consistency, as manifested by the applicant's self-report and the evaluator's clinical observation.

Evaluators and adjudicators must also agree that there is no way to conclusively rule out the possibility of deception. Both sides are better served to focus on the probability of deception, as this is a more realistic and useful lens by which to assist adjudicators to make tough decisions in sometimes ambiguous circumstances.

An example can illuminate this process. A clinician once worked with a semiliterate market woman from West Africa who had suffered multiple traumas in her home country and was suffering from depressive symptoms exacerbated by ongoing separation from her children. The clinician and applicant worked together clinically over fifteen months. The clinician was able to trace a nuanced course in treatment in which the client showed therapeutic gains, but with spikes and troughs that were influenced by external stressors.

During cross-examination, the government attorney pressed the clinician on the possibility that the client was deceiving him. The clinician admitted to this possibility. He then described a scenario in which the woman was actually a gifted actress who was able to give a performance (not just a one-time performance, but a nuanced portrayal over the course of dozens of sessions, – like a Broadway performer). The clinician also posited that the woman might not be a semiliterate market woman but, rather, a highly trained student of psychology, who was able to fabricate a sophisticated and nuanced course in treatment that showed clinical improvement (so as not to appear to be malingering) and also showed the ups and downs associated with external stressors that are associated with long-term recovery from PTSD and Major Depressive Disorder. The clinician fully admitted that it was "possible" that this woman was actually a talented actress and sophisticated student of psychological phenomena. However, based on his experience and clinical judgment, it was clearly more "probable" that she was actually a semiliterate market woman who had suffered the sorts of ongoing abuse that she specified in her testimony.

By admitting the limits of certainty while focusing on what can actually be said with a reasonable level of clinical certainty, the clinician was able to provide contextual information that helped the adjudicator make an informed and appropriate decision in the case. This exemplifies the opportunities and tensions in the dialectical relationship between evaluators and adjudicators. Evaluators cannot be counted on the answer all questions and remove all ambiguity. This should not be the goal of the evaluator, or the expectation of the adjudicator. By focusing on the areas where the evaluation can shed light and provide context, the communication and expectations between stakeholders becomes clearer and more effective in terms of moving the asylum case forward.

One promising development is that as more clinicians are able to shed light on the complicated situations asylum applicants face, adjudicators seem to be increasingly willing to consider the credibility of the applicants within the nuanced context of their past suffering, their potential desperation to never return to those dangerous circumstances; and the possibility that these factors may compel some applicants to exaggerate certain aspects of their stories. An example of this movement is a decision that was handed down by the United States Board of Immigration Appeals (BIA) in September 2013.

It was reported in the Fahamu Refugee Program Legal Aid Newsletter (FRP, January, 2014) that an asylum applicant from Cameroun had testified that he was imprisoned and beaten three times. He also gave the court a fake photo of his injuries. The Immigration Judge initially denied asylum, deeming respondent not credible, in large part because of the fake photo. The BIA reversed and remanded the initial decision, noting that the Immigration Judge had not considered other evidence of record, including country conditions and a medical affidavit from an American physician. The BIA stated that the 'submitted evidence cumulatively may be sufficient to rehabilitate the respondent's credibility or establish independently past persecution or a well-founded fear of persecution. See *Camara v. Ashcroft*, 378 F.3d 361 (4th Cir. 2004)."

So it does seem that the ongoing dialectical processes between asylum applicants, expert witnesses, and adjudicators are making differences – not only in individual cases; but in the ways that these cases are globally considered. We hope that this is a conversation that will continue, and will be joined by many more informed and caring voices.

CONCLUSION

As this chapter clearly illustrates, the path for an asylum applicant to be accorded the status of asylee is not easy. There are cultural, historical and social realities that reinforce accentuate these difficulties for African applicants. The collaborations between mental health professionals and adjudicators have been crucial in the successful adjudication of many asylum processes. This professional activity – helping to shed light on domains of functioning for marginalized clients coming from neglected regions in the world – can actually be a lifesaving endeavor for the applicant. It also serves adjudicators, providing pertinent data and insights to contribute to a most fully informed and well-founded decision on each case.

Beyond that, a proper psychological evaluation (and even more so an ongoing therapeutic relationship) provides support and can contribute to genuine healing for the traumatized, frequently anxious and overwhelmed asylum applicant (Gangsei and Deutsch 2007). No promises can ever be made about the outcome of a case, but applicants may come to realize that they are not alone in this proceeding or, indeed, in the world. Someone is listening intently to their story and bearing witness to their existence.

We conclude with the words of a female torture survivor from Ethiopia. She said, "Consider me like someone who has no home, no country, and nowhere to go – and I am asking if I can stay with you" (Smith 2007). For many survivors of human rights abuses in Africa, the asylum process is just that simple – and just that complicated.

REFERENCES

Dolnick, Sam. 2011. "Immigrants May Be Fed False Stories to Bolster Asylum Pleas." *The New York Times.* http://www.nytimes.com/2011/07/12/nyregion/immigrants-may -be-fed-false-stories-to-bolster-asylum-pleas.html?pagewanted=alland_moc.semityn .www [Retrieved January 15, 2014].

Eligon, John. 2011. "Strauss-Kahn Drama Ends with a Short Final Scene." *New York Times,* p. A-1. http://www.nytimes.com/2011/08/24/nyregion/charges-against-strauss-kahn-dis missed.html?pagewanted=all [Retrieved January 15, 2014].

Fahamu Refugee Legal Aid Newsletter. January 2014. *"Cumulative Credibility Ruling."* Fahamu Refugee Program. Oxford, England. http://www.refugeelegalaidinformation .org/fahamu-refugee-legal-aid-newsletter#January_2014 [Retrieved April 20, 2014].

Gangsei, David and Ana Deutsch. 2007. "Psychological Evaluation of Asylum Seekers as a Therapeutic Process." *Torture* 17.2: 79–87.

Guyer, Jane. 1981. "Household and Community in African Studies," *African Studies Review* XXIV.

HealthRight International. 2011. *Human Rights Clinic: Training Manual for Physicians and Mental Health Professionals.* New York: HealthRight International.

Herlihy, Jane, Peter Scragg, and Stuart Turner. 2002. "Discrepancies in Autobiographical Memories – Implications for the Assessment of Asylum Seekers: Repeated Interviews Study." *British Medical Journal* 324.9: 324–327.

Iacopino Vincent, Ozkalipci Onder, and Schlar Caroline. 1999. The manual on the effective investigation and documentation of torture and other cruel, inhuman or degrading treatment or punishment (the Istanbul Protocol). *United Nations,* 1999. http://www.ohchr.org/Documents/Publications/training8Revien.pdf [Retrieved January 15, 2014].

Jacobs, Uwe, Evans F. Barton, and Patsalides Beatrice. 2001a. "Principles of Documenting Psychological Evidence of Torture – Part I." *Torture, Quarterly Journal of Rehabilitation of Torture Victims and Prevention of Torture.* Vol. 11, No. 3, October, 11 (3): 85–89.

Jacobs, Uwe, Evans F. Barton, and Patsalides Beatrice. 2001b. "Principles of Documenting Psychological Evidence of Torture – Part II." *Torture, Quarterly Journal of Rehabilitation of Torture Victims and Prevention of Torture.* Vol. 11, No. 3, December, 11 (4): 100–102

Jacobs, Uwe and Vincent Iacopino. 2001. "Torture and Its Consequences: A Challenge to Clinical Neuropsychology." *Professional Psychology: Research and Practice* 32 (5): 458–464.

Jacobs, Uwe and Stuart Lustig. 2010. "Psychological and Psychiatric Opinions in Asylum Applications: Ten Frequently Asked Questions by Fact Finders." *Bender's Immigration Bulletin*, August 1, 15:1066–1069.

Knoll, J. and P. J. Resnick. 2006. "The Detection of Malingered Post-Traumatic Stress Disorder." *Psychiatry Clinical North America* 29(3): 629–47.

Lustig, Stuart 2008. "Symptoms of Trauma Among Political Asylum Applicants: Don't Be Fooled." *Hastings International and Comparative Law Journal* 31(2):725–734.

Lustig, Stuart, S. Kureshi, K. Delucchi, V. Iacopino, and S. Morse. 2008. "Asylum Grant Rates Following Medical Evaluations of Maltreatment Among Political Asylum Applicants in the United States." *Journal of Immigrant and Minority Health* 10(1):7–15.

Mehta, Suketa. 2011. "Annals of immigration: 'The asylum seeker'." *New Yorker Magazine*, 32–37.

Physicians for Human Rights. 2001. *Examining Asylum Seekers: A Health Professional's Guide to Medical and Psychological Evaluations of Torture*.

Physicians for Human Rights. 2012. *Examining Asylum Seekers: A Clinician's Guide to Physical and Psychological Evaluations of Torture and Ill Treatment*. New York: PHR.

Resnick, Phillip. 2003. "Guidelines for evaluation of malingering in P.T.S.D." In R. I. Simon, ed., *Posttraumatic Stress Disorder in Litigation*, 194. Washington, DC: American Psychiatric Publishing.

Resnick, Phillip, Sara West, and Joshua Payne. 2008. "Malingering of posttraumatic disorders." In R. Rogers, ed., *Clinical Assessment of Malingering and Deception: Third Edition*, 109–27. New York: Guilford Press.

Smith, Hawthorne. 2007. "Approach to the Client in a Psychological Evaluation." In H. Smith, A. Keller, D. Lhewa, eds., *Like a Refugee Camp on First Avenue: Insights and Experiences from the Bellevue/NYU Program for Survivors of Torture*. New York: Jacob and Valeria Langeloth Foundation, pp. 375–92.

Smith, Hawthorne, and Keller, Allen. 2007. "The Context in Which Treatment Takes Place: The Multi-Faceted Stressors Facing Survivors of Torture and Refugee Trauma." In H. Smith, A. Keller, and D. Lhewa, eds., *Like a Refugee Camp on First Avenue: Insights and Experiences from the Bellevue/NYU Program for Survivors of Torture*. New York: Jacob and Valeria Langeloth Foundation, 1–37.

Smith, Hawthorne, Kuck, Julia, and Beck, Janet. 2011. *Preparing the Mental Health Expert for Testimony*. Presented at the conference "Torture Survivors Seeking Asylum: The Intersection of Forensic Mental Health Evaluation and Legal Representation" sponsored by *the National Consortium for Torture Treatment Programs*, Los Angeles, California.

Souter, James. 2011. "Bogus Asylum Seekers? The Ethics of Truth Telling in the Asylum System." *Open Democracy*. http://www.opendemocracy.net/5050/james-souter/bogus-asylum-seekers-ethics-of-truth-telling-in-asylum-system [Retrieved January 15, 2014].

Sussan, N. 2006. In Session with Phillip J. Resnick, MD: Malingering of Psychiatric Symptoms. *Primary Psychiatry* 13(6): 35–8.

Vaughan, Megan. 1983. "Which Family." *Journal of African History* 24(2): 275–83.

9

Importing Forensic Biomedicine into Asylum Adjudication: Genetic Ancestry and Isotope Testing in the United Kingdom

Richard Tutton, Christine Hauskeller, and Steven Sturdy

When refugees apply for asylum, they have to relate a narrative of their persecution in their country of origin. Evaluating the veracity or otherwise of these narratives is central to the asylum adjudication process. Over the past decade or so, determination of national identity has become vitally important in assessing whether someone claiming the right to asylum is a legitimate refugee or an economic migrant. Border agencies have focused increasingly on the possibility that economic migrants might pose as citizens of particular countries in order to gain access to Britain as recognized refugees. This phenomenon has become known as "nationality swapping." Border control agencies have introduced several methods to eliminate supposed pretend asylum seekers. In this chapter we discuss the Human Provenance Pilot Project (HPPP) conducted in 2009–10 by the U.K. Border Agency (UKBA) that investigated the utility of genetic ancestry and isotope testing as means of corroborating refugees' nationality claims. At its launch, the HPPP was heavily criticized by leading scientists, journalists, and parliamentarians on scientific as well as ethical grounds. In response, the UKBA scaled it back to a small pilot study that came to an end in spring 2010. Over a year later, in June 2011, the UKBA finally announced that the tested techniques would not be introduced into asylum procedures, at least for the time being.[1]

The use of molecular biological techniques for determining nationality – an exclusively political category – is clearly a highly problematic endeavor. The fact that the UKBA should have taken an interest in using such technologies in the first place, and then persisted with trialing them in the face of concerted

[1] ACKNOWLEDGMENT: A different version of this chapter was earlier published as "Suspect Technologies: Forensic Testing of Asylum Seekers at the U.K. Border," *Ethnic and Racial Studies*, 37.5 (2014): 738–52. We are grateful to the editors and publishers for permission to publish the present version.

scientific opposition, appears at first sight to be rather surprising. However, closer analysis reveals that the Border Agency's turn to these technologies is quite in keeping with the increasingly prejudicial tenor of asylum policy and practice within the United Kingdom. As we show in this chapter, the molecular technologies of genetic ancestry and isotope testing had previously been employed for forensic purposes in criminal investigations, and they were imported into asylum adjudication directly from that context. Their adoption by the UKBA is indicative of a growing tendency on the part of the British immigration authorities to adopt forms of expert inquiry and knowledge production developed originally for purposes of criminal investigation, and to redirect that expertise to the work of challenging asylum seekers' personal testimony.

This chapter situates and examines these events in the context of changing immigration and asylum policies in what is often referred to as "Fortress Europe."[2] The entanglement of border control technologies and immigration policies and practices with discourses of race, national identity, and belonging has long been a focus of scholarly interest (Fox et al. 2012). Official and popular attitudes to those who request sanctuary have become dominated by a hermeneutic of suspicion. Public and policy discourse portrays them as mostly 'bogus' refugees who seek admission to the country for economic, not humanitarian reasons. This attitude shapes the practices and technologies of border control. We argue that the HPPP is only one move in a wider campaign to subject vulnerable individuals to biometric and other identification practices established in the treatment of crime suspects. This interpretation is supported by other researchers who have also pointed out how increasingly exclusionary immigration policies, and an increasingly close integration of immigration with criminal law, have tended toward de facto criminalization of asylum seekers in both Europe and North America (Arat-Koc 1999; Miller 2003; Silveira Gorski 2008; Schuster 2011). The importation of forms of expertise developed specifically for the purpose of investigating criminal behavior is part of a wider de facto criminalization of asylum applicants that suspends their basic human rights until proven innocent of lying and nationality fraud. Meanwhile, increasingly exclusionary border controls have fueled the business of human trafficking, because it has become so difficult for refugees to

---

[2] The language of "fortress Europe" is widely used, particularly by critics of E.U. immigration policy. For recent examples, see "Fortress Europe: How the E.U. Turns Its Back on Refugees," *Spiegel Online*, October 9, 2013, http://www.spiegel.de/international/europe/asylum-policy -and-treatment-of-refugees-in-the-european-union-a-926939.html [Retrieved December 20, 2013]; "Fortress Europe 'Miserably Failing' Syrian Refugees," *The Week*, December 13, 2013, http://www.theweek.co.uk/world-news/syria/56501/fortress-europe-miserably-failing-syrian-refugees [Retrieved December 20, 2013].

reach a safe country with minimal risk to personal safety and without loss of identity, dignity and the power of self-determination. While so far unsuccessful, the HPPP contributed to a vicious circle of criminalization and victimization of asylum seekers. The HPPP also shows how asylum seekers' testimonies of persecution, and of why and how they came into the country, are replaced more and more by impersonal methods of assessing eligibility. Border controls rely on new forms of expert testimony that distort the standards and principles originally envisioned by the process of refugee status determination.

THE RECENT HISTORY OF U.K. BORDER CONTROL

Although migration and providing refuge to victims of persecution are different legal, administrative, and moral categories, in the British context asylum and the wider debates about migration have become closely related in public discourse.[3] Both are highly politicized, and their history is worth outlining briefly in order to set the historical context of the HPPP. In the United Kingdom, the 1905 Aliens Act marked the inception of a modern apparatus of border control as a response to growing migration by Jews fleeing persecution in Eastern European countries. This and subsequent measures built up a distinction between British subjects and aliens, individuals who do not owe allegiance to the British crown. In the aftermath of World War II, United Nations Conventions on Human Rights (1948) and the Rights of Refugees (1951) were signed and ratified by the United Kingdom. These conventions enshrine the right to refuge and protection from persecution for all humans. In the 1950s and 1960s, however, the British economy faced a shortage of labor in certain areas and people from the Commonwealth, specifically from the Caribbean territories, were actively encouraged to migrate to Britain as guest workers. Analysis of Cabinet discussions of that time indicates that "colour was at the root of the government's objections to West Indian workers" migrating to Britain in the 1950s (Clayton 2012, p. 9). Despite such objections, tens of thousands of people migrated from Commonwealth states to Britain where they faced varying degrees of hostility. New laws were enforced to counter discrimination, whilst simultaneously a series of legislative interventions aimed at preventing the continued migration of people from certain

---

[3]   The right to seek asylum in another country is enshrined in international law, such as the 1951 United Nations Refugee Convention that defines a refugee as someone who 'owing to a well-founded fear of being persecuted for reasons of race, religion, nationality, membership of a particular social group or political opinion, is outside the country of his nationality, and is unable to, or owing to such fear, is unwilling to avail himself of the protection of that country' (UNHCR 2012).

Commonwealth countries were also enacted. The 1962 Commonwealth Immigrants Act distinguished between persons who were born in the United Kingdom or the Republic of Ireland and held passports issued by those countries and persons who did not. In practice, however, guidance provided to immigration officers indicated that the new law did not apply to white migrants from Australia, Canada, New Zealand, and South Africa who faced fewer obstacles in gaining entry. Subsequent legislation such as the 1968 Commonwealth Immigrants Act, the 1971 Immigration Act, and the 1981 British Nationality Act, led to a fundamental change in the principles on which citizenship and rights of migration were founded, away from place of birth (*jus soli*) to "blood relations" (*jus sanguinis*). The right to family in the Human Rights Convention is one pillar on which the immigration of family members was based, and led to the introduction of genetic testing to confirm biological kinship in the immigration context in Britain in the 1980s.

Since the early 1990s, the legitimacy of those applying for asylum has been a hot political issue and the perennial interest of right-wing tabloid journalism using an aggressive derogatory rhetoric. Journalistic commentators argue that the British tabloid press came increasingly to depict asylum seekers as a separate minority group.

> They have been made into scapegoats for a variety of society's current ills [. . .] To this end, editors have sought to forge a unity of viewpoint between the indigenous white population and second and third generation Afro-Caribbean and Asian immigrants in opposition to asylum-seekers, of whatever race or creed. (Greenslade 2005, p. 6)

In a context in which immigration policy has become increasingly concerned with distinguishing "deserving" from "undeserving" migrants, the status of asylum seekers has become particularly fraught (Flynn 2005; Sales 2005).

There have been various well-publicized interventions to "crack down" on "bogus asylum seekers" by both Conservative and Labour administrations, whose measures have included reducing the benefits given to asylum applicants and a firmer approach to the detention and deportation of rejected applicants (Campbell 2012). Steadily rising numbers between 1990 and 2000, and changes in regulation that prevent asylum seekers from earning their living and make them dependent on state welfare and benefits, led to massively rising public costs. In response, new policies were established including the detention of asylum applicants in detention centers if their claim is considered to be decided quickly. Moreover, under U.K. law, illegal entry into the country is now a criminal act. Consequently, use of the expertise and infrastructure provided by traffickers in order to arrive in a safe country further taints perceptions of migrants' integrity (Koser 2000). Official statistics show that the number of asylum applications to Britain has declined significantly over the last ten years, due in part, one might assume, to the effectiveness of some of these interventions. However, the debate about "bogus asylum seekers" has not lost force in public and policy discourses in a time of economic crisis and austerity measures.

British policies mirror those followed in other European countries (Geddes 2003; Flynn 2005). Developments in E.U. immigration policy since the early 1990s have tended to limit the rights of refugees to enter the E.U. in order to seek asylum, and the policy that visa and entry documents should be applied for in the relevant embassy in the home country prior to travel, rather than upon arrival in the United Kingdom, places additional barriers for those who face indifference, hostility, or persecution from the authorities in their home country (Guild 2010). Asylum seekers are increasingly suspected of illegitimately claiming political persecution (Lynn and Lea 2003) and individuals in need of refuge face bureaucratic procedures that make it more difficult to leave one's country and reach a safe destination. One result of bureaucratization and the tightening of immigration rules in Europe has been an increase asylum seekers' reliance on clandestine methods of entry (Schuster 2011). Those seeking asylum in Europe depend more and more on professional traffickers who are paid for providing transportation and often-forged passports and identity documents. Traffickers are 'experts' on immigration policies, suitable travel routes and border control practice and often choose the country of arrival according to recent policy developments and practicalities. This leads to the separation of families or friendship networks. Asylum seekers report in interviews that they feel a lack of control about which country they go to and how. This weakens their confidence and their chances of integration into a new culture and society (Healey 2006; Korac 2003).

In 2007, the British government reorganized its border control services and formed the U.K. Border Agency. This agency initiated a £1.2 billion "e-borders" program that accelerated the adoption of biometric and other new technologies in order to further enhance border control. The British government claimed that it was involved in "delivering the biggest shake-up of border security and the immigration system in a generation" (Cabinet Office 2009, p. 97). Nick Vaughan-Williams (2010) argues that identity management has become central to how the British Government has conceptualized border control. A 2007 U.K. Home Office White Paper states that "managing identity is fundamental" to effective border security and that the aim of the UKBA is to "fix people's identities at the earliest point practicable" (Anon. 2007). The systematic biometric control of all tourist or business overseas travel aims at combating identity fraud and detecting suspicious movements. The UKBA also introduced a new process for the adjudication of asylum claims, called the New Asylum Model, whereby a UKBA staff member assumes the role of case owner and is responsible for all the decisions taken on an asylum application until the person is granted or denied permission to stay. The case owner will conduct interviews with the applicant. A first interview aims to record details about how the applicant came to arrive in Britain and whether there was a relevant previous application for asylum either in Britain or another EU member state. A second interview, called the "asylum interview," follows in which the applicant has the opportunity to give an account of why she or he wishes to apply for asylum. The overwhelming majority of asylum applications are rejected at this stage. The applicant then has the right of appeal and to be heard by an independent immigration judge. As Anthony Good (2009) argues, the outcome of this process largely depends on the credibility of the applicant's own testimony regarding her or his history and reasons for arrival in Britain to claim asylum:

> When presenting their claims, most asylum applicants cannot produce documentary corroboration of their ill-treatment, and certainly cannot call as witnesses those who have persecuted them. Asylum decisions are therefore heavily dependent upon assessments of the credibility of their accounts, presented to the Home Office and the courts mainly in the forms of asylum interview transcripts and witness statements. (Good 2009:1)

In a context where it is increasingly assumed that a high proportion of applicants do not tell the truth about their reasons for seeking admission to the country, the process is heavily weighted toward finding reasons to doubt the applicant's testimony and reject the application.

Given the uncertainties involved in assessing asylum applicants' testimony, for some time now, the UKBA – along with border agencies in other countries – has sought other methods to inform decision making. A key method, in this respect, is the controversial technique of language analysis (see Kam's chapter in this volume). Since the early 2000s, it has become increasingly common for the UKBA to subcontract commercial firms to analyze the speech of asylum applicants, with the aim of determining whether they actually come from the country they claim (Campbell 2012). Since 2008, language analysis has been applied several thousand times to applicants presenting as Somalian refugees (Campbell 2012). Language analysis can be seen as a "technology of identification" aimed at establishing aspects of an applicant's identity without relying on their personal testimony.

In this context, the HPPP can be seen as an attempt to develop and implement additional technologies of identification that might potentially serve to establish nationality independently of such testimony and documentary evidence as asylum seekers can themselves provide. Justifying its investment in the HPPP, the UKBA indicated that a "significant percentage of asylum applicants" might be engaging in "nationality-swapping," in particular applicants from the East African region. Kenyan nationals were allegedly seeking to pass themselves off as Somalis. The HPPP focused specifically on asylum applicants from that area to determine whether isotope and DNA analysis could help to "identify at the outset of the asylum process those who are claiming under a false nationality" (UKBA 2009).

The HPPP involved two such technologies: genetic testing for biogeographical origins – often referred to simply as ancestry testing – and isotope testing. These technologies were trialed specifically as an additional test to support language testing, which had been shown to be vulnerable to legal challenge in appeal hearings. Genetic ancestry testing and isotope analysis were to be undertaken in cases where personal testimony and language analysis led UKBA officers to suspect that an individual who claimed to be from Somalia might actually be from another country. We now turn to an explanation of these technologies and the contexts in which they have developed.

TECHNOLOGIES OF IDENTIFICATION IN THE HPPP

One important issue that the case of the HPPP highlights is the uncritical way in which technologies that had yet to establish their validity and utility in the context of forensic science and criminal investigation were nonetheless adopted into the asylum context – initially, at least, on the assumption that they could be useful in evaluating 'live' asylum applications. In this section, we focus on the background to how genetic ancestry testing and isotope testing came to be adopted in the HPPP

It is important to understand how the genetic tests employed in the HPPP differ from other genetic technologies of identification. In the immigration context, DNA testing is regularly used to determine biological relationships between individuals. This well-established and well-validated test involves looking at the degree of similarity between the DNA of two individuals to determine whether they are biologically closely related, for instance as parent-child or siblings. Likewise, in forensic applications, routine DNA identification is based on simple matching of DNA profiles obtained from scene-of-crime DNA traces with those from suspects. In contrast, the genetic tests for ancestry and geographical origins trialed in the HPPP were significantly more complex, and the inferences that can be drawn from them far more tenuous.

Genetic ancestry tests emerged in the late 1990s out of decades of basic research on population genetics. They utilize knowledge of how genetic variations arise through mutation and accumulate within more or less isolated populations, which thus come to embody distinctive combinations of gene variants. By analyzing particular genetic variants present in an individual's DNA, it may therefore be possible to infer, with a reasonable degree of probability, that certain of that individual's ancestors were members of a particular biogeographical population. However, there are very clear constraints on the precision and certainty with which such inferences can be drawn. The ability to trace ancestry to any particular population depends upon how precisely that population has been characterized in genetic terms: ancestry tracing is only as good as the genetic reference databases on which it draws. The construction of such databases is informed by prior assumptions about what counts as a population, and biogeographic identities are thus inevitably clouded by ethnic/racial and geopolitical presuppositions. Moreover, because DNA variants are passed on through generations, it is difficult to infer just how recently an individual's ancestors lived in a particular region. Consequently, a biogeographic origin test may show that a particular individual has shared ancestors with members of a population that now lives predominantly in a particular location, but says nothing about that individual's own recent place of residence, and certainly offers no scientific mechanism for establishing her or his nationality.

Despite these constraints, however, genetic testing for ancestry and geographical origins has come to be widely used, not only as a research tool by scientists interested in historical population movements but also as a consumer service (Shriver and Kittles 2004). One important market is among private users interested in tracing their recent genealogical and ancestral history. The idea that genetic testing can help to throw light on an individual's "roots" has been widely popularized in the media. The experiences of individuals who have undergone such testing to discover more about their family histories and geographical origins provide compelling stories of personal identity and social history, and many such stories have featured in newspapers and magazine articles (Harmon 2007) and television programs (such as *Motherland: A Genetic Journey*, broadcast February 2003 on BBC television: see BBC 2003). As a result, hundreds of thousands of consumers have bought genetic ancestry tests over the past ten years (Wolinsky 2006, p. 1073).

The marketing, uptake, and effects of these tests have in turn been examined by social scientists. Some emphasize their scientific untrustworthiness, noting for instance that commercial genetic tests for biogeographical origins often do not take account of the large population movements that have taken place across Africa in the past two to three hundred years, and urging that this may have implications for the truth of the origin and identity stories that consumers build around such tests (Royal et al. 2010; Lee et al. 2009; Scully et al. 2013). Some suggest that such limitations are unimportant, as genetic ancestry testing is little more than a harmless recreational indulgence. Thus U.S. bioethicist Henry Greely concludes that genetic genealogy is "interesting but arguably not very important ... genealogy ... [is] rarely of real significance" (Greely 2008, p. 229). This has been very much the orthodox view: regulators and policy advisors have given little serious consideration to genetic ancestry testing, on the assumption that the ethical issues at stake are far less critical than those related to medical genetics (e.g., Human Genetics Commission 2003).

However, a growing number of social scientists argue that, despite its scientific and technical limitations, the dissemination of genetic ancestry testing into popular culture has the potential to effect far-reaching changes in ideas of identity, belonging, history and race (Bolnick et al. 2007; Elliott and Brodwin 2002; Skinner 2006; Nelson 2008; Tutton 2004; Nash 2004). In particular, they point to instances where genetic ancestry testing is used not just for recreational purposes, but for the express purpose of identifying membership of particular sociopolitical groups. For instance, such testing has been employed by Native Americans in the United States to determine tribal membership in ways that can exclude individuals who have traditionally been part of such tribes (Tallbear 2008; Beckenhauer 2003). In such cases, DNA testing is being used to redraw the boundaries around certain social and political identities, sometimes with profound implications for how individuals and groups think about themselves and for the life choices available to them. Meanwhile, forensic agencies have also taken an active interest in genetic ancestry tests as a possible means of identifying or eliminating suspects in criminal investigations. Notably, in Britain, the Forensic Science Service has looked into the geographical distribution of particular Y chromosome variants, and their association with particular surnames, as a means of using scene-of-crime samples to narrow down the range of likely suspects (Vince 2006).

Although genetic ancestry testing concentrates on tracing the genes of ancestors in contemporary human bodies, isotope testing is based on the way that the different environments in which an individual lives may leave distinctive traces in her or his body. The proportions of different isotopes of various chemical elements present in the environment vary from one locality to another. These elements are ingested in food and drinking water and are incorporated, over time, into body tissues. Consequently, assuming that a person consumes local food, water, and air, the proportions of different isotopes present in her or his tissues will mirror those in the place where he or she lives. Moreover, because different tissues are laid down at different times in a person's life, they embody a record of the person's diet, and her or his movements over time. Adult teeth, for instance, are largely laid down between the ages of four and twenty, and may thus provide an indication of where a person lived as a child or young adult. Bone tissues, by contrast, are replaced over a period of several years, whereas hair and nails are replaced within a matter of months, so provide an indication of a person's habitation or consumption within more recent time frames.

We should note that, since both the number of naturally occurring isotopes and the range of possible variation are small, many different places in the world share similar isotope profiles. Consequently, isotope testing cannot be used to specify a unique location but may be useful as a way of eliminating options from a range of possible locations. These limitations are reflected in the way that archaeologists have used isotope testing to reconstruct the life course and migration of Neolithic and early mediaeval individuals from well-preserved skeletons (Evans et al. 2006; Budd et al. 2004): the confidence with which such reconstructions may be made is greatly aided by the fact that population movements at that time generally occurred over relatively small distances, thus reducing the range of possible places of origin, and that people consumed almost exclusively local food and water.

By the early 2000s, isotope testing was also becoming incorporated into forensic techniques for tracing the origins of biological and chemical substances. Law enforcement agencies in North America and Europe formed networks with academic centers, forensic research laboratories and commercial laboratories to develop ways of applying isotope science to various aspects of law enforcement. Isotope analysis is now routinely used to authenticate the origins of certain imported foods such as honey. More importantly for security purposes, in 1999 the Forensic Explosives Laboratory (FEL) at Fort Halstead in Kent, England, was funded by the British Home Office to examine the utility of isotope ratios in the forensic analysis of explosives, with a view to tracing their movement through international terrorist networks (Doyle 2002).

Crucially for the story of the HPPP, genetic ancestry and isotope testing were used together for forensic purposes in the early 2000s in a rather unusual police investigation that became known as the Thames torso case. In September 2001, the Metropolitan Police began investigating a dismembered body of a young boy found in the river Thames in London. The unknown victim came to be known as "Adam." Within a few months, the police came to focus on the theory that Adam was the victim of a ritualistic killing, which the British media repeatedly reported as an "African ritual murder" (Sanders 2003, p. 58). Although a number of Africanist anthropologists consulted by the Metropolitan Police contested this framing of what happened to the boy, arguing a lack of evidence to support this account, the detectives pursued this line of inquiry (Ranger 2007; Sanders 2003). As well as visiting Nigeria and South Africa, they employed the services of population geneticists and geo-chemists to help them determine the boy's ancestry and place of origin. Mitochondrial DNA analysis indicated that he was probably of West African origin, while analysis of the strontium isotopes in his bones was consistent with him having grown up in a "small area in north-west Africa, probably a rural area near the city of Benin in south-western Nigeria" (in Ranger 2007, p. 272). As a result of a witness coming forward, police now believe they have identified the boy and have spoken to relatives still living in Nigeria (Quinn 2011). Though the perpetrators have never been found, the case generated consid-erable media interest and much of the original investigation was documented by a film crew and shown on British television.

A direct link can be drawn between this case and the HPPP. The detective in charge of the Thames torso investigation was Detective Inspector Will O'Reilly. He is credited with being responsible both for proposing the HPPP and for securing its funding from the British Foreign and Commonwealth Office (FCO) under its Returns and Reintegration Fund, with "full Ministerial support" (Douglas 2009). On retiring from the Metropolitan Police he became the project manager of the HPPP, and – it is claimed – went on to assist in the construction of "isotopic and ancestral DNA databases for the forensic use of law enforcement agencies worldwide" (Anon. 2012). It would appear that the HPPP was directly inspired by O'Reilly's experience of using these new and still relatively untested technologies of identification in the Adam torso case. We now consider whether these new technologies can appropriately be transferred to the assessment of asylum applications.

SUBSTITUTING BIOLOGY FOR NATIONALITY

Recent years have seen a massive intensification in the use of new technologies of identification – including biometrics and networked information technology as well as language analysis – not just for evaluating the credibility of asylum applicants, but for routine purposes of border control. Such technologies are concerned with identity, not as experienced by individuals but as assigned by impersonal, suspicious, and often hostile agencies. As Louise Amoore (2011) has argued, they diminish the agency of all who cross international borders, by depriving them of their right to tell their own stories (*see* also Feldman 2012). The use of biometric and linguistic technologies shifts the evidence from the applicant's personal narrative of persecution to seemingly objective means of assessing certain aspects of identity. However, such technologies of identification do not simply offer more objective means of confirming or disconfirming conventional identity claims. They actually redefine the social categories of identity on which immigration and asylum decisions are based. Thus, genetic family relationship testing replaces the social category of kinship with the biological category of genetic relatedness; as other observers have noted, since biological relatedness does not necessarily map onto kinship, for instance where children are adopted, this may do violence to family relationships and cause renewed distress to those seeking asylum (Heinemann and Lemke 2013). The HPPP went even further in seeking to employ biological categories of ancestry and life history as a proxy for the social category of nationality. Criticism of the HPPP has focused primarily on the viability of this substitution.

With regard to isotope testing, critics pointed out that archaeologists and forensic investigators are typically able to base their inferences about individuals' origins and movements on measurements from a range of tissues, including teeth and bone as well as hair and fingernails. By contrast, UKBA officials could not take tooth or bone samples from asylum applicants, so were limited to observations of hair and fingernails, which only provide information about an applicant's likely diet over a short period of time. This placed very severe limits on what can be inferred from such measurements. Asylum applicants often spend protracted periods away from their home country before arriving at their country of destination. Many Somali refugees, for instance, spend years in refugee camps outside their home country, while those who resort to human trafficking networks may spend long periods being moved from one place to another before being delivered to Britain. Even in instances when individuals come directly to Britain from their home country, their diet in the previous months could often be heavily supplemented with imported food, particularly in countries such as Somalia that receive significant quantities of food aid. All of these factors will mean that the isotopes present in asylum applicants' hair and nails may bear little relationship to those found in their home country. In consequence, it is difficult to see how isotope analysis could provide meaningful information about the origins of asylum applicants subjected to the HPPP It might, however, provide evidence consistent with an individual having recently spent time in another country outside their country of origin – which the UKBA typically sees as sufficient reason to reject an asylum application, as it assumes that the applicant can safely be returned to that other country.

Moreover, the use of isotope testing to indicate whether a person's biological makeup is consistent with them having spent time in a particular region depends on having sufficiently detailed information about the distribution of the relevant environmental isotopes across that region. Such data for Somalia are very sketchy; while the situation there makes it unlikely that accurate mapping will be undertaken in the foreseeable future. Similar objections have been made to the use of genetic ancestry testing under the HPPP. Critics pointed out that there is little detailed information about the genetics of Somali populations; the present political situation effectively prohibits the kind of research that would be necessary to generate such information. Even if such research were possible, significant and often chaotic population movements prompted by the political situation would likely render the resulting data unreliable in a relatively short time. The UKBA sought to get around these problems by compiling information on the genetics of various Kenyan populations, on the grounds that the majority of "bogus" Somali asylum seekers were thought to come from Kenya – but without proper knowledge of the genetic similarities, differences, and overlaps between Kenyan and Somali populations, such information is meaningless.

This leads to another even more fundamental issue: namely, that biological information about population genetics or environmental circumstances has no necessary relationship to the social categories of national identity and citizenship. As the journal *Nature* put it, "the idea that genetic variability follows man-made national boundaries is absurd" (Nature 2009). Exactly the same point can be made about language analysis (Campbell 2013). On the one hand, national borders have often been drawn in ways that cut across existing population groupings – as for instance in Eastern Africa, where ethnic Somalis are found on both sides of the border that divides Somalia from Kenya. On the other hand, national borders rarely represent a complete barrier to human migration and relations, and such migrations may be especially large in war-torn areas such as the Horn of Africa. In sum, genetic testing, and information about probable place of recent residence provide no guide to nationality.

CONCLUSION

The HPPP ended on March 31, 2010. Initially, the UKBA had promised to publish a full review of the project. In the event, no such review was ever conducted. By way of explanation, the UKBA responded to a Freedom of Information request by one of the authors as follows:

Following the conclusion of the pilot, a decision was taken within the U.K. Border Agency not to take forward DNA/Isotope testing for country of origin identification purposes in the foreseeable future. On the basis of this decision, it was agreed that resources would not be devoted carrying out an evaluation of the pilot at this point in time. If a decision to resume Familial DNA or Country of Origin testing is taken in the future, further consideration will be given to the scientific, legal and ethical basis on which it would operate. The Home Office would engage with relevant experts to address any concerns that may be raised regarding the use of this technique. (Martin 2011)

The UKBA response also detailed that 198 familial relationship tests were carried out over 76 family groups, while a total of 38 individuals were tested as part of the "country of origin" element of the HPPP (Martin 2011). It is notable that, while the UKBA states that it has no plans to develop these techniques in the "foreseeable future," it leaves open the possibility that the U.K. government may decide "to resume . . . Country of Origin testing . . . in the future."

At first sight, this appears to be a very odd response. Given that a wide range of experts, including population geneticists and environmental chemists as well as lawyers and social scientists, had argued that the scientific assumptions on which the HPPP was founded are fundamentally flawed, why did the UKBA not acknowledge this criticism by definitively ruling out the possibility of using molecular techniques to determine nationality in future? The answer, we would argue, lies in the way the UKBA frames aims and means of border control more generally. The HPPP was indicative of a broader set of trends by which technologies, practices, and modes of thought from the context of criminal investigation have come to shape the asylum system. The sociologists Robin Williams and Paul Johnson have argued persuasively that the establishment and use by U.K. police of the forensic National DNA Database should be seen as part of a larger paradigm shift in policing: from a criminal justice paradigm, premised on a concern to deliver justice equally to all citizens, to a crime management paradigm, concerned rather with identifying and managing what is taken to be an inherently criminal element within society (Williams and Johnson 2008). According to Williams and Johnson, the routine use of technologies of identification like the National DNA Database has been a vital element in realizing the crime management paradigm, by providing an effective means of both identifying and incriminating that criminal element.

In that light, the HPPP appears to be part of a similar shift in asylum procedures: from a humanitarian paradigm motivated by a concern to provide shelter for the victims of human rights abuses, to a border control paradigm concerned with restricting the movement of would-be immigrants. In the border control case as in the crime management case, new technologies of identification provide a means of identifying and excluding suspect individuals from the rights and privileges enjoyed by ordinary citizens. Moreover, these parallels are more than just accidental, or attributable to some more general shift in government ideology. They also involve direct exchange of technology and expertise between the respective government agencies. The HPPP was actively promoted and subsequently managed by ex-Detective Inspector Will O'Reilly, who had previously employed the same technologies of identification in forensic police work. Moreover, the UKBA anticipated that the results of the HPPP would eventually be evaluated by the Forensic Science Regulator, an ombudsman responsible for ensuring that forensic services meet appropriate standards of scientific quality (Vorhaus 2009). In effect, the HPPP marked a distinct convergence of personnel, technology and practice between policing and border control. Seen in this light, the HPPP was clearly a further step in the de facto criminalization of asylum applicants that we described at the beginning of this chapter.

Once we appreciate this, we can begin to understand why the UKBA remained relatively unmoved by criticism from scientists and others. What matters, from a border control perspective, is not so much the need to distinguish legitimate from illegitimate asylum applicants, but rather the need to manage and control the flow of individuals into the country. The UKBA's attitude toward the new molecular technologies of identification trialed in the HPPP reflects this perspective. Faced with concerted criticism of the scientific viability of the HPPP, the UKBA responded, not by mobilizing contrary scientific arguments, but by raising a very different point: whatever the scientific case, the HPPP had at least proved to be an effective deterrent, as measured by a significant reduction in the number of asylum claims during the time it was in operation.[4] This response is telling. It is of course impossible to say how many of those deterred by the additional barriers imposed under the HPPP were legitimate applicants and how many were bogus. But as far as the UKBA was concerned, that seems to have been beside the point. What mattered was that application numbers had fallen. This has implications for what was expected of the new technologies of identification. In order to be of use in restricting the influx of asylum seekers, it was not necessary for those technologies to provide an accurate or reliable means of determining the nationality of any individual. All that was required was that they be effective in challenging and undermining the personal testimony on which

---

[4] Will O'Reilly from the UKBA made this claim at a meeting with members of the Human Genome Commission (HGC) in Hinxton, Cambridge, in February 2010 (HGC 2010).

asylum applications are based. Given the presumption that most asylum seekers are illegitimate, the policy aims to deter all those from applying who may find their prospect of being accepted improved elsewhere, independent of whether or not they are genuine refugees.

In effect, these molecular biotechnologies and other tests only serve as "technologies of suspicion" (Campbell 2004), without having to meet the higher standards of technical certainty required of technologies of truth in science and judicial proceedings. That the UKBA and the forensic experts with whom they worked chose not to engage with the criticisms of external scientific experts suggests that it was the former standards that they worked to, not the latter.

The priorities behind the introduction of the HPPP are evident: it was motivated at least as much by a desire to discourage asylum seekers from applying as by any concern to identify and provide refuge for legitimate refugees. The use of new technologies of identification under the HPPP and the highly selective attitude toward different forms of technical expertise demonstrated by the UKBA were entirely in keeping with this orientation. In the event, it appears that concerted and sustained criticism ultimately led the Border Agency to shelve the use of genetic and isotope testing for country of origin. But as we have seen, the Agency also declined to foreclose the possibility that such use will be revived in the future. Meanwhile, the political impetus to further restrict immigration into the United Kingdom, including admission of asylum seekers, persists – and, with it, the motivation to adopt new technologies of identification to challenge the testimony of asylum applicants. Consequently, the HPPP stands as a salutary warning of the ways in which new technologies are increasingly being used at international borders as means of disempowering the vulnerable. But more than that, the way that the UKBA has responded to criticism by scientists and other external experts serves as a reminder that expertise and the salience of technical arguments depends on context: within the context of U.K. border control, certain kinds of argument and expertise clearly count for more than others. If the use of new technologies to deny the rights of refugees is to be countered, that context, and its implications for the politics and deployment of expertise, needs to be understood.

REFERENCES

Amoore, Louise. 2011. "Data Derivatives." *Theory, Culture & Society* 28(6): 24–43.
Anonymous. 2007. "Securing the U.K. Border: Our Vision and Strategy for the Future." London: The Home Office.

Anonymous. 2012. "Will O'Reilly." Speaker biography, International Association of Women Police. http://www.iawp2012.org/conference/speakers.html [Retrieved September 1, 2013].

Arat-Koc, Sedef. 1999. "Neo-Liberalism, State Restructuring and Immigration: Changes in Canadian Policies in the 1990s." *Journal of Canadian Studies* 34(2):31–56.

BBC. 2003. "Long Lost Roots of Black Britons Revealed by Groundbreaking BBC TWO Documentary." http://www.bbc.co.uk/pressoffice/pressreleases/stories/2003/02_february/05/motherland.shtml [Retrieved February 13, 2013].

Beckenhauer, Eric. 2003. "Redefining Race: Can Genetic Testing Provide Biological Proof of Indian Ancestry?" *Stanford Law Review* 56:161–90.

Bolnick, Deborah A., Duana Fullwiley, Troy Duster, Richard S. Cooper, Joan H. Fujimura, Jonathan Kahn, Jay S. Kaufman, Jonathan Marks, Ann Morning, Alondra Nelson, Pilar Ossorio, Jenny Reardon, Susan M. Reverby, and Kimberly TallBear. 2007. "The Science and Business of Genetic Ancestry Testing." *Science* 318(5849):399–400.

Budd, Paul, Andrew Millard, Carolyn Chenery, Sam Lucy, and Charlotte Roberts. 2004. "Investigating Population Movement by Stable Isotope Analysis: A Report from Britain." *Antiquity* 78(299):127–41.

Cabinet Office. 2009. "The National Security Strategy of the United Kingdom: Update 2009, Security for the Next Generation." London: The Stationary Office.

Campbell, Nancy D. 2004. "Technologies of Suspicion: Coercion and Compassion in Post-Disciplinary Surveillance Regimes." *Surveillance & Society* 2(1):78–92.

Campbell, John. 2012. "Language Analysis in the United Kingdom's Refugee Status Determination System: Seeing Through Policy Claims about 'Expert Knowledge'." *Ethnic and Racial Studies* 36(4):1–21.

Clayton, Gina. 2012 *Textbook on Immigration and Asylum Law* (5th ed.). Oxford: Oxford University Press.

Martin, Douglas. 2009. "Letter to stakeholders: Human Provenance Pilot Project." Croydon: U.K. Border Agency.

Doyle, Sean. 2002. "Stable Isotope Ratio Profiling: The Challenge and the Vision." *Network Developing Forensic Applications of Stable Isotope Ratio Mass Spectrometry Conference*. Brands Hatch, UK, pp. 5–6.

Elliott, Carl and Paul Brodwin. 2002. "Identity and Genetic Ancestry Tracing." *British Medical Journal* 325(7378):1469–71.

Evans, Jane, Nick Stoodley, and Carolyn Chenery. 2006. "A Strontium and Oxygen Isotope Assessment of a Possible 4th Century Immigrant Population in a Hampshire Cemetery, Southern England." *Journal of Archaeological Sciences* 33(2):265–72.

Feldman, Gregory. 2012. *The Migration Apparatus: Security, Labor and Policymaking in the European Union*. Stanford, CA: Stanford University Press.

Flynn, Don. 2005. "New Borders, New Management: The Dilemmas of Modern Immigration Policies." *Ethnic and Racial Studies* 28(3):463–90.

Fox, Jon E., Laura Moroşanu, and Eszter Szilassy. 2012. "The Racialization of the New European Migration to the U.K." *Sociology* 46(4):680–95.

Geddes, A. 2003. *The Politics of Migration and Immigration in Europe*. London: Sage.

Good, Anthony. 2009. "The Taking and Making of Asylum Claims: Credibility Assessments in the British Asylum Courts." Keynote Lecture, *Seeking Refuge:*

Caught Between Bureaucracy, Lawyers, and Public Indifference, ESRC-funded Conference, School of Oriental and African Studies, London, April 17, 2009.

Greely, Henry T. 2008. "Genetic Genealogy: Genetics Meets the Marketplace." In Barbara Koenig, Sandra Soo-Jin Lee, and Sarah S. Richardson, eds., *Revisiting race in the genomic age*. New Brunswick, NJ: Rutgers University Press, pp. 215–35.

Greenslade, Roy. 2005. *Seeking Scapegoats: The Coverage of Asylum in the U.K. Press.* London: Institute for Public Policy Research.

Guild, Elspeth and Didier Bigo. 2010. "The Transformation of European Border Controls." In Bernard Ryan and Valsamis Mitsilegas, eds., *Extraterritorial Immigration Control: Legal Challenges*, edited by Leiden: Martinus Nijhoff, pp. 257–80.

Harmon, Amy. 2007. "Genetic Testing + Abortion = ???" *New York Times*, May 13. http://www.nytimes.com/2007/05/13/weekinreview/13harm.html [Retrieved February 13, 2013].

Healey, Ruth L. 2006. "Asylum Seekers and Refugees: A Structuration Theory Analysis of their Experiences in the U.K." *Population, Space and Place*, 12.4:257–71.

Heinemann, Torsten and Thomas Lemke. 2013. "Suspect Families: DNA Kinship Testing in German Immigration Policy." *Sociology* 47(4):810–26.

Human Genetics Commission. 2010. "Minutes of Meeting Between the HGC and Officials from the UK Border Agency, 10 February 2010." http://webarchive.nationalarchives.gov.uk/20110504083424/http://www.hgc.gov.uk/Client/document.asp?DocId=273&CAtegoryId=8 [Retrieved June 24, 2014].

Korac, Maja. 2003. "Integration and How We Facilitate It: A Comparative Study of Settlement Experiences of Refugees in Italy and the Netherlands." *Sociology* 37(1):51–68.

Koser, Khalid. 2000. "Asylum Policies, Trafficking and Vulnerability." *International Migration* 38(3): 91–111.

Lee, Sandra Soo-Jin, Deborah A. Bolnick, Troy Duster, Pilar Ossorio, and Kimberly TallBear. 2009. "The Illusive Gold Standard in Genetic Ancestry Testing." *Science* 325(5936): 38–9.

Lynn, Nick and Susan Lea. 2003. "'A Phantom Menace and the New Apartheid': The Social Construction of Asylum-Seekers in the United Kingdom." *Discourse Society* 14(4): 425–52.

Martin, Douglas. 2011. "Response to Freedom of Information request." London: UKBA

Miller, Teresa A. 2003. "Citizenship and Severity: Recent Immigration Reforms and the New Penology." *Georgetown Immigration Law Journal* 17: 611–16.

Nash, Catherine. 2004. "Genetic Kinship." *Cultural Studies* 18(1): 1–33.

Nature. 2009. "Editorial. Genetics Without Borders." *Nature* (October 8) 461: 697.

Nelson, Alondra. 2008. "Bio Science." *Social Studies of Science* 38(5): 759–83.

Quinn, Ben. 2011. "Police to Fly to Nigeria Following New Lead in Thames Torso Case." *The Guardian*, March 29.

Ranger, Terence. 2007. "Scotland Yard in the Bush: Medicine Murders, Child Witches, and the Construction of the Occult: A Literature Review." *Africa* 77(2): 272–83.

Royal, Charmaine D., John Novembre, Stephanie M. Fullerton, David B. Goldstein, Jeffrey C. Long, Michael J. Bamshad, and Andrew G. Clark. 2010. "Inferring Genetic Ancestry: Opportunities, Challenges, and Implications." *The American Journal of Human Genetics* 86(5): 661–73.

Sales, Rosemary. 2005. "Secure Borders, Safe Haven: A Contradiction in Terms?" *Ethnic and Racial Studies* 28(3): 445–62.

Sanders, Todd. 2003. "Imagining the Dark Continent: The Met, the Media and the Thames Torso." *Cambridge Anthropology* 23(3): 53–66.

Schuster, Liza. 2011. "Turning Refugees into 'Illegal Migrants': Afghan Asylum Seekers in Europe." *Ethnic and Racial Studies* 34(8): 1392–407.

Scully, Marc, Turi King, and Steven D. Brown. 2013. "Remediating Viking Origins: Genetic Code as Archival Memory of the Remote Past." *Sociology* 47(5): 873–90.

Shriver, Mark D. and Rick A. Kittles. 2004. "Genetic Ancestry and the Search for Personalized Genetic Histories." *Nature Reviews Genetics* 5(8): 611–18.

Silveira Gorski, Héctor C., Cristina Fernández, and Alejandra Manavella. 2008. "A Right-Based Approach to Migration Policies in a Context of Emergencies: 'Expelling States' and Semi-persons in the European Union." Barcelona: University of Barcelona. http://www.libertysecurity.org/IMG/pdf_deliverable _dic_2008.pdf [Retrieved 13 February 2013].

Skinner, David. 2006. "Racialised Futures: Biologism and the Changing Politics of Identity." *Social Studies of Science* 36(3): 459–88.

Tallbear, Kimberly. 2008. "Native-American-DNA.coms: In Search of Native American Race and Tribe." In Barbara Koenig, Sandra Soo-Jin Lee, and Sarah S. Richardson, eds., *Revisiting Race in a Genomic Age*. New Brunswick, NJ: Rutgers University Press, pp. 235–52.

Tutton, Richard. 2004. "'They Want to Know Where they Came From': Population Genetics, Identity, and Family Genealogy." *New Genetics and Society* 23(1): 105–20.

UKBA. 2009. "Nationality Swapping – Isotope and DNA Testing (Annex B)." http://www.genomicsnetwork.ac.uk/media/nationality-swapping-DNA-testing.pdf [Retrieved September 24, 2013].

Vaughan-Williams, Nick. 2010. "The U.K. Border Security Continuum: Virtual Biopolitics and the Simulation of the Sovereign Ban." *Environment and Planning D: Society and Space* 28(6): 1071–83.

Vince, Gaia. 2006. "Y Chromosomes Give the Name Away." *New Scientist – Science in Society*. http://www.newscientist.com/article/dn8757-y-chromosomes-give-the-name -away.html [Retrieved February 13, 2013].

Vorhaus, Dan. 2009. "The Human Provenance Project Attempts to Unring the Bell." *Genomics Law Report*, October 7. http://www.genomicslawreport.com/index.php/ tag/human-provenance-pilot-project/ [Retrieved September 24, 2013].

Williams, Robin and Paul Johnson. 2008. *Genetic Policing: The Use of DNA in Criminal Investigations*. Cullompton: Willan Publishing.

Wolinsky, Howard. 2006. "Genetic Genealogy Goes Global." *EMBO Reports* 7(11): 1072–4.

10

"Health Tourism" or "Atrocious Barbarism"? Contextualizing Migrant Agency, Expertise, and Medical Humanitarian Practice

Benjamin N. Lawrance

A TALE OF TWO KIDNEYS

On July 24, 2013, Roseline Onoshoagbe Akhalu was celebrating. She had just won her second appeal against deportation to Nigeria by the United Kingdom Border Agency (UKBA). Judge Southern, on behalf of the Upper Tribunal, stated, "the circumstances here were, if not truly unique, so exceptional as to stand out from the ordinary run of cases where a claimant complains of being disadvantaged by a comparative lack of medical care in his or her own country" ([2013] UKUT 400 (IAC) §53).[1] Removal to Nigeria was deemed "disproportionate," and a result it is now likely that Akhalu will be able to remain permanently in the United Kingdom, and continue her life. The relationships established with her physicians and the "ongoing therapeutic relationships" with National Health Service (NHS) providers were reckoned significant enough that she had a right, under Article Eight of the European Convention on Human Rights (ECHR), to a private life, thus safeguarding her claim to residency and continued medical care (Toal 2014).

Akhalu's victory was a remarkable conclusion to a long sequence of medical and legal ordeals. Akhalu first came to the United Kingdom in 2004 with a financial scholarship for a Masters degree in International Development. She left behind in Nigeria no immediate family; her husband had died of a brain tumor several years earlier, and they were childless. But while undertaking her studies, she was diagnosed with kidney failure. Several years of treatment ensued, concluding, or so she thought with a successful transplant in 2009. But, like many transplant patients, Akhalu is destined for a lifetime

---

[1] [2013] UKUT 400 (IAC). July 24, 2013. http://www.bailii.org/uk/cases/UKUT/IAC/2013/%5B2013%5D_UKUT_400_iac.html [Retrieved January 20, 2014].

of immunosuppressant pharmaceuticals. Whereas she won her appeal to remain in 2012, the UKBA challenged the ruling, and argued that it was not the responsibility of the United Kingdom to provide health care to aliens. Akhalu's legal team marshaled vital country conditions reports to argue that comparable medical treatment would be difficult to obtain in Nigeria, and beyond the means of a person with such a limited earning capacity, and that removal would constitute a "disproportionate" burden.

Akhalu's experience differed greatly from that of Ama Sumani only six years earlier. On March 19, 2008, Sumani died in Korle Bu Teaching Hospital, Accra, Ghana, from renal complications caused from bone cancer. She was forty-two years old. Sumani, a mother of two, first came to the United Kingdom in 2003 with a visitor's visa with hopes of obtaining a degree in economics. She soon applied for change of status to a student visa and attempted to stay in the United Kingdom by enrolling in a banking course in Cardiff, Wales. Her poor English skills and low educational level prevented her from enrolling. Upon returning from a brief trip to Ghana in 2005 to attend a memorial for her late husband, Sumani learned that her student visa had been revoked because she had violated reporting requirements.

In January 2006, Sumani was diagnosed with myeloma, an aggressive cancer affecting the bone marrow. By January 2008, the cancer replicated and led to serious health problems, including kidney failure. After forgoing a medically recommended transplant, doctors began kidney dialysis in order to prolong her life. At the same time, however, efforts were untaken to remove her to Ghana. Despite the pleas of lawyers and doctors, the predecessor of the UKBA, the Borders and Immigration Agency (BIA), decided that because Sumani had knowingly overstayed her visa, she was to be removed from the country (Travis 2008). Whereas Sumani's legal counsel confirmed that Sumani conceded her removal was fair, publically her advocates pleaded for consideration under Article Three of the ECHR prohibiting cruel and unusual punishment, a claim falling outside remit of the refugee conventions. They sought "humanitarian consideration" for permission to access medical treatment. They argued that to deport her was effectively a death sentence. They noted that she could not afford dialysis treatment in Ghana, which cost more than £8,000 (approximately $13,000 in 2014) a year, but presented no compelling country conditions data. By contrast, Lin Homer, the BIA Chief Executive, observed that Sumani's case was "not exceptional" (Ford 2008). And to the very last, BIA officials insisted her forced migration was not a "deportation" because her expired visa voided any legal status in the United Kingdom (BBC 2008).

INTRODUCTION

Akhalu's and Sumani's narratives may be viewed as two provisional bookends to a drama continuing to unfold in the United Kingdom, and indeed throughout the European Union, concerning attempts by African migrants seeking protection and the right to reside temporarily or permanently in order to access medical care. At one extreme, the Nigerian Akhalu prevailed with an Article Eight "proportionality" claim and is now able to reside in the United Kingdom and continue her life-sustaining medical therapies. At the other extreme, the Ghanaian Sumani failed with an Article Three "exceptionality" claim, was subsequently removed from the United Kingdom and from life-preserving medical care, and promptly died. What made it possible for Akhalu to win her claim? Why did Sumani fail? To be sure, they made distinctive claims, their personal circumstances differed greatly, and they faced different judges; but importantly Akhalu presented detailed country conditions evidence to support her claims.

This chapter attempts to understand the different paths taken by these two women, and how they arrived at remarkably different outcomes, by focusing on the vital role of expert evidence in non convention human rights-based claims routinely adjudicated by the same judges who consider refugee claims. The legal terrain surrounding human rights-based claims, a sibling of asylum and refugee claims governed by the refugee conventions, is rapidly evolving. Rulings in U.K. and European courts are transforming rights ideology, and indeed the enforcement and protection of rights more broadly. Like asylum and refugee claims, concealed at the heart of many human rights–claim determinations, such as those of Akhalu and Sumani, are observations about country conditions based on reports that interpret the specific biomedical needs of claimants within the context of medical provision in countries of origin. Here I argue that in engaging the capacity of country conditions experts to interpret and contextualize specialized medical and psychiatric knowledge, *transnational medical emergencies argued as human rights-based claims* offer a fruitful avenue to dialog with the current state of scholarship about medical humanitarianism.

Previously I explored how human rights claimants become *detached* from the biomedical narration of their own deteriorating conditions in the context of their attempts to remain in the United Kingdom, and how expert testimony *re-tethers* specific claims (Lawrance 2013). I employed the term "detachment" to explain the process whereby, in the context of the adversarial nature of protection claim adjudication, claimants, such as Sumani, are separated from the biomedical specificities of real and present illnesses. To counteract detachment, a carefully crafted country conditions report "re-tethers" the personal claimant's narrative to the bodily-lived reality of the claimant.

By examining the nature of medical or psychiatric treatments and the actual capacity of the origin state to provide the prescribe care plans envisioned by licensed physicians, the country conditions expert serves a powerful function documenting the empirical basis for a human rights–based claim.

In this chapter, I further develop this argument by considering two real-life examples of individuals who advanced human rights claims, one of which prevailed with the assistance of country conditions expertise. I first contemplate how political rhetoric and news media about individuals who seek humanitarian medical care by advancing human rights claims mirror contemporary debates in the scholarship of medical humanitarianism. Whereas advocates for Sumani and others like her may decry the removal of ailing migrants as "atrocious barbarism," the British authorities responsible for border securitization and migration enforcement, and a considerable sector of the public and news media, routinely portray such individuals as "health tourists." I then consider the current legal state of play for gravely ill migrants in the United Kingdom, and parse the language of judicial determinations pertaining to "exceptionality" and "proportionality" in the consideration of human rights-based claims, including that of Akhalu. I draw on several recent anonymous examples of human rights-based claims seeking humanitarian medical access for which I provided expert country conditions evidence to make sense of the type of detail and argument required, and the nature of the empirical evidence for a country conditions report.

RHETORICAL MIRRORS OF MEDICAL HUMANITARIAN DEBATES

As a critical scholarly subfield, medical humanitarianism has experienced an upsurge of attention in recent years. Whereas medical humanitarianism was viewed until quite recently by some rather cynically as a militarized outgrowth of the "new humanitarianism" made possible by the collapse of the Cold War status quo, a variety of new approaches to define the terrain offer important avenues for scholarly intervention (Chandler 2001). The metaphorical "book-ends" presented by the attempts by Sumani and Akhalu to frame their human rights-based claims as humanitarian medical emergencies open an important transnational and rights-based set of issues that dialog with medical humanitarian scholarly debate, news media, and political rhetoric.

At least two somewhat diverging views have arisen over the course of the past decade as efforts to define medical humanitarianism have accelerated. First, there are scholars who see medical humanitarian action as a "reflection" of sociopolitical factors structuring health risks prior to crisis or emergency (Farmer 2003; Chung 2012). Early work in this vein examined the historical evolution of humanitarian medicine with the perspective of a practitioner (Fox 1995). More recently this approach highlights the "moral imperative" informing the medicine of humanitarian action (Ticktin 2011, p. 85). As Miriam Ticktin states, "humanitarianism is about the exception rather than the rule, about generosity rather than entitlement" (2006, p. 45). This approach unpacks humanitarian medical act(s) to expose a variety of ironies, inequalities, inadequacies, and insecurities. It recognizes the political action embodied in humanitarianism, beyond the myopia of international human- itarian law focused on war and civil conflict (de Torrente 2004). With an outside perspective, looking in, this approach explores the range of motiva- tions that drive physicians to provide care (Castañeda 2011) as the complexity of humanitarian claims alters the medical landscape.

Not quite in opposition are a second group of scholars who scrutinize the "application" of care (Abramowitz and Panter-Brick 2014, p. 1). Still building on the narrower empiricism of practitioners, such as Brauman (2009), who view medical humanitarianism as medicine for "marginalized people" hit by "crisis" or "deprived of access," this second camp focuses on the "delivery" of "health-related services" by NGOs and other agencies in the context or post- context of "complex emergencies" involving massive refugee displacement (Lewando Hundt et al. 2004). The dynamism of this branch of medical anthropological scholarship today owes much to a rich ethnography of humanitarian practice conveying an internal perspective looking out. The comparative method at the core of ethnographic practice functions as a "distinct space of inquiry," and as a window to the wider social and cultural meaning of health and welfare (Abramowitz and Panter-Brick 2014, p. 2).

This dichotomy in medical humanitarian scholarship finds an unlikely mirror in prevailing news media accounts, public reactions, and political rhetoric. The removal of Sumani was routinely cast by critics in the media and the public at large as a reflection of the immorality of the United Kingdom's immigration regime and a disavowal of a long-standing British tradition of humanitarian care and social responsibility. Before her deporta- tion, an editorial in the leading British medical journal sharply criticized the action as "atrocious barbarism" (*The Lancet* 2008, p. 178). Petitions, signed by hundreds of doctors, called on the government to reject proposed regulations abolishing the right of failed asylum seekers to seek medical help from the NHS (Jackson 2008).[2] Church leaders decried the "moral example" conveyed

---

[2]   See, for example, Editorial, "Treating failed asylum seekers in the NHS" *BMJ* (2009) 338: b1614; and letters received in response; BMA Ethics Department, "Access to Health Care for Asylum Seekers and Refused Asylum Seekers." (September 2008): 1–2. http://www.bma.org.uk/ images/asylumhealthcare2008_tcm41-175519.pdf [Retrieved March 29, 2013].

by such a "breach of basic human rights" (Wales Online 2008). *The Guardian* noted, with dramatic irony, that Sumani had died "two hours before friends rang with the news that they had found a U.K. doctor willing to treat her" (Gray 2008). Reactions to attempts to remove Akhalu echoed this moral framework. The OpenDemocracy.net blog, "Our Kingdom," reprinted a letter from Akhalu detailing how she was denied access to a bathroom by a private contractor on her way to Yarl's Wood detention facility, forced to urinate in her pants, and then made to sit in wet clothes, resulting in a urinary tract infection (Madill 2012). Journalistic accounts focused on the "repugnant" desire to remove an ailing widow to "a certain and lonely death" (White 2013).

By contrast, the "application of care" medical humanitarian paradigm advanced by Abramowitz and Panter-Brick (2014) is mirrored by fraught political rhetoric decrying Sumani and Akhalu as classic examples of "health tourism." Without regard for the facts that Akhalu entered the United Kingdom on a student visa, and that in November 2012 First-Tier Tribunal Judge Saffer concluded that "there is nothing to suggest she was aware of her illness before she came here or that she is a health tourist," "Our Kingdom" blog public comments leapt to untenable conclusions (Saffer cited in ([2013] UKUT 400 (IAC) §19)). For example, one public commentator questioned whether "any seriously ill person who manages to set foot in Britain should be cared for at taxpayer's expense for life," and whether "British taxpayers [are] obliged to pay the medical bills of any visitor who falls ill while here, for the rest of their lives" (MacDougall 2013). Such attitudes resonate in news media "sensationalism" (Stevens 2010, p. 369).

The broader national context is also instructive. Unsubstantiated allegations of widespread "health tourism" have provoked policy changes in the United Kingdom. In late 2013, the U.K. Home Secretary, Theresa May, announced that a "new health surcharge" would be applied to tourists (BBC 2013). Although May provided no concrete data evidencing the dimensions of the purported "health tourism" problem, her rhetoric implied that migrants were accessing resources to which they were not entitled (Cohen 2013). May's public comments mirrored the discourse of her predecessor, John Reid, a decade earlier. But evidence supplied by Reid actually "pointed to the opposite conclusion" (Stevens 2010, p. 367). Indeed, empirical evidence about the practice globally is shaky at best (Hopkins et al. 2010; Johnson et al. 2010). Although there is considerable scholarly disagreement about the nature of health tourism, intentional "medical tourism" (entirely unlike Sumani's or Akhalu's predicament) appears to be an international "growth industry" (Connell 2013; Thompson 2008, 2011; Reisman 2010; Carrera and Bridges 2006, p. 447).

Although it is beyond the scope of this chapter to grapple with the contours of medical humanitarian debates in depth, the narratives of Sumani and Akhalu offer two challenges that pertain directly to the broader concerns of this anthology with the issues of expertise in asylum adjudication and the related problem of how adjudicators distinguish large-scale persecution from individual cases of persecution pertaining to political view or membership of a particular social group. The first concerns how scholars find or *see* medical humanitarianism, and the preference for the macro-lens. Even a brief survey of the literature reveals the centrality of large-scale "crisis" and "emergency" to many formulations of medical humanitarianism (Redfield 2012; Calhoun 2010). By focusing on crises and emergencies, whether in post-earthquake Haiti or post-tsunami Indonesia, however, it is all too easy to lose sense of the bias of scale (Wagner 2014; Good, Grayman, and DelVecchio-Good 2014). A personal medical crisis, however episodic and individual, may speak with equal power to medical humanitarian issues. Whereas macro emergencies routinely provide the valuable added dimension of the engagement of NGOs and intergovernmental organizations, the discreet expressions of medical choice speak no less powerfully to the mobilization of advocacy and empirical research.

The second challenge this narrative recommends concerns what is overlooked by a focus on biomedical practices as the wellspring of humanitarian praxis. While it is undoubtedly the case that biomedicine, in the broadest possible sense, resides at the heart of medical humanitarian interventions, it is all too simple to elide biomedical practices with the activities of medical practitioners, to the exclusion of other disciplinary perspectives on humanitarianism and human rights. The contributions both of nonmedical personnel and nonmedical fora to advocating and accessing emergency medical provision remain poorly understood. Just as the activist medical anthropology characterized by the engaged humanitarian projects and health policy debates of Paul Farmer, Jim Y. Kim, and others paved the way to rich critiques of global health interventions and modern humanitarianism, the time is ripe to reflect on the expanding role of nonmedical expertise and nonmedical space in medical humanitarian debates (Fassin and Padolfini 2010).

As the chapter by Anthony Good in this volume reveals, expert testimony in asylum claims addresses political, cultural, and social conditions in countries of origin, and the degree to which a refugee or asylum seeker may be endangered if forcibly returned. Good (2004, 2008) demonstrates how specific forms of testimony operate within defined parameters. Judges, for example, may call upon experts when the documentary evidence about persecution is inadequate or an identity is in question, as Noé Kam's chapter in the volume explains. Asylum lawyers turn to experts to translate a claimant's narrative of "personal trauma into an act of political aggression" (Shuman and Bohmer 2004, p. 396). Experts interpret domestic statutes (such as nationality and citizenship laws, for example), and apply it to claims, such as statelessness (Lawrance forthcoming). Country conditions experts level the playing field (Kerns 2000). But the tasks accorded them are expansive and "should be broadly defined" (Malphrus 2010, p. 8).

Akhalu's and Sumani's ordeals point to how important ideas are brought to the table when medical humanitarianism intersects with legal regimes (Willen 2011; Gottlieb, Filc, and Davidovitch 2012). Along with the chapter in this volume by Richard Tutton, Christine Hauskeller, and Steve Sturdy, Akhalu's and Sumani's experiences highlight how interactions with the UKBA give rise to new strategies and technologies. Requests for continuation of emergency medical care framed as human rights–based claims draw attention to the important role of expert testimony in the contextualization of highly specialized biomedical knowledge. Expert testimony is a relatively recent feature of asylum, refugee, human rights–based decision making, and humanitarian law (Rose 1956; Rosen 1977; Thuen 2004). As Galya Ruffer and I observed in the introduction to this volume, until the 1980s, asylum operated within a climate of "trust" and the asylum seekers were "presumed to be telling the truth" (Fassin and d'Halluin 2005, p. 600). Today, however, refugees must represent their concerns within "a climate of suspicion," and indeed reside in a space characterized by a public rhetoric reinforcing the idea that "the asylum seeker is seen as someone trying to take advantage of the country's hospitality," clearly exemplified by Secretary May's comments (Fassin and d'Halluin 2005, p. 600).

THE SHIFTING LEGAL TERRAIN OF HUMAN RIGHTS CLAIMS

Ailing migrants who pursue protection in the United Kingdom under the ECHR invoke the poor quality and limited accessibility of medical and psychiatric treatments in their home countries as grounds for temporary refugee status or permanent protection. But depending on the nature of the claim, different tests are applied by adjudicators. Human rights claims pertaining to health may be lodged by citing Article Three (the absolute right not to be subjected to cruel or inhuman treatment or torture) or Article Eight (the nonabsolute right to a private life weighed against society's broader needs). Article Three claims generally need to be considered "exceptional" if they are to prevail and are weighed against extensive jurisprudence. Article Eight claims must be weighed for the test of "proportionality," but appear to have more space for intervention, for all parties. Both tests are adjudicated by the same individuals who evaluate asylum claims and refugee petitions, and, as siblings to the same, both lend themselves to the deployment of expert country conditions information.

Dallal Stevens (2010, p. 375) argues that, "human rights arguments" can "rarely reverse" negative asylum determinations. A carefully composed health care provision report by a country conditions expert, however, may provide important empirical anchors to a human rights claim challenged on appeal (Lawrance 2013, p. 278). In adjudicating the "exceptionality" and "proportionality" of claims, adjudicators may base their decisions on a variety of sources, including information about known conditions and facilities in home countries, and reports from medical, psychiatric, and country conditions experts. In the context of a human rights claim, the burden falls on the claimant to establish the danger encumbered by removal.[3] But the legal terrain for the success of these claims is rapidly shifting in the United Kingdom and Europe generally. As the avenue for Article Three claims appears to be narrowing, lawyers are paying greater attention to Article Eight and advancing sophisticated arguments about proportionality.

The decision to deport Sumani stemmed directly from knowledge that dialysis was available in Ghana. A U.K. government spokesperson reportedly claimed that, "part of our consideration when a person is removed is their fitness to travel and whether the necessary medical treatment is available in the country to which they are returning" (Mason 2008). By contrast, the attempt to remove Akhalu was moderated by a concession from the government lawyer that the requisite medical care was unavailable in Nigeria or beyond her means. Since a 2005 ruling, the UKBA has consistently invoked the very high standard of "exceptional circumstances" in asylum claims invoking medical and psychiatric issues (*N (FC) v. SSHD* (2005) UKHL 31 at §53–54). The UKBA insists that effectively enforcing immigration policy is a legitimate goal that must be weighed against the specificities of human rights claims.[4] Several U.K. and European rulings have bolstered the authority to adjudicate applications case-by-case.[5]

Until quite recently the preferred avenue for claims pertaining to health issues was Article Three of the ECHR, which reads, "no one shall be subjected to torture or to inhuman or degrading treatment or punishment." Since 1978,

---

[3]   *Regina v. SSHD (Appellant) ex parte Adam (FC) (Respondent) Regina v. SSHD (Appellant) ex parte Limbuela (FC) (Respondent) Regina v. SSHD (Appellant) ex parte Tesema (FC) (Respondent) (Conjoined Appeals)*, §55.

[4]   The role of the UKBA (formerly BIA) in the adjudication of immigration cases involving evaluating the private life of the applicant versus the national objectives of an immigration policy was upheld as compatible with the ECHR in *Nnyamzi v. U.K.* (2008).

[5]   Beginning with *N (FC) v. SSHD* (2005) UKHL 31.

the distinction between torture and inhuman or degrading treatment has been interpreted to "derive … principally from a difference in the intensity of the suffering inflicted" (*Ireland v. U.K.* (1978) 2 EHRR 25 at §167). To advance an Article Three claim, the individual must make a strong case about the severity of the suffering caused by removal.[6] To engage the U.K.'s Article Three obligations, on the basis of medical treatment, the individual must meet three conditions. The individual must demonstrate that there is a complete absence of the appropriate medical treatment for the illness. Credible medical evidence must demonstrate that return would significantly reduce life expectancy and lead to acute physical or mental suffering and/or a painful death. The individual must additionally demonstrate that the United Kingdom has provided the individual with appropriate medical or psychiatric treatment for an appreciable amount of time to the extent that the United Kingdom can be regarded as having *assumed the responsibility for care.*

The significant burden on migrants making Article Three claims about the withdrawal of access to care became clearer after 1997, when a ruling established the general principle that persons cannot avoid deportation based on the fact that they should continue to benefit from state-provided assistance.[7] Since then, at least according to British barrister Colin Yeo, the "U.K.'s domestic courts have been seeking to distinguish" this landmark case "as being all but unique" (Yeo 2013). Only in "very exceptional circumstances" may special considerations be invoked. In 2005 this principle was entrenched when the U.K. House of Lords stated that what must be considered is "whether the applicant's illness has reached such a critical stage" that it would be "inhuman treatment to deprive him of care" and send "him home to an early death" unless similar care is available "to meet that fate with dignity" (*N (FC) v. SSHD* (2005) UKHL 31 §18). While medical and psychiatric claims are constantly litigated, these rulings are withstanding scrutiny (Sawyer 2004; Chalmers 2010; Bettinson and Jones 2009; Mantouvalou 2009). Today asylum seekers are not considered "ordinarily resident" for the purpose of access to health care; discretion is the order of the day.[8]

---

[6] The history of the application of human rights law to resist removal from the United Kingdom originated with *Soering v. U.K.* (1989) 11 EHRR 439. A German national was able to resist extradition to the United States to face a capital murder charge on the grounds that there was a real risk he would be exposed to the death penalty, and that such treatment constituted inhuman or degrading treatment. See Lillich (1991).

[7] *D v. U.K.* (1997) 24 EHRR 423 the European Court of Human Rights held that it would be a violation of Article 3 if D, who suffered from advanced HIV complications, were removed to his home country of St. Kitts, where he faced a rapid death with no medical or other support whatsoever.

[8] See, for example, *R (on Application of YA) v. SSHD* [2009] EWCA Civ. 225.

Article Eight claims are qualitatively different and increasingly attractive to lawyers in the United Kingdom because they are newer, the jurisprudence is still developing, and there appears space for innovation. It is surely also not insignificant that the nonabsolute nature of the right lends itself to, among other things, the introduction of empirical data and expert testimony. Article Eight contains two clauses, and conveys a right to a private life in a conditional context. It reads:

1. Everyone has the right to respect for his private and family life, his home and his correspondence.
2. There shall be no interference by a public authority with the exercise of this right except such as is in accordance with the law and is necessary in a democratic society in the interests of national security, public safety or the economic well-being of the country, for the prevention of disorder or crime, for the protection of health or morals, or for the protection of the rights and freedoms of others.

One of the first attempts to engage Article Eight argued that, "removal would have a severely damaging effect on his private life in the sense of his moral and physical integrity." Lawyers for Abdel Kader Bensaid contended that the NHS had been "responsible for his treatment" since 1996 and that withdrawal of treatment would be disproportionate insofar as the "risk" of "a deterioration in his serious mental illness," involved "symptoms going beyond horrendous mental suffering" (*Bensaid v. UK* (2001) 33 EHRR 10 §44). Although unsuccessful, it opened the door to claims weighing the "proportionality" of the damage inflicted by removing the individual against the behavior and conduct of the claimant, the cost of the claimants needs to the public at large, and the interest of public policy. Subsequent decisions have determined that the "threshold for engagement" of Article Eight is not "specially high" (*AG (Eritrea) v. SSHD* [2007] EWCA Civ. 801 §28), which almost appears to be inviting further challenges.

Expert testimony operates as one such challenge whereby this test can be weighed and the claim adjudicated. Akhalu's legal team submitted two expert reports. A leading renal consultant surgeon in Nigeria authored one report. He assessed medical conditions in the country, and how much it would cost to adhere to the prescribed regimen of care for Akhalu's post-transplant condition, and the type of lifestyle necessary to avoid infection. The report concluded that the regimen of care prescribed was likely beyond the current provision of the Nigerian state, and that the lifestyle necessary to maintain health would be difficult and expensive. A second report by a leading Nigerian economist evaluated the socioeconomic background of Akhalu. It posed a series of questions, including would she be able to command the kind of salary to make it possible for her privately to adhere to her medical regimen and maintain a healthy lifestyle. The report demonstrated unequivocally that the necessary treatments did not likely exist in Nigeria at the public expense, and that Akhalu's limited earning capacity would make it impossible that she could afford them privately (Toal 2014).

Akhalu's successful appeal permitting her to remain in the United Kingdom indefinitely was based on the understanding that the private life right engaged stemmed from the "ongoing therapeutic" relationships she had established in the United Kingdom (Toal 2014). Medical cases argued under Article Eight are "only" likely to succeed when "there is an additional factor" beyond the inadequacy of medical provision in the origin country, to be weighed in the balance (*MM (Zimbabwe) v. SSHD* [2012] EWCA Civ. 279 §23). Perhaps ill-advisedly, the UKBA accepted the expert country conditions evidence submitted by Akhalu's lawyers. Nonetheless, the UKBA echoed an earlier European precedent to the effect that the United Kingdom "cannot afford to be the world's hospital" (*JA (Ivory Coast) ES (Tanzania) v. SSHD* [2009] EWCA Civ. 1353 §16). In Ronan Toal's prevailing Article Eight claim, he drew on the same precedent to argue that the threshold for Article Eight is lower than for Article Three, because the right is not absolute but is subject to a proportionality test. Furthermore, unlike Sumani, who was in violation of the terms of her student visa during her ordeal, the burden of Akhalu's proportionality test was mitigated by the fact that she was a "continuously lawful entrant" in the United Kingdom, placing her in a different class for whom the threshold was lower (*JA (Ivory Coast) ES (Tanzania) v. SSHD* [2009] EWCA Civ. 1353 §25).

Decisions about humanitarian protection citing medical or psychiatric issue are complex, and the jurisprudence is constantly in flux. The European Court ruled that "actual bodily injury or intense physical or mental suffering" could involve issues "flowing from conditions of detention, expulsion or other measures, for which the authorities can be held responsible" (*N v. U.K.* 26565/05 [2008] ECHR 453 §29).[9] The assessment of severity is relative and includes many variables, but abandoning a seriously ill schizophrenic patient on the streets of Freetown, Lagos, or Accra may conceivably reach such a threshold.[10] But whereas Article Three applies principally to prevent deportation where the risk of ill treatment emanates from *intentionally* inflicted acts

---

[9] §29 cites *Pretty v. U.K.*, 2346/02, §52, ECHR 2002-III; *Kudła v. Poland* [GC], no. 30210/96, §94, ECHR 2000-XI; *Keenan v. U.K.*, no. 27229/95, §116, ECHR 2001-III; *Price v. U.K.*, no. 33394/96, §30, ECHR 2001-VII). The interpretation of "severity caused by ill-treatment" extends to mental health.

[10] *Jalloh v. Germany*, no. 54810/00, §67, ECHR 2006.

by public authorities unable to afford the applicant appropriate protection or treatment, claims based only on the lack of adequate care in a specific country prevail with decreasing incidence today. Article Eight claims offer a different equation for the evaluation of medical issues, and U.K. courts appear to be "explicitly" inviting new arguments (Yeo 2013) "in light of Akhalu" (*Okonkwo (legacy/Hakemi; health claim)* [2013] UKUT 401 (IAC) §48). As the rhetoric of "health tourism" intensifies, expert country conditions evidence submitted for deliberation as part of the Article Eight "proportionality" test has emerged as an important lifeline to medical humanitarian consideration.

EXPERT TESTIMONY IN THE CONTEXT OF LEGAL FLUX

Among the most powerful tools employed in Akhalu's successful appeal against removal were two expert reports that dovetailed with the medico-legal reports about her renal condition. Tessa Gregory, a solicitor formerly of Public Interest Lawyers, was able to produce expert reports from a consultant renal surgeon and an economist. For Akhalu, expertise from an economist was a fundamental element to establishing that she "would die within weeks … not because appropriate treatment and living conditions are not available," but "because she would not be able to afford them" ([2013] UKUT 400 (IAC) §6).

In general, a claimant's legal counsel privately contracts expert reports of this nature and sends instructions about the specific matters to be addressed. Reports are addressed to the court, not to the claimant, and must supply "objective unbiased opinion," subject to standards established by *Ikarian Reefer* test ([1993] 2 Lloyd's Rep 68), and other regulations Good addresses in his chapter in this volume. In the United Kingdom, government-funded legal aid is sometimes available to individuals making human rights claims, subject to various residency and means tests. Precisely why Sumani's case did not include similar expertise is unclear, but a survey conducted by the asylum seeker and migrant advocacy charity, Bail for Immigration Detainees, suggests that many human rights claimants never receive the necessary legal advice that would lead to the solicitation of expert testimony.[11]

There is no Istanbul Protocol international equivalency for expert country conditions testimony. There are no internationally established rules or regulations regarding who is an expert, or under what conditions such expertise should be factored into adjudication. It is widely appreciated, that "those

---

[11] See "BID & ICAR survey shows 19% of detainees interviewed never had any legal advice while in detention." February 16, 2011. http://www.biduk.org/471/news/bid-icar-survey-shows-1937-of -detainees-interviewed-never-had-any-legal-advice-while-in-detention.html [Retrieved February 28, 2014].

charged with making" asylum decisions, or "providing expert medical evidence, are unlikely to be experts on the wider political, cultural and socio-economic environments of the many and diverse countries from which asylum seekers come." To be sure, it would be "unreasonable" to expect an adjudicator or physician to have "more detailed knowledge of the availability, and accessibility, or medical and psychiatric services" (Wallace and Wylie 2014, p. 763). But beyond these observations, little exists presently by way of guidelines.

The International Association of Refugee Law Judges (IARLJ) identifies eight reasons for which an expert country conditions report may be necessary (Wylie 2012). Expert country evidence may be obtained for one or more of the following reasons:

(a) To substantiate claims of persecution on return;
(b) To provide firsthand knowledge of the country and/or region, and whether an individual or particular group of persons may be at some specified risk if returned;
(c) To provide the political or conflict analysis or the security situation, and possibly potential future developments;
(d) To contextualize the claimant's case within the situation of the country in question;
(e) To analyze the national laws and the judicial system, including law enforcement and assess whether basic human rights are respected;
(f) To explain cultural and religious practices, ethnicity, language, geography, topography and history of a country;
(g) To evaluate documentary country of origin information;
(h) To convey information the expert has gained from his/her own sources.

Although medical issues are unmentioned, all eight of these general reasons may be relevant when drafting a country conditions report that engages with specific medical or psychiatric issues.

Expertise not only resides within every field and profession, experts can be asked to respond to an infinite spectrum of questions. Good experts are nimble, and respond to challenges. As the pseudonymous narratives of Akua and Kwame demonstrated, U.K. officials with no medical training have no "qualms questioning the medical directives of qualified clinical professionals" (Lawrance 2013, p. 276). Cognizant of the risk of straying into advocacy, effective experts might, for example, provide new, innovative, and alternative strategies substantiated by facts, data, and evidence. But just as fine-tuned expertise may re-tether the specificities of a claim, expert knowledge may also have the consequence of reifying complex social, cultural, and political realities (Speed 2006; Bloomaert 2009; Fassin 2012).

From my perspective, I think of the remit of country conditions expertise somewhat differently to that laid out in the IARLJ position paper. I first seek to understand the nature of the asylum, refugee, or humanitarian protection claim. In order to accomplish this, I review the expert medical and expert psychiatric evidence carefully. I then research evidence of national medical provision, including evidence of pharmaceutical availability, dosage, cost, and supply. Domestic medical provision is a capacious category, and in response to previous adjudicators' comments about the nature of and content of my first reports, I have continued to expand this type of data. Depending on the matter in question, I look at relevant legislation, constitutional protections and mandates, organization of the national health service, if one exists; organization of national health insurance, if relevant; the availability of hospital beds; physician-to-patient ratios; nurse-to-patient ratio; provision of specialists; provision of specialized medical equipment; exclusions on particular treatments; sanitation conditions of facilities; and physical proximity to the claimant's home or family.

Medico-legal reports usually contain specific treatment regimens. My country conditions reports address domestic pharmaceuticals. I consider relevant pharmaceutical regulation and legislation; the prevalence of brand name drugs versus generic alternatives; the existence of official treatment guidelines; the adoption and implementation of World Health Organization Essential Medicines Lists; the availability of a prescribing authorities and qualified supervision; the availability of choice; and the implications of cost, supply, and physical conditions of transportation and storage. Psychiatric care is also subject to specific and tailored inquiries. I research the standards in psychiatric hospitals; the presence of licensed psychiatrists, psychologists, social workers, pharmaceuticals, local preferences for "traditional" treatments; and, particularly any evidence of human rights violations, such as the chaining of patients.

Country conditions reports pertaining to health care provision are qualitatively different to medical and psychiatric expertise because they document real and present clinical realities, not idealized or prescribed scientific provisions. Only when I have a sense of these matters, do I turn to evidence of country conditions, and identify news media, NGO reports, and scholarly articles that support preliminary conclusions. Medical reports must adhere to rigorous objectivity standards and resist partisan instincts (Jones and Smith 2004; Meffert et al. 2010). Instructed health care provision reports addressed to asylum adjudicators, however, offer more scope for reflection, nuance, and interpretation, especially where it concerns the capacity of a particular individual to access care. In this way, they more closely resemble political reports accompanying asylum claims than the reports of clinicians or physicians they shadow. In other ways, however, they are distinct. Although the "exclusionary logic" of securitization that reinforces protocols and judicial determinations remains present, questions about alleged fraud and related impediments, which may disrupt asylum hearings, rarely feature (Squire 2009; Terretta 2015). My experience has been that this form of expert reporting interacts less with the narratives of claimants compared with other forms of country conditions expertise. And I never try to "wear two hats," by befriending or personally contacting the claimant during a pending case (Ross 2001).

Before concluding, several examples from recent West African cases may help illustrate these issues and the navigation of evidence. In late 2013 a lawyer representing an Ivorian woman victim of human trafficking and forced prostitution approached me about an expert report about country conditions as they pertained to trafficking, the risk of re-trafficking, and the provision of specialized medical, psychological, and psychiatric for the post-traumatic stress disorder and suicidal tendencies. My report addressed the absence of appropriate medical and pharmaceutical care, as stipulated in the medico-legal reports of her physicians. I focused on the absence of mental health legislation, and the lack of minimum standards for treatment. I concluded that she would likely fall into destitution, live on the street, or wind up embroiled in the trafficking web in which she was originally ensnared, because she would be unable to access medical and psychiatric help. In granting her appeal under Article Three *and* Article Eight grounds, First-Tier Tribunal Judge Pygott accepted the expert evidence that there were inadequate facilities to continue the woman's highly specialized medical and psychiatric care.

In another 2013 case, from Ghana, a thirty-three-year-old woman claimed that she and her U.K.-born daughter would be subjected to female genital cutting (FGC) if forced to return to Ghana. The woman had been brought to the United Kingdom by Ghanaians as a house servant, mistreated, passed on to another Ghanaian family, and then abandoned. Her daughter was diagnosed with sickle cell anemia (SCA), and a consultant pediatric hematologist managed her care. Her solicitor instructed me to address the risk of FGC, the narrative of trafficking, and the likelihood that the child's care could be maintained in Ghana. On the face of it, the FGC claims and the trafficking narrative were relatively easily found to be consistent with publically available objective evidence. Based partly on my expert report, Judge Law of the First-Tier Tribunal determined that the risk of retrafficking was "a live issue and potential threat."

The SCA matter was more complicated, however. The UKBA produced a medico-legal report from a MedCOI, an agency based in the Netherlands, to support the claim that the medications needed both for managing SCA *and* malaria were readily available in Ghana.[12] But as the child had never resided outside the United Kingdom, she had not been exposed to malaria. In Ghana, 95 percent of children under the age of five years contract malaria, and SCA resulted in reduced immunity to infection. My report zeroed in on the hematologist's observation that there is currently no antimalarial prophylaxis approved for long-term use. The nonspecific MedCOI report submitted by the UKBA ultimately undermined its own argument, because it affirmed the endemic nature of malaria and exclusive use of short-term prophylaxes. To *send* (and importantly not *return*) a child to live permanently in Ghana would be to mandate her exposure to malaria, and the almost certainty of infection. Judge Law granted protection based on Articles Three *and* Eight because of the child's medical condition and both individuals' vulnerability upon return.

Another pediatric anemia case on appeal was ultimately withdrawn and not contested with the result that the family now resides in the United Kingdom. In 2012, the UKBA attempted to remove two parents and three children to Sierra Leone. I produced two separate reports. The first addressed the risk of FGC to the two girl children. The second report focused on the prevalence of medical provision for severe chronic pediatric SCA. The youngest of three children, a boy of five, presented with SCA, cerebrovascular disease, and severe complications, including damaged cerebral blood vessels. The consultant pediatric hematologist described his condition as more serious than 90 percent of all infected with SCA, and one that presents in only 10 percent of his current patients. The boy required blood transfusions every two or three weeks, and probably for the rest for his life; regular iron chelation; regular medication, including penicillin; and he was awaiting surgery for a portacath implant to facilitate transfusion.

My report addressed Sierra Leone's national blood transfusion policy, the blood supply, the essential medicine lists, and the provision of pediatric specializations in the country. I consulted extensive publically available objective evidence. Whereas I found that penicillin is likely available, I reported that there were at the time no registered licensed pediatric hematologists in Sierra Leone; the blood transfusion is dramatically undersupported in Sierra Leone; there is a chronic undersupply of blood products in Sierra Leone; and that medical professionals in Sierra Leone do not have confidence

---

[12] MedCOI is a project to increase cooperation and harmonization among European asylum services with respect to the research and use of medical country of origin information. The Immigration and Naturalization Service of the Netherlands maintains a database with specific medical information about countries of origin. The project is funded by the Community Activities of the European Refugee Fund.

in the blood supply or pharmaceutical supply. Furthermore, there is no facility for iron chelation therapy, and there is no provision for the supply of pharmaceuticals for iron chelation. As sending the child to Sierra Leone would likely result in death with a matter of weeks, it was no surprise when the deportation order was withdrawn before the appeal was heard.

One pending case is also instructive. In early 2014, I was approached by a lawyer for a severely ill Ghanaian male who suffered from schizophrenia that tended to reoccur in response to inadequate support and monitoring. His voluminous medical and psychiatric reports encompassed over two hundred pages. His comprehensive care plan and regimen included regular antipsychotic medication, appropriate psycho-education and psychotherapy, and regular community mental health team monitoring. My report addressed the history of psychiatric care in Ghana, based on a review of the scholarly literature. Drawing on published peer-reviewed studies and a 2013 Human Rights Watch report, I addressed allegations of maltreatment and human rights abuse including chaining, enforced fasting, and beatings. I confirmed that the individual's prescribed medication, Quetiapine, is not currently part of Volume Six of the Ghanaian 2010 Essential Medicines List. And I engaged with the direction, by the consultant psychiatrist, Dr. Cornelius Katona, for a "team of mental health experts," pertaining to the management of his condition. As there are twelve psychiatrists, fifteen clinical psychologists, and one occupational therapist, all of which must collectively deal with a population of twenty-five million, I concluded that it was hard to see how this was even remotely feasible under current conditions.

In countries that are emerging from political or sectarian conflict, such as Sierra Leone and Liberia, where hospitals are crumbling, and pharmaceutical distribution is piecemeal, publically available NGO reports may readily substantiate claims. In countries that briefly flirted with universal health care or national insurance, such as Côte d'Ivoire, government policy specifically dismantling such programs demonstrates the significant burden a claimant may face upon return. But perhaps paradoxically, countries that are the site of significant advances and improvements in public medical provision in recent years, such as South Africa, or experiments in national health insurance provision or mental health reform, such as Ghana, require qualitatively different reports.

CONCLUSION

It is impossible to know definitively why Akhalu succeeded and why Sumani failed. I would like to believe that each and every case is considered on its merits. And it would be unwise to find a connection between the two women's cases beyond a simple similarity with respect to the medical diagnoses. But when examined as transnational medical emergencies argued as rights-based claims these narratives offer a fascinating entrée into debates about contemporary medical humanitarianism. Akhalu's and Sumani's stories demonstrate how two discrete expressions of medical choice speak powerfully to the broader mobilization of advocacy and empirical research. They also highlight the contributions of nonmedical personnel and nonmedical fora to advocating and accessing medical provision. Precisely how the divergence in their outcomes accurately reflects the current state of play regarding Article Three and Article Eight claims is still unclear. But claims under the latter mantle are increasing, possibly because advocates seek new avenues to shape jurisprudence, while Article Three claims more often than not fail to advance because of adverse precedent.

The inconspicuous spaces where medical humanitarianism intersects with legal regimes spawn important strategies. Human rights protection requests and human rights–based claims citing medical care highlight the important role of expert testimony in the contextualization of highly specialized biomedical knowledge. Expert testimony has emerged to fill a legal niche in the context of asylum adjudication and "assessing" credibility (Lawrance et al. 2015; UNHCR 1979). Medico-legal reports constitute fact-based accounts of current medical and psychiatric conditions and care tailored to specific individuals, accompanied by supporting documentation, or "the evidence of truth" (Fassin and d'Halluin 2005, p. 598). But whereas the medical expertise informing the authorship of medico-legal reports has come under increasing scrutiny, the deployment of country conditions expertise to interpret and apply the conclusions of medico-legal reports to conditions on the ground is a relatively new phenomenon (see Chelidze et al., this volume; Wallace and Wylie 2014, p. 758–9).

Charles Watters predicted at the turn of the millennium that asylum seekers would continue to have "less and less control over their own lives" as a consequence of migration policy (2001, p. 1712). Indeed, Akhalu and Sumani may be classic exemplars of what Giorgio Agamben (2003) described as a "state of exception," wherein the capacities of citizenship and individual rights are forfeited and the government holds ultimate power over life and death. Indeed, renal conditions continue to be an intense site of legal contestation in the United Kingdom.[13] Notwithstanding these observations,

---

[13] See Yeo 2013. Yeo notes the case of GS *(Art. 3 – health exceptionality) India* [2011] UKUT 35 (IAC), in which it was held that a diabetic undergoing dialysis would die within two weeks of removal in great pain. GS's legal team appealed the tribunal's decision and the case was remitted by the Court of Appeal to the Upper Tribunal by consent with the UKBA to consider the legal test in *N v. U.K.* against the specific medical issues thrown up by removal of a patient dependent on dialysis to sustain life.

however, expert country conditions reports provide a vehicle with which asylum seekers, refugees, and protection claimants can navigate the complex and shifting legal terrain of human rights-based claims.

Author's Note: The author would like to acknowledge the insight and feedback of Sharon Abramowitz, Kristin Doughty, Tobias Kelly, Kristine Krause, and Sjaak van der Geest on this and related work.

REFERENCES

Abramowitz, Sharon and Catherine Panter-Brick, eds. 2014. *Medical Humanitarianism: Ethnographies of Practice*. Philadelphia: University of Pennsylvania Press.

Agabem, Giorgio. 2003. *Stato di Eccezione. Homo Sacer, 2,1.* Turin: Bollati Boringhieri Trans. Kevin Attell as State of Exception (2005).

Anand, S., F. Peter, and A. Sen, eds. 2004. *Public Health, Ethics, and Equity*. Oxford: Oxford University Press.

BBC News. 2008. "Cancer Patient Loses Visa Battle." January 9. http://news.bbc.co.uk/2/hi/uk_news/wales/7178416.stm [Retrieved January 20, 2008].

BBC News. 2013. "Theresa May: Health Tourism 'Not Fair'." October 10. http://www.bbc.com/news/uk-24471679 [Retrieved February 1, 2014].

Bettinson, V. and Jones, A., 2009. "The Integration or Exclusion of Welfare Rights in the ECHR: the Removal of Foreign Nationals with HIV After *N v. UK*." *Journal of Social Welfare and Family Law* 31: 83–94.

Bloomaert, Jan. 2009. "Language, Asylum, and the National Order." *Current Anthropology* 54.4: 415–441.

Brauman, Rony. 2009. *Humanitarian Medicine*. Paris: Crash/Fondation Médecins Sans Frontières.

Calhoun, Craig. 2010. "The Idea of Emergency: Humanitarian Action and Global (Dis)order." In Fassin, Didier, and Mariella Pandolfi, eds., *Contemporary States of Emergency: The Politics of Military and Humanitarian Interventions*. New York: Zone Books, 29–58.

Carrera, Percivil M. and John F. P. Bridges. 2006. "Globalization and Healthcare: Understanding Health and Medical Tourism." *Expert Review of Pharmacoeconomics & Outcomes Research* 6(4): 447–54.

Castañeda, Heide. 2011. "Medical Humanitarianism and Physicians' Organized Efforts to Provide Aid to Unauthorized Migrants in Germany." *Human Organization* 70(1): 1–10.

Chalmers, James. 2010. "Legal Responses to HIV and AIDS." *Legal Studies* 30(2): 334–7.

Chandler, D. 2001. "The Road to Military Humanitarianism: How the Human Rights NGOs Shaped a New Humanitarian Agenda." *Human Rights Quarterly* 23:678–700.

Chung, Ryoa. 2012. "A Theoretical Framework for a Comprehensive Approach to Medical Humanitarianism." *Public Health Ethics* 5(1): 49–55.

Cohen, Nick. 2013. "In Theresa May's Surreal World, Feelings Trump Facts." *The Guardian*, October 12, 2013. http://www.theguardian.com/commentisfree/2013/oct/12/theresa-may-health-tourism-facts [Retrieved January 12, 2014].

Connell, John. 2013. "Contemporary Medical Tourism: Conceptualisation, Culture and Commodification." *Tourism Management* 34: 1–13.

Daniels, Norman. 1985. *Just Health Care*. New York: Cambridge University Press.

Daniels, Norman. 2008. *Just Health: Meeting Needs Fairly*. New York: Cambridge University Press.

de Torrente, Nicolas. 2004. "Humanitarian Action Under Attack: Reflections on the Iraq War. *Harvard Human Rights Journal* 17(1): 1–29.

Eastmond, Marita. 1998. "Nationalist Discourses and the Construction of Difference: Bosnian Muslim Refugees in Sweden." *Journal of Refugee Studies* 11(2): 161–81.

Fassin, Didier. 2012. *Humanitarian Reason: A Moral History of the Present*. Berkeley: University of California Press.

Fassin, Didier and Estelle d'Halluin. 2005. "The Truth from the Body: Medical Certificates as Ultimate Evidence for Asylum Seekers." *American Anthropologist*, 107(4): 597–608.

Fassin, Didier and Mariella Pandolfi. 2010. *Contemporary States of Emergency: The Politics of Military and Humanitarian Interventions*. New York: Zone Books.

Feldman, Ilana and Miriam Ticktin, eds. 2010. *In The Name Of Humanity: The Government of Threat and Care*. Durham, NC: Duke University Press.

Ford, Richard. 2008. "Cancer Deportation 'Not Exceptional'." *The Times*, January 16, 2008.

Fox, Renée C. 1995. "Medical Humanitarianism and Human Rights: Reflections on Doctors Without Borders and Doctors of the World." *Social Science and Medicine Volume 41*, Issue 12: 1607–16.

Good, Anthony. 2004. "'Undoubtedly an Expert'? Anthropologists in British Asylum Courts." *Journal of the Royal Anthropological Institute* 10: 113–33.

Good, Anthony. 2008. "Cultural Evidence in Courts of Law." *Journal of the Royal Anthropological Institute* 14 (April).

Good, Byron J., Jesse Grayman, and Mary-Jo DelVecchio Good. 2014. "Humanitarianism and 'Mobile Sovereignty' in Strong State Settings: Reflections on Medical Humanitarianism in Aceh, Indonesia." In Sharon Abramowitz and Catherine Panter-Brick, eds., *Medical Humanitarianism: Ethnographies of Practice*. Philadelphia: University of Pennsylvania Press.

Gottlieb, N., D. Filc, and N. Davidovitch. 2012. "Medical Humanitarianism, Human Rights and Political Advocacy: The Case of the Israeli Open Clinic." *Social Science and Medicine* 74 (6): 839–45.

Gray, Sadie. 2008. "Deported Ghanaian Dies of Cancer." *The Guardian*, March 20. http://www.guardian.co.uk/uk/2008/mar/20/immigration.immigrationandpublicservices [Retrieved March 15, 2013].

Gruskin, S. et al., eds. 2005. *Perspectives on Health and Human Rights*. New York: Routledge.

Harrington J. and M. Stuttaford, eds. 2010. *Global Health and Human Rights: Legal and Philosophical Perspectives*. Abingdon, UK: Routledge

Hopkins, L., Labonté, R., Runnels, V., and Packer, C. 2010. "Medical Tourism Today: What Is the State of Existing Knowledge?" *Journal of Public Health Policy* 31: 185–98.

Jackson, G. 2008. "Ama Sumani: Avoidable Death of a Deportee." *International Journal of Clinical Practice* 62(6): 84.

Johnston, R., Crooks, V., Snyder, J., and Kingsbury, P. 2010. "What Is Known About the Effects of Medical Tourism in Destination and Departure Countries? A Scoping Review." *International Journal for Equity in Health* 9: 24.

Jones, David Rhys and Sally Verity Smith. 2004. "Medical Evidence in Asylum and Human Rights Appeals." *International Journal of Refugee Law* 16(3): 381–410.

Kerns, Susan K. 2000. "Country Conditions Documentation in U.S. Asylum Cases: Leveling the Evidentiary Playing Field." *Indiana Journal of Global Legal Studies* 8(1): 197–222.

Lawrance, Benjamin N. 2013. "Humanitarian Claims and Expert Testimony: Contestation over Health Care for Ghanaian Migrants in the United Kingdom." *Ghana Studies* 15–16: Special Double Issue, "Health and Health Care," 251–86.

Lawrance, Benjamin N. et al. 2015. "Introduction: Law, Expertise, and Protean Ideas about African Migrants." In Iris Berger, Benjamin N. Lawrance, Tricia Redeker Hepner, Meredith Terretta, and Joanna Tague, eds., *African Asylum at a Crossroads: Activism, Expert Testimony, and Refugee Rights*. Athens: Ohio University Press.

Lawrance, Benjamin N. Forthcoming. "De jure? De facto? Denied, Deported: State-Effected Statelessness." In Benjamin N. Lawrance and Jacqueline Stevens, eds., *Citizenship-in-Question: Evidentiary Encounters with Blood, Birthright, and Bureaucracy*. Philadelphia: University of Pennsylvania Press.

Lewando Hundt, Gillian, Chatty, Dawn, Thabet, Abdel Aziz, and Abuateya, Hala. 2004. "Advocating Multi-Disciplinarity in Studying Complex Emergencies: The Limitations of a Psychological Approach to Understanding How Young People Cope with Prolonged Conflict in Gaza." *Journal of Biosocial Science* 36(4): 417–31.

Lillich, Richard B. 1991. "The Soering Case." *The American Journal of International Law* 85(1): 128–49.

MacDougall, William. 2013. "Our Kingdom" blog, OpenDemocracy.Net, by "William MacDougall." In response to a repost of Alan White's New Statesman article. http://www.opendemocracy.net/ourkingdom/alan-white/trials-of-roseline-akhalu [Retrieved February 1, 2014].

Madill, Esmé. 2012. "Roseline's Journey: A Kidney Transplant Patient Meets UK Border Agency Contractors." OpenDemocracy.Net May 12, 2012. http://www.opendemocracy .net/ourkingdom/esme-madill/roseline's-journey-kidney-transplant-patient-meets-uk -border-agency-contracto [Retrieved January 12, 2014].

Malphrus, Garry. 2010. "Expert Witnesses in Immigration Proceedings." *Immigration Law Advisor* 4(5): 6–10.

Mantouvalou, V. 2009. "N v. U.K.: No Duty to Rescue the Nearby Needy?" *Modern Law Review* 72: 815–28.

Mason, Barry. 2008. "Britain: Terminally Ill Ghanaian Woman Deported and Denied Medical Care." World Socialist Website. January 18. http://www.wsws.org/en/ articles/2008/01/depo j18.html [Retrieved March 29, 2013].

McColl, Helen and Johnson, Sonia. 2006. "Characteristics and Needs of Asylum Seekers and Refugees in Contact with London Community Mental Health Teams: A Descriptive Investigation." *Social Psychiatry and Psychiatric Epidemiology* 41: 789–95.

Meffert, Susan M., Karen Musalo, Dale E. McNiel, and Renée L. Binder. 2010. "The Role of Mental health Professionals in Political Asylum Processing." *Journal of the American Academy of Psychiatry Law* 38(4): 479–89.

Musalo, Karen. 1996. "In re Kasinga: A Big Step Forward for Gender-Based Asylum Claims." *Interpreter Releases* 73 (July): 853–67.

Musalo, Karen. 1998. "Ruminations on *In re Kasinga*: The Decision's Legacy." *USC Review of Law and Women's Studies* 7: 35–7.

N. A. 2008. "Migrant Health: What Are Doctors' Leaders Doing?" *The Lancet* 371 (9608): 178.

Piot, Charles. 2007. "Representing Africa in the Kasinga Asylum Case." In Ylva Hernlund and Bettina Shell-Duncan, eds., *Transcultural Bodies: Female Genital Cutting in Global Context*. New Brunswick, NJ: Rutgers University Press.

Redfield, Peter. 2012. *Life in Crisis: The Ethical Journey of Doctors Without Borders*. Berkeley: University of California Press.

Reisman, David A. 2010. *Health Tourism: Social Welfare Through International Trade*. Cheltenham, UK: Edward Elgar.

Rose, A. M. 1956. "The Social Scientist as an Expert Witness." *Minnesota Law Review* 40: 205–18.

Rosen, Lawrence. 1977. "The Anthropologist as Expert Witness." *American Anthropologist* 79(3): 555–78.

Ross, J. 2001. "Can an Expert Wear Two Hats?" *New Law Journal* (2001): 1646–9.

Sawyer, C. 2004. "Insufficiently Inhuman: Removing AIDS Patients from the UK," *Journal of Social Welfare and Family Law*. 281–8.

Shuman, Amy and Carol Bohmer. 2004. "Representing Trauma: Political Asylum Narrative." *Journal of American Folklore* 117: 394–414.

Speed, Shannon. 2006. "At the Crossroads of Human Rights and Anthropology: Towards a Critically-Engaged Activist Research." *American Anthropologist* 108(1): 66–76.

Squire, Vicki. 2009. *The Exclusionary Politics of Asylum*. Basingstoke, UK: Palgrave-Macmillan.

Stevens, Dallal. 2010. "Asylum Seekers and the Right to Access Health Care." *Northern Ireland Legal Quarterly* 61(4): 363–90.

Terretta, Meredith. 2015. "Fraudulent Asylum-Seeking as Transnational Mobilization: The Example of Cameroon." In Iris Berger, Benjamin N. Lawrance, Tricia Redeker Hepner, Meredith Terretta, and Joanna Tague, eds., *African Asylum at a Crossroads: Activism, Expert Testimony, and Refugee Rights*. Athens: Ohio University Press.

Thompson, Charis. 2008. "Medical Tourism, Stem Cells, Genomics: EASTS, Transnational STS, and the Contemporary Life Sciences." *East Asian Science, Technology and Society* 2: 433–8.

Thompson, Charis. 2011. "Medical Migrations Afterword: Science as a Vacation?" *Body and Society*, 17: 205–13.

Thuen, Trond. 2004. "Anthropological Knowledge in the Courtroom: Conflicting Paradigms." *Social Anthropology* 12(3): 265–87.

Ticktin, Miriam. 2006. "Where Ethics and Politics Meet: the Violence of Humanitarianism in France." *American Ethnologist* 33(1): 33–49.

Ticktin, Miriam. 2011. *Casualities of Care: Immigration and the Politics of Humanitarianism in France*. Berkeley: University of California Press.

Toal, Ronan. 2014. Interview with Ronan Toal, Ms. Akhalu's barrister, conducted by the author, February 26, 2014.

Travis, Alan. 2008. "Immigration Chief Defends Deportation of Cancer Patient." *The Guardian*, January 15. http://www.guardian.co.uk/uk/2008/jan/16/immigration.poli tics [Retrieved March 14, 2013].

UNHCR. 1979. *Handbook and Guidelines on Procedures and Criteria for Determining Refugee Status Under the 1951 Convention and the 1967 Protocol Relating to the Status of Refugees* [Reissued December 2011, HCR/1P/4/ENG/REV. 3, http://www .refworld.org/docid/4f33c8d92.html accessed April 17, 2013].

Wales Online. 2008. "Bishops' Appeal Over Cancer Patient Row." January 18. http:// icwales.icnetwork.co.uk/news/cardiff-news/2008/01/17/bishops-appeal-over-cancer -patient-row-91466-20361834/ [retrieved January 12, 2014].

Wagner, Laura. 2014. "Professionals, Providers, and Profiteers? Haitian Doctors Amid the Influx of Foreign Humanitarian Volunteers." In Sharon Abramowitz and Catherine Panter-Brick, eds., *Medical Humanitarianism: Ethnographies of Practice*. Philadelphia: University of Pennsylvania Press.

Watters, Charles. 2001. "Emerging Paradigms in the Mental Health Care of Refugees," *Social Science and Medicine* 52: 1709–18.

White, Alan. 2013. "The Trials of Roseline Akhalu: Why Is the Home Office Continuing a Cruel and Ludicrous Campaign Against a Woman Who They Have Accepted Will Definitely Die If Returned to Nigeria?" *New Statesman*, January 15, 2013. http:// www.newstatesman.com/alan-white/2013/01/trials-roseline-akhalu [Retrieved January 21, 2014].

Willen S. S. 2011. "Do 'Illegal' Im/migrants Have a Right to Health? Engaging Ethical Theory as Social Practice at a Tel Aviv Open Clinic." *Medical Anthropology Quarterly* 25(3): 303–30.

Woodcock, J. 1995. "Healing Rituals with Families in Exile." *Journal of Family Therapy* 17: 397–409.

Wylie, Karen. 2012. "The Use of Expert Country Evidence." IARLJ Discussion Paper circulated at the IARLJ 9th World Conference, Bled, Slovenia, September 7–9, 2011. http://www.iarlj.org/general/images/stories/BLED_conference/papers/WP_ECE _-_K_Wylie.pdf [Retrieved February 2, 2014].

Yeo, Colin. 2013. "Human Rights, Expulsion and Medical Treatment Cases: A Review." Free Movement blog, November 27. http://www.freemovement.org.uk/ 2013/11/27/human-rights-expulsion-and-medical-treatment-cases-a-review/ [Retrieved November 30, 2013].

Afterword

Lisa Dornell[1]

An asylum applicant speaks of his experiences during his nation's long and vicious civil war at an asylum hearing and refers to how he suffered at the hands of the "rebels." The attorney for the Department of Homeland Security argues that the applicant was himself a "rebel" who associated himself with a faction to the fighting which engaged in the persecution of others, such that he would be disqualified from asylum as a matter of law.

A woman seeks protection from family members in her rigid, conservative and patriarchal society. She is fleeing a forced marriage and certain forced mutilation of her genitalia. An issue is raised at the hearing regarding her availability to relocate away from her family in order to avoid the danger.

Practicing Christians do not wish to worship in the church sanctioned by their government. Instead, the family wishes to worship in their traditional church, which has an age-old tradition of answering to a hierarchy outside of the country of their nationality.[2] These are some of the issues faced by Immigration Judges on a daily basis as we seek to adjudicate justly and fairly within the rule of law.

How is an adjudicator to determine who was a "rebel" in a civil war? How might a judge in the United States become familiar with the cultural, economic, and other societal norms that might impact the ability of an unmarried woman to relocate within her country of citizenship in order to avoid mutilation and forced marriage? What are the true implications for worshippers who do not wish to worship in a government sanctioned house of worship?

---

[1] The author, Lisa Dornell is a sitting U.S. Immigration Judge. Disclaimer: The views expressed are her own, and do not necessarily represent the views of the Department of Justice, the Attorney General of the United States, EOIR or the Chief Immigration Judge of the United States. 5 CFR 2635.807(b)(2).

[2] These are hypothetical examples that do not relate to any specific, past or present cases before the Court.

U.S. Immigration Judges are learned in U.S. law. However, given the broad variety of cases that are presented to immigration courts, there are specific areas in which the process benefits from the insertion of a particular expertise. The U.S. system lends itself to the use of expert witnesses. Judges, motivated by the quest to enact justice, work under congressional mandates, which lend themselves to the use of special expertise. For example, The U.S. Congress has emphasized the importance of using Country of Origin Information (COI) through its enactment of the International Religious Freedom Act, which mandates some important requirements that directly relate to the mission of Immigration Judges. One important feature of the legislation is the requirement that the U.S. Department of State, in addition to its annual reports on human rights practices, issue a separate, annual International Religious Freedom Report. These reports contain invaluable COI that addresses specifically the status of religious freedom, or the lack thereof, in nations throughout the world.

The statute also provides, in part, that Immigration Judges must receive training annually on the "nature of religious persecution abroad, including country-specific conditions."[3] The statute specifically mandates that the annual training include "governmental and nongovernmental methods of persecution employed, and differences in the treatment of religious groups by such persecuting entities." And, in fact, during annual conferences, Immigration Judges have been treated to panel presentations by a number of knowledgeable individuals, who are experts in the field of religious freedoms, from organizations such as the Hebrew Immigrant Aid Society, the U.S. Commission on International Religious Freedom, and the Institute on Religion and Public Policy.

In addition to statutory mandates on the use of COI, federal regulations contain numerous provisions that require the consideration of COI in a variety of contexts. For example, regulations governing applications for asylum indicate that an applicant is not required to demonstrate that he or she would be singled out for persecution if it can be demonstrated that there is a pattern or practice of persecution on account of any of the protected grounds against a group or category of persons similarly situated to the applicant and the applicant belongs to or is identified with the persecuted group, such that a reasonable person in the applicant's position would fear persecution.[4] A determination of a pattern or practice of persecution cannot be made in the absence of COI.

For asylum applicants basing their claims on a fear of future persecution, regulations may stand as an impediment to establishing asylum eligibility if

---

[3]   The International Religious Freedom Act, Pub. L. 105–292, SEC. 603 (1998).
[4]   8 CFR §1208.13(b)(2)(iii)(A); 8 C.F.R. §1208.13(b)(2)(iii)(B).

the applicant could avoid persecution by relocating to another part of the applicant's country of nationality or, if stateless, the applicant's country of last habitual residence, and if under all the circumstances it would be reasonable to expect the applicant to do so. Indeed, the regulations further direct an examination of additional factors in the assessment of whether internal relocation is a viable alternative and provide that:

> For purposes of determinations adjudicators should consider, but are not limited to considering, whether the applicant would face other serious harm in the place of suggested relocation; any ongoing civil strife within the country; administrative, economic, or judicial infrastructure; geographical limitations; and social and cultural constraints, such as age, gender, health, and social and familial ties. Those factors may, or may not, be relevant, depending on all the circumstances of the case, and are not necessarily determinative of whether it would be reasonable for the applicant to relocate.[5]

Without COI, immigration judges are not in a position to assess the possibility and the reasonability of internal relocation.[6] For example, COI might reflect that in certain clan-based, conservative, patriarchal societies, unmarried women simply do not have the option of relocating away from their families – it just is not done – they would not be able to independently secure housing or employment or to otherwise live safely and securely outside of their own family circle in a society that does not perceive unmarried women as worthy or capable of living outside of the confines of a male-dominated family circle.

Given that none of the factors set forth in the regulations can be accurately or fairly assessed in the absence of COI, it is important to consider how judges might appropriately use COI to eliminate the use of "armchair logic."[7] In fulfilling the obligation to appropriately utilize COI, Immigration Judges cement the view that, in the United States, all applicants will receive a fair adjudication of applications for asylum and withholding of removal and, thereby, avoid the perception of what has been labeled disparagingly as the "Asylum Lottery" or "Refugee Roulette."[8]

[5] 8 CFR § 1208.13(b)(3) and (2)(ii).
[6] For those who base a claim for protection on past persecution, the prospect of internal relocation may be used to rebut a presumption of a well-founded fear of future persecution. 8 CFR §1208.13(b)(1)(i)(B).
[7] Law Society of South Africa. Undated. "LSSA Says Asylum Seekers' Review Unjust." Internet. Accessed from http://www.lssa.org.za.
[8] BBC News. March 1, 2010. "Big Rise in Afghan Child Migrants." URL: htpp://news.bbc.co.uk/2/hi/southasia (addressing the uneven application of laws to protect refugee laws in the European Union); Philip G. Schrag, et al., *Refugee Roulette: Disparities in Asylum Adjudication and Proposals for Reform* (2008).

Although documentation from well-known, credible sources, such as the U.S. State Department's Report on Human Rights Practices, reports from Amnesty International or Human Rights Watch, may be sufficient to explain general country conditions, there are circumstances under which more up-to-date and specific information is needed. Although there is no legal requirement, for example, that an asylum applicant "corroborate his corroboration" of country conditions, expert testimony may help to clarify those conditions in the context of a particular claim.[9] This additional information may be useful in assisting a court to determine the impact of country conditions as they relate to the unique and specific aspects of an applicant's claim and may serve as a bridge between specific facts and the inferences and conclusions to be drawn by the Court.[10] This is particularly important given directives from higher courts that Immigration Judges should not draw improper inferences from changed country conditions and should not engage in speculation.[11]

Given the restrictions imposed on the ability of Immigration Judges to draw inferences from changes in country conditions, particularly very recent changes, expert testimony can be particularly useful. Typically, the reports received from the U.S. Department of State cover events from the preceding year. Expert testimony might be essential to help the Court understand, for example, the current impact of the cessation of hostilities between warring factions or nations in a situation that might be evolving daily. Such timely information would assist a judge in deciding whether conditions have evolved such that an applicant can safely return home or take advantage of an opportunity to relocate internally. Either party might also use the information to rebut inferences that may be drawn about changed conditions.[12]

Although possessing expertise in a relevant field is certainly a critical factor, knowledge of how to prepare and how to present expert testimony can be just as important. Witness testimony can be presented orally or in writing. A party may seek to introduce an affidavit or report of an expert in lieu of presenting live testimony. One potential downside to written instead of oral testimony is

[9] *Marynenka v. Holder*, 592 F.3d 594 (4th Cir. 2010).

[10] In *Matter of S-M-J-*, 21 I&N Dec. 722 (BIA 1997), the appellate Board stated that an applicant should provide "supporting evidence, both of general conditions and of the specific facts sought to be relied on by the applicant, where such evidence is available." The REAL ID Act of 2005 has codified this corroboration rule.

[11] *See, e.g., Del Valle v. INS*, 776 F.2d 1407, 1413 (9th Cir.1985) (reversing a decision where improper inferences drawn); *Tewabe v. Gonzales*, 446 F.3d 533, 538 (4th Cir.2006) (reversing a decision where fact-finder engaged in speculation).

[12] *See Castillo–Villagra v. INS*, 972 F.2d 1017, 1028 (9th Cir.1992) (requiring parties to be given the opportunity to rebut inferences drawn regarding changed country conditions).

that there might be an objection to admissibility of the submission based on the lack of opportunity by the other side to cross-examine the expert. However, federal regulations provide that evidence is admissible if it is material and relevant.[13] It is therefore not likely that such an objection would lead to an outright exclusion of the information provided in an expert affidavit or report. However, in the absence of live testimony, particularly if there are areas where there are ambiguities or unanswered questions, in the end, the court may find that the expert's information is worthy of less probative value or evidentiary weight. The absence of an accompanying curriculum vitae might further detract from the probative value of an expert report.

With regard to the content of the report, care must be taken to ensure that conclusions reached by experts are limited to the scope of the expertise and are conclusions and opinions that are supported by foundational information provided in the written submission. Opinions that are offered without a sufficient factual predicate or opinions expressed that extend beyond the area of expertise may be attributed no weight in the final assessment of facts by the Court.

The live testimony of experts raises additional considerations. In the absence of a stipulation (an agreement reached between the parties), the decision to allow or disallow testimony of an expert is generally made following a *voir dire*.[14] Although it is important for experts to know how to survive a *voir dire*, it is also incumbent on experts to work with the lawyers who engage them to ensure that their evidence and testimony make it to the *voir dire*. For this reason, pretrial preparation is essential.

Procedural rules designed to facilitate the orderly flow of the proceeding can become procedural hurdles if there is inadequate or noncompliance. As with courts everywhere, U.S. Immigration Courts operate under national rules that govern the filing of documents and other evidence. For example, there are rules relating to how long before the trial evidence has to be served on the other party and filed with the court. One rule directs the parties to file a list of witnesses to be called and requires certain specific information to be provided about the witnesses, including identifying information, the estimated length of testimony and a summary of the testimony to be offered.[15] The rules allow some flexibility in this regard and authorize judges to mandate the filing of an

---

[13] 8 C.F.R. 1240.7(a); Immigration Court Practice Manual section 3.3(g).

[14] The term "voir dire" means "to speak the truth" and involves a preliminary examination to determine the competency of a witness. Merriam Webster Dictionary Online. Accessed from http://www.merriam-webster.com.

[15] Immigration Court Practice Manual section 3.3(g).

affidavit executed by the witness, in addition to the witness list, before the witness is permitted to testify.

Although the lawyers are charged with knowledge and compliance with the rules of court, the putative expert witness must assist by turning over any written reports or materials to be submitted into evidence, a curriculum vitae and other requested information to the lawyer in a timely fashion so that the lawyer can meet procedural requirements, including filing deadlines. Failure to meet procedural requirements will draw an objection from opposing counsel and likely lead to a ruling by the Court that the witness will not be permitted to testify and that any materials provided by the expert will be excluded from evidence.

Assuming that proper procedural rules are adhered to, at this point, the expert witness is now positioned for preparation for a *voir dire* and ultimately for full testimony before the Court on the area of his or her expertise. Although it is incumbent upon the lawyers to make sure that procedural rules of court are adhered to, experts should be proactive in preparing for their testimony. Preliminarily, expert witnesses should consult with the party who seeks to call them to testify in order to ensure that there is a plan to use their expertise wisely. It is appropriate, for example, for an expert witness to question whether their particular area of expertise is germane to the issue or issues being litigated.

Inadequate pretrial preparation may lead to a ruling by the Court that the expert lacks the appropriate expertise and to the exclusion, not only of the testimony but also possibly of any accompanying written report. Lack of adequate pretrial preparation might also lead to a finding that the witness should not be permitted to testify because of unreliability due to real or perceived bias or due to a finding by the Court that the area the putative expert witness has come to testify about is not an area or issue that is actually an issue that is contested by the parties.

By the time the day of trial arrives, comprehensive pre-trial preparation should have been completed. Witnesses should keep in mind the adversarial nature of Immigration Court proceedings and should understand that challenges to expertise are not personal. Rather, a challenge to expertise, in the context of litigation, is a part of the process of ferreting out the truth. Ultimately, even after a withering cross-examination on *voir dire*, the lawyers may reach an agreement on expertise. Even in the absence of an agreement between the parties, the Court may, nonetheless, permit the witness to testify after being satisfied by the testimony elicited through the *voir dire* that the witness is truly an expert in his or her field. Just as the *voir dire* process ought to be understood by putative witnesses, so should other courtroom procedures.

Tensions may arise potentially between lawyers and academics, reflecting the very different academic and legal cultures and communication styles. In U.S. courts, the model of communication between lawyers and witnesses and judges and witnesses is for questions to be asked and for those questions to be answered directly and specifically.[16] This style of communication may differ from an academic environment where answers may be presented at greater length, with greater depth in one sitting, and often with fewer interruptions or challenges.

Unless specifically invited by the court, answers provided during the course of testimony should not be presented in the form of lengthy narratives. Rather, testimony should be directly responsive to specific questions posed by the lawyers or by the court. The clearest advice I often give to individuals about to present expert testimony is as follows: listen carefully to the question, answer the question, and be sure to answer the actual question asked. Failure or inability to answer questions in this fashion may lead to a finding of evasiveness and ultimately to an adverse credibility finding that will lead to some or all of the testimony being discredited. Judges and lawyers are acutely attuned to phrases that signal nonresponsive testimony.

Communication styles must be adapted to fit the forum, or the important message to be delivered may be lost in a sea of objections. Expert witnesses should be prepared in advance of their testimony to cease testimony if an objection is lodged – in other words, if an objection is lodged, they must wait for a ruling from the bench before continuing their testimony or answering the question that has been objected to. In addition to the adaption of communication styles, experts ought to be prepared to adapt behavior and expectations to the courtroom forum. Demeanor and body language are important. Witnesses should avoid appearing defensive or angry in response to questions. These behaviors may create the impression that there might be some factor that may indeed undermine expertise or impartiality and may create a distraction from the main purpose of the hearing, which is to maintain the integrity of the proceeding by obtaining sufficient credible and probative information. The interruption of testimony by the Court or by lawyers should not be perceived as discourtesy. Courts recognize that experts have a wealth of information but the lawyers and the judge know what specific facts are needed to meet legal requirements. Expert witnesses should be prepared to provide explanations in layman's terms to assist the Court in understanding and applying the expert information and opinions provided.

---

[16] See, e.g., *Flores-Calderon v. Gonzales*, 472 F.3d 1040 (8th Cir. 2007) (noting that objective evidence presented must be credible and direct and specific).

A general understanding of the process and patience as the proceeding unfolds are important. Experts ought to be cognizant that, notwithstanding their credentials and time and effort devoted to preparation, they may not actually be called to the witness stand. There might be a variety of reasons for this. In some cases, reports provided by experts may be so complete and informative, that there are no further questions to be asked and no further information needed to reach a just resolution of the case.

The Court recognizes that most experts are engaged in other activities that may impact their availability to appear in court on a given date. In many instances, the Court has the ability and the flexibility to accommodate an expert's schedule to facilitate participation in the hearing. Experts should inform the attorney who has engaged them of any scheduling conflicts and should feel free to request through the lawyer accommodations that might facilitate their appearance. In some cases, particularly where distance or expense or scheduling might otherwise serve as an impediment, telephonic appearances may be appropriate. In other cases, it might be possible for testimony to be presented via televideo equipment. Other accommodations, for example, permitting expert witnesses to be called first and to leave immediately after their testimony, may facilitate the presentation of testimony.

Expert testimony in Immigration Court proceedings is an important, and oftentimes essential, component of the administration of justice. Given that thousands of cases are heard by Immigration Courts around the nation every year, the effective utilization of such witnesses provides an important avenue to fairness and justice.

Index

abuse: child, 85, 158; domestic, 85; sexual, 32, 95. *See also* rape; sexual and gender-based violence; torture; violence

Action of Christian Activists for Human Rights, 85

adjudicators: agenda of disbelief among, 44; and the complexity of rape, 87–8; consideration of mitigating factors by, 50; on the credibility of applicants, 198–9; erroneous conclusions reached by, 41; evidence considered by, 1, 49, 236; expectations of, 39–40; relationship with experts, 6, 8, 15, 19, 28, 180, 182; rigidity of, 31. *See also* Immigration Judges

Advisory Panel on Country Information (APCI), 126

affidavits: concerning LGBT individuals, 148; concerning persecution, 98–9; concerning trauma history, 154; from experts, 157–9, 157n16, 159n19, 161–3, 248–50; medical, 17, 169, 199; medico-legal, 167, 171, 183; training for writing, 172–3

Africa: asylum seekers from, 180–1, 191–4, 199; documentation problems in, 4, 29. *See also* individual countries by name

Akhalu, Roseline Onoshoagbe, 221, 223–4, 226–9, 231–3, 238–9

aliens, resident, 48. *See also* asylum seekers

Aliens Act (U.K.), 204

American Bar Association Rule of Law Initiative, 91–2

Amnesty International, 248

anthropology and anthropologists, 12, 54, 64, 77, 133–4, 140; medical, 225

anxiety disorders, 171. *See also* post-traumatic stress disorder

applicants. *See* asylum seekers

Armed Forces of the Democratic Republic of Congo (FARDC), 90

Asia, documentation problems in, 4, 29. *See also* China

Assessing Credibility in Asylum and Human Rights Claims, 50

assessment measures and methodology. *See* credibility, assessment of

Assessment of Credibility in Claims for Refugee Protection (IRB), 49

asylum adjudication: British system of, 7, 14, 124–6, 204–6, 239; Canadian system of, 7, 49; European system of, 5, 203, 206; in the Netherlands, 57, 59–62, 74, 80; in Sweden, 58; U.S. system of, 3, 7, 47, 48, 246, 249–52. *See also* refugee and asylum adjudication process (RSD); refugee determination process

Asylum Aid, 127

asylum and immigration experts, 10

Asylum and Refugee Law Advocacy Clinic, 28, 30

asylum cases: database of, 174; denial rates of, 1; examples of, 140–1; gender as factor in, 47

asylum claims: assumed to be bogus, 9–10; human-rights based, 223–4, 228–30, 238–40, 244–5; importance of detail to, 124

asylum hearings, 36; pretrial preparation for, 249–50; procedural requirements for, 249–50; review procedures for, 1; transcripts compared to audio recordings of, 33–4

asylum laws, 1, 10, 172, 174. *See also* immigration laws